D1204091

KILLERS IN COLD BLOOD

KILLERS IN COLD BLOOD

by
RAY BLACK
RODNEY CASTLEDEN
GORDON KERR
IAN AND CLAIRE WELCH

Futura

A *Futura* Book

First published by Futura in 2007

Copyright © Omnipress 2007

ISBN: 978-0-7088-0612-8

Produced by Omnipress, Eastbourne

Printed in India

Futura
An imprint of
Little, Brown Book Group
Brettenham House
Lancaster Place
London WC2E 7EN

Photo credits: Getty Images

CONTENTS

PART FOUR: VICTIMS OF ASSASSINATION

PART FIVE: ATROCITIES

PART SIX: ORGANISATIONS

PART SEVEN: COLD-BLOODED MEN

INTRODUCTION

The news is always full of stories of horror whether it is the brutal killing of an individual or mass killings under a political guise. There are those who murder for profit, those who murder for the sheer thrill of it, or those who are motivated by rage. These are the people who inspire the horror movies, but usually the fictional stories are nothing in comparison to the truth. For example, Ed Gein, whose particularly bizarre and morbid crimes shocked the world, was the inspiration for countless books and films, including Robert Bloch's Psycho and Tobe Hooper's *Texas Chainsaw Massacre*. *The Amityville Horror* was based on the character of Ronald DeFeo who killed his parents and siblings one by one as they slept, blaming his actions on the malevolent force of an evil spirit living in the house. Whatever the reason for these cold-blooded killings, as we read about yet another death, it sends a shiver down the spine – or at least for the average person.

Killers in Cold Blood looks inside the dark side of the criminal mind. These are the men and women who commit heinous acts with a gruesome disregard for human life. They do not conform to what society considers to be 'normal' standards, they seem to act purely for self gratification in their own little world of perversion. The difficulty in bringing these monsters to justice is proving whether they are just bad or mad, whether in fact the individual is mentally ill or whether they are fully aware of what they have done. Ed Gein was always thought to be a mild-mannered bachelor who had been held back by his domineering mother. He shocked the world when police raided his home and found a vest made out of human skin and a hoard of body parts. The question that came to the forefront in this case was, is he clinically insane or a cold-blooded killer with a hatred of women? Charles Manson and Jeffrey Dahmer are fine examples of men who killed in cold blood. They knew exactly what they were doing, they knew right from wrong, and yet they still committed their crimes.

The motive behind a cold-blooded killing can probably be differentiated by different labels, i.e. hatred, passion, profit, revenge, fear, power or domination, opportunism, contract killing, desperation, racist, compassion and ritual. For example, Hitler's desire to cleanse Germany of the Jews was because he believed that they were his powerful enemies and he was bent on destroying them. Hitler believed that he was the greatest German and military leader to have ever lived and his paranoia and delusions drove him to commit one of the world's greatest atrocities.

Pol Pot who was the famous leader of the Khmer Rouge

in Cambodia was also paranoid about his supposed enemies, which resulted in a reign of terror. He launched a bloody purge in an attempt to purify the Cambodian race killing hundreds of thousands of innocent people with a complete disregard for pain and suffering.

There has been a considerable amount of research carried out on the criminal mind, but still it causes considerable concern and puzzlement as to how a person could commit a cold-blooded, senseless killing and yet maintain a normal existence. Friends, families and work-mates are totally unaware of the sexual or sadistic side to the person who they thought they knew so well. Ted Bundy is representative of a serial killer who was polite, smart and well-liked and yet underneath this facade was a man who had an addiction to hard-core pornography which fuelled the terrible crimes he committed.

The most feared killers must be those in the medical world. They are people who we are often alone with, and who we trust implicitly even when we are in a weakened state. They have trained for years to try and make us feel better, and yet occasionally one may have macabre plans. For example, medic Donald Harvey claims to have killed fifty of his patients out of mercy, to put them out of their suffering. However, his psychiatrist thought otherwise, calling him a sadistic and compulsive killer who murdered to satisfy his needs. Nurse Beverley Allitt, dubbed the

'Angel of Death' was convicted of killing four children and injuring eleven others, but her motives were completely different. Allitt, who showed signs of Munchausen's Syndrome by Proxy, craved attention and by injecting helpless babies with lethal doses of insulin and then attempting to revive them in front of her colleagues, this is exactly what she got. On the outside, Allitt appeared to be a caring, loving nurse, but on the inside she was really indifferent to the children's pain. Harold Shipman, who everyone thought was the friendly family doctor, was responsible for the worst murder spree in British history, killing as many as 260 people.

Other killers may have had a long history of being institutionalised in juvenile and adult correctional facilities. In some cases this has greatly impaired their ability to live in the community, often lacking both social and work-related skills. Many show signs of aggression and feel they are not really part of normal society. By killing they get the sense of importance, many often revisiting the scene of the crime in the hope of getting caught.

In the case of mass and serial murders, the killer achieves an immense amount of satisfaction as he momentarily gains control of his or her life by controlling others. Whilst serial killers generally try to elude detection so that they can continue to kill for weeks, months and often years, mass murderers are usually either caught by the police, commit suicide or turn themselves in to the authorities. It is very rare that we ever hear of a mass murderer who has had the opportunity to carry out a second crime. Serial killers will often keep a trophy of their victim and display it proudly in their home. They rarely show any emotions to their family or friends and it is very rare that they know their victims. A serial killer will also often develop some sort of 'trademark' which becomes more elaborate with each murder.

When dealing with serial killers, the question of sanity almost always arises and an insanity plea is usually used when the case goes to court. This defence claims that the defendant is unable to appreciate the error of his ways due to a severe mental disease or defect. Because a person who is insane is not considered to be capable of killing with wilful intent, they cannot be charged with wilful murder. However, for this defence to be successful in court, the defendant's insanity has to be convincingly proved.

Another type of killer that can come under the general term of serial killer, is the mission killer, who wishes to purge the world of people who they believe are undesirables or worthless. For example, they may target prostitutes, homosexuals, paedophiles or drug addicts as in the case of Jack the Ripper who terrorised London in 1888 slaying prostitutes before removing their organs. Usually this killer is not considered to be psychotic or sexually motivated, they just single out their victims as being a burden to society.

Society would like to believe that killers are suffering from some sort of mental disorder, it is far too disconcerting to believe that they are really 'ordinary' people who simply lead a Jekyll and Hyde existence. As mentioned before, the caring, attentive nurse who secretly murders sick children, or the builder who enjoys torturing and killing young women and then burying them under his home, as in the case of Fred West.

Women who kill are not usually associated with sexual attacks, tortures or violence against their male counterparts, but of course there are always going to be those that break the rules as in the case of Aileen Wuornos. She has been dubbed America's first female serial killer as her killing spree left seven men dead. However, there will always be the question was she a cold-blooded killer or a tragic victim of violence and abuse who was just fighting back? Female killers are usually more careful, precise, methodical and quiet in committing their crimes and their preferred choice of weapon is poison.

Black Widows are famous for systematically killing spouses, partners or members of their families and they generally start their criminal career in their mid- to late-twenties. Again poison is the preferred weapon of choice with the aim of collecting life insurances or inheriting large sums of money. The first 20th-century Black Widow was Belle Gunness who killed 49 people, including husbands, suitors, ranch workers and her own children. She managed to lure husband after husband by advertising for suitors, asking them to bring large sums of cash to prove their worth and sincerity. Mind you the money was the only thing that survived, the husbands ended up as corpses wrapped up in rough sacks.

Ruth Ellis became famous for her *crime passionel* (crime of passion), when she killed her allegedly cruel boyfriend. She made history as the last woman to be executed in England and Wales. The crime of passion is not a new form of crime, in fact it is believed to be one of the first crimes ever committed in the killing of Abel by his brother Cain in Genesis, Ch. 4 in the Old Testament. This type of crime is quite unique in that the offender is very unlikely to have had a previous criminal history, not are they likely to ever offend again. It is generally a spur of the moment crime that is usually brought about by a rage of jealousy.

Assassination differs from other forms of murder in that the victim is usually a political figure, as in the case of Kennedy, or a popular public figure, for example, John Lennon. When interviewed, the majority of assassins are able to give a rational reason to justify their act. The reasons usually involve political values or money, as in the case of a contract killing, revenge against an individual or an act of espionage at the request of a government. Assassins often believe that they have the moral right to kill, some even say they were instructed by God. An assassin's so-called 'work' is completely separate from other aspects of their lives, usually leading a normal, healthy family life. Because it is just a business to them, they work quickly and leave the scene of the killing as fast as possible. Killing does not normally excite an assassin and they would consider killing anyone, other than their target, as very unprofessional.

Sadists are probably the most dangerous of our cold-blooded killers, as they gain great satisfaction out of inflicting pain and suffering upon another human being. The word was derived from Marquis de Sade, who was a French philosopher and author of sadistic novels and probably the most famous sadist in history. The serial killer Harvey Glatman was decidedly strange from an early age and his masochism soon turned into sadism. He had begun torturing himself at a very young age and it wasn't long before these urges completely took over his life. His frustration led him to molest and murder women because he feared and hated what they represented.

The infamous Texas killer, Kenneth Allen McDuff, earned himself the tag of predator and monster after years of committing ghastly murders. The sheer enormity of his evil forced the US government to bring about much-needed reforms on state legislature – he is believed to be the only US criminal ever to go to death row for one murder, get out of jail, then be sent back to death row for a completely different crime.

Killers in Cold Blood takes a chilling look at all these different types of crime. It exposes cases where the cold-blooded brutality and devious scheming behind a killing takes it to a new dimension – that of horror and disbelief. Many psychologists believe that many of us possess the animal instinct to kill to survive, but the only thing that stops us from carrying out this act is logic and our ability to reason. The stories in this book are all the stuff of nightmares and the depravity of these killers is beyond most people's comprehension. It is only the murderer who knows why they have chosen a particular victim or victims, why they opted for strangulation over shooting and why they left the body in such an explicit position. It is therefore the job of the investigators to try and get inside the sinister recesses of the brains of the cold-blooded killer.

PART ONE

ANCIENT MURDERERS

ATTILA THE HUN

During World Wars I and II the allies referred to the Germans as 'the Hun'. This was partly because the Huns were a pre-medieval Eastern European people whose empire included the area that became Germany. Also the Huns had a fearsome reputation for cruelty towards their neighbours from whom they stole lands and possessions.

King of the Huns during their heyday was Attila, who lived circa AD 406–453. Among historians he divides opinion. Some see him as the aggressive driving force behind the rape and pillage that the Huns delivered to those who stood in their way. Others see him as the driving force for Hun empirical expansion at a time in history when the whole of Europe was populated by warlike tribes.

By the time the Huns first came to prominence, in the fourth century, Europe had entered a period popularly known as the Dark Ages. The Ancient Roman Empire had reached critical mass and fragmented around AD

150, leaving the way open for nomadic tribes, such as the Huns, to begin establishing themselves without the Roman hand of repression. The Huns began to make their presence felt on the European stage by late third century. They moved into eastern central Europe and began a concerted campaign to oust or conquer existing populations. In fear for their lives, Germanic tribes began pouring westward from AD 406, which happens to have been the time when Attila was born into the world.

Until AD 434, the Huns were ruled by Rugila. Upon Rugila's death his two nephews Attila and Bleda took control. The Hunnic Empire was now on the up and up, comprising many conquered peoples who swore allegiance to the Huns. Attila and Bleda set their sights on taking as much territory as they could. They became the scourge of the two remaining factions of the former Ancient Roman Empire – the Western Roman Empire and the Byzantine Empire.

Attila and Bleda took many Roman prisoners and negotiated high ransoms for their safe return. They then turned their attentions to Persia, in the Middle East, with a five-year-long campaign, but they suffered a defeat in Armenia which served to divert their attentions back to Europe. Once more they rampaged their way through lands ruled by the Byzantine emperor Theodosius II, who was forced to agree to their demands.

Theodosius got his chance to reinforce his defences when Attila and Bleda took a sabbatical in AD 442. A year later they were back though, razing civilisations to the ground until they reached Constantinople, the capital of the Byzantine Empire. They failed to breach the city walls because they lacked the technological know-how to construct siege equipment. Despite this, Theodosius capitulated and paid an enormous sum in gold to make them leave him in peace.

Having sated their appetites for wealth and destruction, the two Hun kings retired to their heartlands in about AD 445. At this point, Bleda met with his death, at the hands of Attila according to legend, but it could have been due to any number of causes. By AD 447, Attila was back on the campaign trail, riding towards the Byzantines as sole king of the Huns and with unfinished business to attend to, having failed to take Constantinople four years earlier.

All attempts to halt Attila's onslaught failed until he reached the very walls of Constantinople. Once again, they proved too well built and defended for him to enter and sack the city. Nevertheless he forced negotiations with the Romans and, after three long years, got what he wanted – tributes to be paid in gold and the evacuation of vast swathes of land to add to his empire. Having failed in the east and succeeded in the south, Attila now tried his luck in the west.

Unlike the Byzantine ruler, Attila got along with the heads of the Western Roman Empire. General Flavius Aetius had defeated the Huns, earning him the title 'The Last of the Romans' and earning the respect and allegiance of Attila. Aetius had only been de facto ruler until Valentinian III was old enough to take to the throne. He too became Attila's ally, enabling the Huns to plan an attack on the Visigoths, whose kingdom comprised the area around Toulouse, in modern-day France.

Just as everything was set to invade the Visigoths, Valentinian's sister Honoria put a spanner in the works. She had been facing an arranged marriage to a Roman senator, to which she objected. She posted her engagement ring to Attila along with a message asking for his intervention. Attila interpreted her actions as an offer of marriage and accepted with a condition that he receive half of the Western Roman Empire as dowry.

When Valentinian discovered the plot he hit the roof and came close to having Honoria executed, but he settled for exile when their mother Galla Placidia made her feelings felt. Valentinian then sent message to Attila explaining that the whole thing had been a big mistake, but Attila was in no mood to hear it.

As a result, the Huns and Romans became sworn enemies. Attila amassed an enormous army of 500,000 troops and marched westwards. Aetius, whose loyalties lay with Valentinian, amassed his own army to defend the Western Roman Empire. The Visigoths were persuaded to join forces with the Romans and an almighty battle ensued at a place called Chalons, east of Paris.

Attila was defeated at the Battle of Chalons. He retreated eastwards with what remained of his army and never returned to the western front of his empire. The following year though, in AD 452, he decided to reawaken his claim to Honoria's hand in marriage and used it as his excuse to invade Italy.

To avoid the Alps, his army moved into the north of Italy over the Adriatic Sea. The town of Aquileia was sacked and razed to the ground by fire, causing many to flee to the safety of nearby islands, where they established Venezia, often known as Venice.

Aetius now reappeared on the scene, using his army to slow the southward advance of Attila. The Huns then came across the great River Po, which forms a natural defence east-to-west across the Italian peninsula. Having reached this impasse, Attila received a party of peacemakers, including Pope Leo the Great and a number of Roman dignitaries. Attila evidently realised the game was up as he decamped and headed north, having relinquished his claim to both Honoria's hand and any territories that might have come with it.

Historians are of the opinion that Attila gave in without further bloodshed because his army had become demoralised by a combination of factors. Aetius' relentless wearing down of his forces wouldn't have helped, but famine and plague seem to have been the key ingredients. He knew that his army would only become steadily depleted if he continued, so he made the strategic decision to evacuate while he still could.

Attila made his way back to his palace across the River Danube, in modern day Hungary, and before long was planning a third attempt at taking Constantinople. This is where Attila's story ends however, for he died in early AD 453.

The circumstances of his death are not entirely clear, but a number of theories exist. It seems that he may have died from a haemorrhage brought on by natural causes or excessive drinking. Alternatively, he may have been knifed by his seventh wife, Ilico. The only consistent detail is the mention of blood.

It seems unlikely that his wife was involved though, for she would certainly have been executed, such was Attila's following. Also, it is said that his horsemen sang a dirge, declaring that they couldn't describe his dying as a true death because there was no one to blame. In other words, he hadn't died in battle or under suspicious circumstances.

There is another theory that the new ruler of the Eastern Roman Empire, Marcian, had conspired to have Attila killed. It is conceivable that he may have haemorrhaged due to poisoning, but it seems unlikely.

Attila's body was apparently buried beneath a river named the Tisza. His most devoted soldiers dammed and diverted the flow before interring his coffin into the river bed. They then volunteered their lives so that the exact location would remain a secret. Legend has it that the coffin was made from iron and embellished with gold and silver.

When Attila died his legacy was fought over by his sons. With a lack of cohesion the Hunnic Empire became immediately vulnerable. It came to an end at the Battle of Nedao in AD 455, when an Ostrogoth-Gepid alliance annihilated the Hunnish army.

The reputation of Attila the Hun is based on his ruthlessness when it came to conquest. He seems to have been quite reasonable to those whom he genuinely got on with or who complied with his rules and demands. He clearly, however, had a disregard for the value of human life, which showed itself in the field of battle and while on the warpath. If commoners didn't manage to flee, then they would be slain without mercy. Similarly, enemy soldiers would be taken prisoner and executed if ransoms were not paid for their release.

It would be fair to say though, that life was cheap to everyone in that period of history. Different tribes fundamentally believed themselves to be superior to all others, so they though nothing of killing every last man, woman and child – genocide as we now call it. As a matter of fact, it has been suggested that atrocities committed in the Balkans recently stem from a tribal mentality that has survived in the area since the time of the Huns.

In addition, the Ancient Roman Empire had compressed barbarian populations into a relatively small part of Europe. This inevitably created a melting pot of warlike tribes vying for available resources and space. This was the social environment that Attila was born into. If you didn't become the aggressor and dominate, then someone else would. It was really a matter of survival.

Part of the myth and legend surrounding Attila also stems from the fact that the Roman world was one of burgeoning Christianity at the time. The Romans aspired to notions of being civilized, which meant recognising the value of human life in the eyes of their new omnipotent god.

So, Attila fell victim to the propaganda machine. He was portrayed as the Antichrist, intent on the destruction and extortion of his fellow humans because he wasn't civilized enough to know any better. Much the same thing happened to other leaders of barbarian tribes, as demonizing was a useful way of exaggerating the differences between holiness and unholiness in a Europe about to emerge from the Dark Ages.

GENGHIS KHAN

Originally named Temujin, after his place of birth, the man who would later become Genghis Khan was born into the Mongol clan known as the Borjigin in circa AD 1162. He became khan, or ruler, in AD 1206 and died in AD 1227. His legacy was the largest homogeneous empire in world history – that is to say, it comprised a contiguous area of territory, stretching from modern-day Korea in the east to the Black Sea in the west, and Russia in the north to Afghanistan in the south.

The secret behind Genghis Khan's success was his uniting of all the Mongolian tribes into a single Mongol Empire. He also created an army where promotion and position were merit related – a meritocracy – as opposed to accident of birth and wealth – an aristocracy. This did wonders for military morale and ambition, so that the whole force remained loyal to his cause.

Genghis Khan had to learn to fend for himself from a very early age. While still a child his father was murdered. He and his family were then cast out and thereby exiled from their clan as Genghis was successor to his father as clan leader, but deemed too young for the position. That experience taught him to lead and protect his immediate family, but to distrust others and seek vengeance. His family had to adopt a nomadic existence, hunting and gathering to survive.

His first act of murder was performed on his older half-brother Bekhter, whom he shot with an arrow. Genghis had promoted himself to head of the family by taking the life of another. It was to set the pattern for the remainder of his life.

Sometime later Genghis was captured by another tribe and humiliated with a device named a cangue, which is a form of wooden stock that is carried on the shoulders. He was assisted in his escape by the father of a man who would later become a general in his army. This experience taught him the value of friendship and alliance.

By the time he reached adulthood, he was of toughened character, able to survive in the harshest of conditions and kill if necessary, but also able to win friends and influence people. He already had the makings of the great and ruthless leader he would eventually become.

Genghis' masterstroke was to negotiate a confederation between many of the Central Asian tribes – the beginning of his Mongol Empire. This had a double purpose: it brought to an end much of the intertribal warring that had characterised Central Asia for hundreds of years and it enabled Genghis to amass a good sized army.

In order that every member of the confederation remained obedient to the greater cause, a code of Mongol laws was drawn up, called the Yassa Code. The key incentive for everyone to comply was the promise of untold wealth from the spoils of conquest. In addition, the Yassa Code made it clear that civilians and warriors would benefit from an egalitarian philosophy. That meant that all individuals would be treated as equals and thus they were all rewarded according to the merits of their conduct and achievements.

At that time, Genghis was still known as Temujin, and he was in charge of only his own tribal division within the confederation. So, he too had to prove himself if he wanted to earn additional power within the meritocracy.

Perhaps inevitably, tensions arose between tribes in the confederation as different khans jostled for power and influence. One thing led to another, so that different khans fell by the wayside following civil conflicts. Eventually, it came down to Temujin and an old friend, turned enemy, Jamuqa who had adopted the title Gur Khan (Universal Ruler).

Jamuqa was eventually captured and imprisoned following a battle with Temujin's forces. Temujin offered

Jamuqa the chance for reconciliation and a place in his army but he chose execution. As he wasn't to die in the field of battle Jamuqa elected to have his back broken as an honourable death as it meant that his blood wouldn't have been spilled for no reason.

This is the point in history when Temujin adopted the title Genghis Khan (Ruler of All). It also marked the point when all tribes joined the confederation to become known as one people: the Mongols. It was the year AD 1206 and the Mongol Empire was on the map. Genghis Khan was omnipotent leader of about a 250,000 people and he had plans!

The Mongol Empire was boxed in by two Chinese Dynasties: immediately to the east was the Western Xia Dynasty of the Tanguts, to the south-east and the south there was the Jin Dynasty of the Nuzhen. Genghis set his sights on conquering the former as his opening gambit. He briefed his army for an invasion and made his move.

He had predicted that the Jin would fail to help the Western Xia, partly because of the difficult geography involved, but mainly because the Jin emperor was relatively young and naive to the potential threat of the Mongols. This was, in part, because the Jin had a history of lording it over the Mongolian tribes and therefore underestimated the change brought about by Genghis Khan.

Having also defeated a tribe called the Jurchen, who were sworn enemies of the Mongols, Genghis Khan had taken control of the Western Xia territory by ad 1209. He was now poised for vengeance over the Jin.

His campaign began in ad 1211 with a massacre at a place called Badger Pass. A Jin messenger had defected with some counter-intelligence that the Jin army was waiting in ambush. Genghis Khan trapped the Jin Army and mercilessly slaughtered all those who failed to escape. This atrocity was perhaps the event that cemented his reputation as a cold-blooded killer. Not least because the bones of the Chinese dead littered the floor of the pass for many years afterwards. Four years later Genghis Khan had reached the capital of the Jin Dynasty – modern-day Beijing. He besieged the city before capturing and sacking it.

Genghis Khan now set his sights westward, on the Khwarezmid Empire, which covered an area that roughly equates to modern-day eastern Iran, Turkmenistan, Uzbekistan, Tajikistan, southern Kazakhstan, western Afghanistan and Kyrgyzstan. In those days, the area comprised Persia and Transoxiana. As a matter of fact, Genghis Khan originally set out to establish a trading relationship with the Khwarezmians, who were a Muslim people, but his efforts were rejected in no uncertain terms.

Firstly a 500-man Mongol trading caravan was massacred and then a group of ambassadors received an unorthodox welcome. They all had their head's shaved before being beheaded. Just one was allowed to live and travel back to Genghis Khan with the insulting news. Not surprisingly, Genghis Khan gave the Khwarezmians what was coming to them. His army marched on the city of Otrar and defeated the defending army. The governor of the city was then executed by Genghis Khan in person as retribution for his insults. He had molten silver poured into his eyes and ears.

The Mongol force then brutally murdered the citizens of Otrar. They took lives as readily as they took the spoils of war, until nothing was left to take. Then Genghis Khan sent two of his generals to hunt down the Shah, who had fled the scene to avoid surrender. He eventually died in hiding on an island and with his demise the Khwarezmid Empire was gone forever. The year was AD 1220.

For the remainder of Genghis Khan's life he focussed on maintaining his empire and launching further campaigns against the Chinese, for whom he had a particular dislike. He sent generals west to advance on territory west of the Caspian Sea – namely modern-day Georgia, Armenia, Azerbaijan and part of Russia (Volga–Bulgaria) – but the Mongol Empire had reached its limit of expansion.

On August 18, 1227, Genghis Khan died while on a military campaign against his old adversaries the Tanguts of the Western Xia Dynasty. Details are unclear, but it seems that his advancing years got the better of him when he was thrown by his horse. A funeral escort took his body back to his homeland, where he was buried in secret. Just like Attila the Hun, it is rumoured that his remains lie beneath a river bed, except that this time a river was diverted to flow over the site.

Much has been written about the supposed cruelty and destruction wrought by Genghis Khan. In truth, it seems that most of it stems from propaganda issued by the Persians and the Chinese, who found themselves at the receiving end of his aggression. Clearly though, they played a part in antagonising him, simply because they were warlike nations themselves. It can therefore be argued that Genghis Khan was simply making a good job of ensuring that they would no longer pose a threat.

It is well documented that he preferred to give nations the chance to become part of his empire without a fight. If they refused to submit and comply with his conditions, then would he come down with a heavy fist. Only when he had lost his respect and patience would he turn to meting out severe punishments, such as exterminating entire populations. However, this was done because it made no tactical sense to allow an insurgent population to continue living within the bounds of the Mongol Empire.

Genghis Khan has been blamed for countless millions of deaths in China, but it is likely that many can be attributed to the Black Death, which was a pandemic of bubonic plague that coincidentally originated in Central Asia at that time and eventually swept its way across most of the Old World.

Of course, pestilence and disease often come in the wake of warfare anyway, due to the presence of corpses and the resulting lack of infrastructure that can mean low standards of hygiene and so on. So any number of causes may have contributed to the Asian deaths.

Interestingly, there is evidence to suggest that Genghis Khan was a spiritual man. In his twilight years, he developed a fascination for Taoism. A monk named Ch'ang Ch'un came to meet him at the Afghanistan border, but Genghis Khans motive for summoning him soon became apparent. He asked the monk for a potion to make him immortal.

Even though he was disappointed that the monk wasn't a magician or shaman, Genghis Khan decreed that Taoists should be exempt from paying his taxes. He was noted for his tolerance of all religions, just as long as the followers were compliant. If his trust was betrayed however, then their places of worship were razed to the ground to teach them a lesson.

In conclusion, Genghis Khan certainly seems to have been something of a despot and his Mongol Empire a totalitarian regime. Nevertheless, people could choose their fate. If they accepted the rules of Mongol oppression then they could live quite happily and safely. If they rebelled against those rules, then they could expect to be treated with short shrift and cut down in cold blood. 'You takes your pick' might have been Genghis Khan's motto.

VLAD THE IMPALER

When it comes to cold-blooded killers Vlad the Impaler must surely take the prize. He ran up a list of atrocities as long as your arm. As his name suggests, he had a predilection for impaling people on wooden stakes. His preferred method was to insert a sharpened and greased pole through the rectum and run it through the torso until it exited through the mouth. This was done while the unfortunate victims had their legs pulled apart by two horses. They were then hoisted into an upright position and left to die in agony, which sometimes took three or four days.

Vlad's reputation was such that he became the stuff of horrifying folk tales that served to warn children of the dangers of misbehaving and disobeying their parents. In 1897, the Irish author Bram Stoker found enough inspiration in the tales to invent the story of Count Dracula, an immortal vampire who feasted on the blood of his victims. The fictitious Dracula had a morbid fear of the holy cross and could be killed by being impaled with a wooden stake through the heart. Vlad was in fact known in Eastern Europe as Dracula as it is derived from the word 'dracul', which translates as 'devil', 'demon' or 'dragon'. This was because his father had been a member of the Order of the Dragon and given the surname 'Dracul'.

He was a Wallachian (Romanian) prince in real life. His real name was Vlad Tepes, or Vlad III, as his father and grandfather had also been named Vlad. He was born in 1431 and spent his formative years witnessing constant persecution of his family and clan by the Ottoman Turks and Hungarians. This was the root of his behaviour in later years, as he grew hell-bent on retribution.

Even though he was a prince by birth the Romanian system dictated that the new leader be elected by the aristocracy, who were known as boyars. That meant getting the boyars on side, which all depended on the political situation at the time.

His father, Vlad II Dracul, had become prince of Wallachia in 1436 but then been removed from power six years later due to gerrymandering over a war between the Ottomans and Hungarians. He regained the throne 1443–47 but was then assassinated on the orders of the regent of Hungary, Hunyadi. The method of death was quite unsavoury, for he had his face cut around the edges and then ripped off while still alive and conscious.

Vlad was born in Wallachia, but was raised in exile in Transylvania. His father was murdered when he was at the impressionable age of sixteen. Before this Vlad and his younger brother Radu had suffered at the hands of the Ottomans who held them hostage to force their father into siding with the them against the Hungarians, which is why he ultimately died at the hands of the latter.

While a hostage, Vlad was locked in a dungeon and harshly treated while Radu was favoured. Vlad developed a deep seated mistrust of family. His brother had sided with the Ottomans and his father had left him to rot to save his own skin.

His luck changed slightly following his father's death when the Ottomans placed Vlad on the throne of Wallachia as a puppet ruler – Vlad III. His reign was brief as the Hungarians then invaded, but Vlad was at least free, so he fled to Moldavia, where he lived in exile with his uncle, Bogdan II, until 1451.

The next chapter saw his uncle assassinated. Vlad was left between a rock and hard place and fled to the Hungarian court. There he met Hunyadi, the very man who had killed his father. He might have been killed on the spot, but he impressed the Hungarians with his knowledge of the Ottoman court, having lived there for a number of years. Hunyadi saw the potential in having Vlad repositioned on the throne of Wallachia as an ally, so allowed him his life and freedom. He was pardoned and became political advisor to Hunyadi.

By now Wallachia was no longer in Hunyadi's hands, so Vlad would have to wait for the right opportunity to return. That opportunity came in 1456. The Hungarians launched a campaign against the Ottomans to remove them from Serbia. Vlad took an army and simultaneously invaded Wallachia while the Ottomans were busy against the Hungarians. He became Vlad III once more and began a reign of terror for six years.

Vlad found himself surrounded by potential enemies, both real and imagined. He set about eliminating anyone who might pose a threat to his rule: namely the Ottomans, the Hungarians and his fellow Wallachian nobility, the boyars. He had enemies without and enemies within. That meant that just about everyone was in the firing line, as even the commoners and peasantry might very well side with an enemy if push came to shove. He should have been dubbed 'Vlad the Paranoid' such was his suspicion that no one could be trusted.

In one incident, he had a number of boyars impaled and then forced their families into hard labour, building his new castle. They toiled away until they died from sheer exhaustion and were simply replaced by others.

Vlad became something like Joseph Stalin in his relentless obsession with watching his back. Thousands of people – men, women and children – died by impalement. Many were simply thrust onto erect stakes that stood on the perimeters of cities. The sight of putrefying corpses on poles became familiar to anyone who lived within the Wallachian kingdom. Inevitably, Vlad's attempts at omnipotence only served to degrade further the infrastructure of the nation he ruled. Anarchy and crime took hold, so Vlad had no choice but to deliver punishments to restore a semblance of law and order. With social chaos he would have been vulnerable to invasion by external enemies, so he found himself in a vicious cycle.

During the first few years of his reign, Vlad had paid a tribute to the Ottomans to prevent them from invading his territory. In 1459, the Hungarians began plans to attack the Ottomans, so Vlad stopped his payments and formed an alliance with the Hungarians. He then took an army across the River Danube and ransacked the lands between the Black Sea and Serbia. It is reckoned that he left around 20,000 dead in his wake.

His revenge on the Ottoman Turks backfired on him. In 1462, the Ottomans launched a counter-offensive with a 60,000 strong army. Vlad had less than half that number of troops and failed to prevent the Turks from taking his capital city Targoviste. He had no choice but to resort to guerrilla-style tactics. By organising relentless ambushes and raids, he eventually encouraged the Turks to leave, but they had a trick up their sleeve. They installed Vlad's younger brother Radu as ruling monarch of Wallachia. He quickly gathered support in light of the atrocities committed by Vlad, who was chased into exile again in Transylvania.

Eventually, Vlad was caught and 'imprisoned' by the Hungarians. For the next twelve years he actually lived in the Hungarian court, where he married and had children. The Hungarians always viewed him as an ally, so they protected him with a view to eventually re-turning him to the Wallachian throne.

Interestingly, he became a Catholic Christian during this period of his life. Nevertheless, he could not let his old habits die with his new found faith. To entertain his need to inflict suffering, he would torture and impale birds and mice to watch their agonising death throes. This would suggest that Vlad had become a sadist, unable to correct his behaviour even with the teachings and guidance of the Bible.

Come 1475, Vlad had regained his freedom and pre-pared to reclaim the Wallachian throne. By now his brother Radu had died and Basarab – another Ottoman ally – was ruler of Wallachia. Vlad managed to usurp

Basarab quite easily, but his Hungarian army returned home once he was back in power, so that his position was vulnerable.

Vlad found that the Wallachian boyars and peasants alike had had enough of his depravity towards them, so they naturally reasoned that continued rule by Basarab would be a better option. The Ottomans sent in an army to find Vlad with barely 4,000 defenders of his throne.

Vlad didn't stand a chance and met his death in 1476. No one knows exactly how he died, but his head was removed and preserved in honey. It was then sent to Istanbul (Constantinople until 1453), where it was displayed by the Sultan as proof that the scourge of the Turks was dead – Kazikli Bey, as they called him. Appropriately enough, his head was exhibited impaled on a wooden stake.

There can be little doubt that Vlad the Impaler's compulsion to torture, maim and kill his fellow humans was the result of a personality flaw. He seems to have practised just about every form of cruelty available to him and been the inspiration for the phrase 'man's inhumanity to man'.

The list includes: blinding, boiling and burning, scalping, skinning and strangling, removal of ears, noses, lips and limbs, mutilation of sexual organs, impalement with wooden stakes and nails, and exposure to the elements and wild animals.

Ironically, his interest in Christianity and eventual conversion to Catholicism may have encouraged his cruelty. The reason is that Christianity holds with the idea of an afterlife, so Vlad may have reasoned that he was doing nothing more than freeing people's souls from the shackles of their earthly existence. Catholicism also offers confession, so that the absolution of sins is achieved. In other words, he gave himself license to become Dracula the monster in the name of Christianity itself.

It seems that a number of internal and external agents came together in Vlad the Impaler. The result was a human with an absence of compassion for his species or any other. The act of inflicting suffering on others became the very lifeblood on which he voraciously fed, so perhaps that is the notion that Bram Stoker had of him when he metamorphosed Vlad into Count Dracula the supernatural vampire.

CESARE BORGIA

Fratricide is the term used to describe the act of murdering one's own brother. That was the kind of crime that Cesare Borgia thought nothing of committing to get what he wanted from life, but then his whole family were no saints.

The Borgias are famed for their patronage of Renaissance artists in Italy, including Michelangelo and Leonardo da Vinci. The family actually originated from Spain, and they became leading players in the game of wealth, power and political influence in Renaissance Europe, which was centred on Italy. They used plenty of underhand tricks to secure and maintain their position, such as poisoning rivals. The family spoke Valencian to one another as a means of privacy and security to ensure that outsiders had difficulty in obtaining intelligence about their dealings.

Cesare Borgia was born in 1476. He was the younger and favoured son of Pope Alexander VI. He initially became Archbishop and then Cardinal of Valencia – an area on the eastern coast of Spain – in his early twenties, thanks to the nepotism of his father. In 1497, he was implicated in the murder of his elder brother Giovanni, the Duke of Gandia. It seems that his motive was to acquire the undivided attentions of the pope, as he was envious of Giovanni's position and wanted to free himself from his ecclesiastical duties to pursue a secular career. He duly resigned in 1498 and embarked on his new journey.

The pope made Cesare the papal legate (ambassador to the pope) in France, where he formed a political alliance with King Louis XII. Before long he was made Duke of Valentinois in south-east France. By 1499, he had married the sister of the king of Navarre, a Basque region in north-east Spain. He now took advantage of the Second Italian War, which saw the French invade Italy, to take control of the Romagna region in north-east Italy. By 1501, the Pope had made him Duke of Romagna. He then added to his territory by taking areas to the south, including Urbino, Elba, Piombino and Camerino. In order to make certain of his position, he rounded up many of his political rivals and had them summarily murdered by strangulation at the Castle of Senigallia.

Having done all he could to assert his power Cesare was dealt a blow. In 1503, his father was killed by poison and then he too was poisoned. Cesare managed to recover, but the political landscape had suddenly changed, leaving him vulnerable. The new pope, Pius III, had Cesare arrested, but died under suspicious circumstances after a pontificate of only twenty-six days. Things got worse for Cesare. While he was still weak from poisoning, an enemy of his named Giuliano della Rovere tricked his way into the papacy to become Pope Julius II, who would become known as the 'Warrior Pope'. To make things worse, King Louis XII of France now turned against Cesare, leaving him compromised and in decline.

Cesare had his titles and lands taken from him. He was then arrested in Naples and extradited to prison in Spain as the result of an agreement between Julius II and the monarchs of Spain, Ferdinand and Isabella. He escaped from prison in 1506 and fled to Navarre, where his brother-in-law King John III gave him refuge. Cesare died only a year later in battle defending Viana.

Cesare Borgia relied on the nepotism of his father, Pope Alexander VI, to achieve all of his aims in life – papal patronage. This was made abundantly clear when his career dramatically came to an end with the death of the pope. He evidently failed to forge a reputation for being a self-made man as a result of this assistance, which is why his enemies immediately went in for the kill as soon as he no longer enjoyed the protection of the Catholic Church. If anyone ever needed an illustration of what people really think about nepotism then they should look no further than Cesare Borgia. In essence, he was nothing more than a spoilt child given licence to cheat his way into power. That power shrivelled away like a burst balloon once his father was no longer there to keep it inflated.

Given Cesare Borgias credentials, it may seem odd that in some quarters he is thought of as something of a hero. The reason for this is that he happened to be rather handsome and cut a fine figure. This made him something of a ladies' man and inspired historians to see him as something more than the wing-hider that he really was. None more so than a contemporary of his named Niccolo Machiavelli.

Machiavelli was an Italian statesman and political philosopher who was completely taken in by Borgia's charms when he met him in person and stayed at court over the winter 1502–3. He began by writing admiring reports of Borgia's exploits and despatching them to Florence. In 1532, he published a book titled The Prince, which was modelled on Cesar Borgia. The book was a work of philosophy in which he advised that it is necessary to employ unethical practises to acquire power and then use it effectively. Basically, the message was to imitate Borgia.

In modern-day language, we use the term 'Machiavellian' to describe people who are unscrupulous, corrupt and scheming in their political dealings. Machiavelli and Borgia would have considered those qualities to be virtues, but the term is used as a pejorative term in this day and age. An example is the way in which certain governments in Russia think it is perfectly acceptable to remove political enemies by killing them, rather than tolerating their opposing points of view. Truly democratic and ethical governments consider this to be Machiavellian, which amounts to saying that they are lacking in ethical substance and are politically primitive in their conduct.

To Cesare Borgia's credit, he did personally employ Leonardo da Vinci at one point, although not as an artist, but as a military engineer and architect. Da Vinci joined Borgia in 1500 and worked for him over a five-year period. He travelled with his patron to different parts of his territory, helping to improve Borgia's defences. An example of this collaboration was the design of the port at Cesenatico on the Adriatic coast.

Borgia's reputation as a cold-blooded killer stems from his general behaviour. He was always unnecessarily cruel and unsympathetic towards the peoples that he invaded and readily resorted to murder to manipulate the political situation. For example, he had his own brother-in-law, the Duke of Bisceglie, assassinated because he had had a quarrel with Borgia and was related to enemies of his father, the pope. He was the third husband of the famous Lucrezia Borgia. In fact, the first assassination attempt left him fighting for his life, so Cesare sent in the assassins again to finish the job.

On another occasion he double-crossed the Lord of Faenza, Astorre Manfredi, while on a military campaign in Romagna. Manfredi agreed to surrender on condition that his life be spared. Borgia immediately broke his word and had Manfredi put to death.

It is fair to say that Cesare Borgia was really something of a cad, for he would take whatever road he deemed necessary to achieve his goals without any sense of honour or shame. As is often the case with cads though, he was apparently rather charming and affable as a personality, which helped him to beguile people into a false sense of security before taking their lives.

He may have thought that he was somehow blessed by his abilities and skills until it became abundantly clear that he had none and no one really trusted him or liked him once his father was removed from the picture. In the end, it came down to the adage 'be nice to people on the way up, as you might meet them again on the way down'. Clearly his journey down was spectacularly precipitous because he found that he had no allies to speak of.

He had failed to inspire friendship or loyalty in anyone and was treated like a common criminal – the exact opposite of what he evidently aspired to be.

HENRY VIII

When King Henry VIII came to the throne in England the year was 1509. Pope Julius II (Warrior Pope), the man who had destroyed Cesare Borgia in Europe, would remain in power for another four years. The relationship between England and the Catholic Church had already become strained under the rule of Henry VII, and things were about to get a lot worse. Henry VIII was what people now term a 'control freak'. He liked to live according to his own rules and found the rulings of the Vatican more than he could bear.

In 1502, Henry became Prince of Wales and heir to the English throne because his elder brother Arthur had died. In the same year that he became king, Henry married his brother's widow Catherine of Aragon, who happened to be the daughter of Ferdinand and Isabella of Spain, who had imprisoned Cesare Borgia until his escape. Catherine was, of course, a devout Catholic and Henry married her out of a sense of duty to his family and nation. He was eighteen years of age and ruggedly handsome, while his first wife was twenty-four and no oil painting.

For the next two decades Henry ran a successful court and excelled at his duties as head of state. He had an athletic physique and an alert mind, making him effective both in the field of battle and in matters of government. That part of his reign was dominated by political dealings abroad with the French, Spanish and Italians, who were always at war over territory. This did much to propagate his annoyance at the Catholic Church, to which the foreigners all looked for instruction and guidance.

He was even more intolerant of the teaching of Martin Luther, who promoted a version of Christianity called Protestantism, so called because it 'protested' at the extravagancies of the Catholic Church. Henry played his part in attacking Luther by publishing a written assault titled the *Assertio*. In reaction, followers of Luther would used the term 'catholic' to denote an undiscerning mind, as in the phrase 'catholic tastes', alluding to the Catholic Church's liking for gaudy decorations and embellishments.

Ironically, Henry was accorded the title 'Defender of the Faith' by Pope Leo X as recognition of his work against the Protestants. With his newfound papal favour, Henry began to consider approaching the Vatican about the possibility of divorcing Queen Catherine. Their only surviving child was female – Mary (I) – and Henry wanted a male heir to the throne. Catherine was too old to produce more children, so Henry decided that a new wife was in order.

Henry had his eye on a potential new queen named Anne Boleyn, so he instructed his politicians to negotiate an annulment of his marriage to Catherine. The Pope refused and tensions began to ferment between Henry and the Vatican. After eight years of political wrangling, Henry finally had enough and declared his marriage null and void in 1533. He then married Ann Boleyn in secret. When the pope discovered the truth he excommunicated Henry from the Catholic Church. Henry simply responded by declaring himself head of the Church of England. Anne Boleyn happened to be a Protestant, so the new church followed those lines, although still retaining some Catholic vestiges.

Having married Anne Boleyn, something had changed in Henry. He had grown omnipotent in temperament and fickle with it. After three years Anne had only produced another daughter – Elizabeth (I). He chose to trade Ann in for a new model in 1536. To escape his second marriage, he trumped up charges of infidelity and had Ann beheaded before marrying Jane Seymour. She gave birth to his short-lived heir Edward VI, but died following childbirth.

Henry married his fourth wife Anne of Cleves in 1540, but wanted out before the year was finished, so applied for his second divorce. His fifth wife Catherine Howard was married in the same year and lasted two more years before becoming the second wife to lose her head. His sixth wife Catherine Parr became the only one to avoid both divorce and beheading, but only because she outlived Henry, who died in 1547.

When Henry turned his back on the Catholic Church in 1533 he had to deal with the many Roman Catholics still living in England at the time. There were many monasteries scattered over the country, so Henry encouraged their persecution and repression. By 1536, he was ready for a more proactive approach to the Catholic problem, so he initiated a period in English history called the Reformation. It was so-called because it resulted in the dissolution of the monasteries so that the religious infrastructure was 'reformed' into one of Protestant values. In 1539, Henry ordered that the surviving monasteries be razed to the ground, signalling the end of Roman Catholicism and diverting total control of ecclesiastical affairs to the Crown.

It would be an exaggeration to say that Henry VIII was a ruthless monarch. It is true that he chose execution as a means of dealing with certain members of court, including Anne Boleyn and Catherine Howard, but it was in part because of the law at the time. His chief minister Thomas Cromwell was a famous example of this.

Cromwell had been instrumental in the downfall of Anne Boleyn, but he also arranged Henry's marriage to Anne of Cleves following the untimely death of Jane Seymour. His marriage to Anne remained unconsummated because Henry couldn't bring himself to arousal as she was so unattractive. Cromwell had shown Henry a portrait of Anne by Hans Holbein in which she had a pleasant appearance, so he agreed to the marriage. He was duly shocked when he met her in person, but had to go ahead with the betrothal for political reasons. Henry's embarrassment eventually caught up with Cromwell, who was arrested on the charge of treason and executed as a traitor to the king.

Anne Boleyn's downfall began when she miscarried a son and heir to the throne. A number of male courtiers and aristocrats were arrested by Cromwell on the charge of having affairs with the queen. It is not clear whether the queen actually did commit adultery, but the king clearly wanted to end the marriage, so she went to trial without any prospect of being found innocent. She was executed along with the accused men, who included her own brother George Boleyn, accused of incest.

Catherine Howard's story was slightly different, in that she definitely did have an affair. Before she caught Henry's eye she began a relationship with a courtier named Thomas Culpepper. That relationship continued behind Henry's back. As rumours surfaced Catherine attempted to silence people by appointing them positions in court. Francis Dereham was among those shown favour and he turned out to have had an affair with Catherine before Henry had met her. Catherine, Culpepper and Dereham all went to the block.

The fall of the axe was a common punishment in Tudor times, so Henry would have regarded it a reasonable sentence. He was omnipotent as monarch at that point in history, so any behaviour that saw him betrayed or embarrassed was punishable by death. His actions probably had greater impact on the many Roman Catholics in his kingdom. The dissolution of the monasteries and the reformations of the Church would have caused widespread upheaval across the land. In 1534, a Treason Act was passed that to deny Royal Supremacy over the Church was to commit high treason and so punishable by death.

Thomas More, Lord Chancellor to Henry VIII, was a Roman Catholic who refused to acknowledge the king's claim to being the head of the Church of England and paid with his life by the axe in 1535. Another victim of the new law was William Tyndale. He was a Protestant reformer who translated the Bible into English and distributed it under Henry's nose. His punishment was partial strangulation followed by burning at the stake.

These two examples demonstrate clearly that Henry showed equal distain towards both the Catholic and Protestant faiths, which is why his new Church of England was something of a hybrid of the two. Interestingly the faiths of his six wives had been a mix, so perhaps that played a part in Henry's decision to settle at a compromise. That way all of his people would grow to accept it rather than rise up in rebellion as some had done in certain parts of the country. Civil war was thus avoided at that stage in English history.

An intriguing consequence of Henry's actions against the Catholic Church was that Britain grew to be the leading light in scientific progress. In turn, it would become the dominant force in industrial modernisation. Elsewhere in civilized Europe scientists would face Catholic inquisitions and charges of blasphemy for daring to suggest that natural laws dictated and explained the way things work. While scientists such as Copernicus and Galileo would be persecuted on the continent, Newton and others would be celebrated in England.

IVAN THE TERRIBLE

You'd have to have a pretty bad reputation to earn the epithet 'the Terrible', so what was so terrible about Ivan? Well, the answer is that he went one better than Cesare Borgia, who famously killed his own brother. Ivan actually killed his own son – also called Ivan – in a fit of blinding rage during a row. This act of filicide, as it is technically known, removed the heir to the throne. As it happened the argument was catalysed by the fact that Ivan, the elder, had beaten his daughter-in-law, causing her to miscarry. So, he had in fact removed two possible heirs to the throne in one fell swoop of madness. When he died his kingdom was left to his younger son Feodor, who was wholly unfit to reign and childless to boot.

Ivan the Terrible was properly known as Ivan Vasilyevich, or Tsar Ivan IV of Russia. In truth his popular name arose due to a whole list of atrocities during his reign, topped off by killing Ivan the younger. His reign formally began when he was aged just three years, but he didn't actually assume the role of tsar until he was fourteen. His formative years had been spent being generally mistreated and neglected by the people charged with looking after him – families of aristocrats, or boyars, known as the Shuiskys and Belskys. Consequently, he grew into a young man with an intrinsic hatred of boyars and a malicious streak that was expressed by his cruelty to animals. The signs for his lack of mental stability in later years were already there as a teenager, just like Vlad the Impaler.

Despite his burgeoning penchant for cruelty, Ivan spent the first nine years of his reign in positive and constructive mood. He did much to expand the realm of Russia, turning it into the multiethnic region it remains today with its mix of races and religions. This included the conquest of Siberian and Tatar (Central Asian, Mongolian and Turkic) regions, to the north-east and east of Russia.

Things started to go wrong though when Ivan fell seriously ill in 1553. His wife Anastasia died at the same time and Ivan suspected the boyars of having murdered her with poison. This was in part because they has refused to swear an oath of allegiance to his infant son – Ivan the younger – in case Ivan died of his illness. When Ivan eventually recovered his health the boyars had hell to pay.

He wrought vengeance on the boyars so that many were brutally murdered whether guilty or innocent. By

1565, Ivan was so paranoid about his position that he had formed a police state called the Oprichnina in which he was omnipotent, so that the boyars held no sway over his power. His personal guard were known as the Oprichniki. They dressed in black and had a ruthless reputation, something like that of Hitler's SS.

The latter years of Ivan's reign saw his mental health progressively deteriorate. At the same time, he set his sights on expanding his kingdom westward so that he might establish sea trade links with Western Europe and elsewhere via the Baltic Sea. This resulted in prolonged periods of warfare with Scandinavian and Eastern European nations who resisted his attempts at invasion. Added to the terrors of war there came the plague, which swept through the region leaving economic collapse in its wake as already beleaguered populations were decimated.

Ivan became more and more introspective within his policed realm. He seems to have suffered from severe manic depression, or bipolar condition as it is now called, for his periods of mania were punctuated by periods of calm. He was known to fluctuate from orgies of sexual depravity and violence to locking himself away in a monastery for the purpose of prayer and fasting. Lithium tablets were unavailable in his day, so his illness progressed until he became a liability to himself – by now he was both mentally and physically impaired by his horrible affliction.

Without a stable and coherent leader the Oprichniki fell into disarray. Their leader Malyuta Skuratov let the power go to his head and took matters into his own control. Before long they were committing atrocious massacres wherever and whenever they came across resistance to their regime. The depopulation of areas resulted in famine and disease so that Russia became a fragmented nation. One of the worst atrocities occurred at a place called Novgorod. The city had already lost about 10,000 people to the plague. Now it lost tens of thousands more as the Oprichniki did their worst.

By the 1580s, Ivan had metamorphosed into a raving maniac. This was when he lashed out at his daughter-in-law, for wearing immodest clothing it is said. One thing led to another and Ivan ended up guilty of two counts of manslaughter – his eldest son and unborn grandchild were dead, killed by him in a state of thoroughly diminished responsibility. The final years of his life were spent flying in and out of fearsome rages, earning him a reputation as a monster capable of rape and murder.

Ivan the Terrible finally died in 1584 at the age of fifty-four. Legend has it that he died setting up a chessboard in the company of Bogdan Belsky, a member of one of the boyar families he had loathed from childhood. His remains were disinterred in the 1960s for scientific analysis, and it was discovered that he had high levels of mercury in his body. It is possible that the Belskys had gradually poisoned him with the mercury, but he may also have been taking a mercury compound as a treatment for syphilis. Either way, the mercury would certainly have played its part in his madness, as would the syphilis if he had had that, too.

It seems likely that Ivan the Terrible was probably not quite so terrible after all, rather just suffering from madness brought about by a combination of mental illness, prescribed treatments and possible poisoning. The reason why poisoning was so popular was because it was so difficult to prove as a method of murder in those days. Unlike now, there were no chemical tests that could be done to detect the presence of poisons, so cause of death was often recorded as an illness that best suited the symptoms.

A number of letters or epistles have been attributed to Ivan the Terrible, which were sent to various men under his rule. They reveal a sharp-minded, intelligent man who used his writing skills to make his point in no uncertain terms. He was particularly scathing of the boyars and monks whom he saw as hypocrites, for they claimed to live ascetic lives but did anything but. This riled him in particular because they were openly critical of his own way of life, which was characterised by all forms of indulgence. He saw himself as more honest, as he would indulge and then periodically repent for his sins so that he could start again with a clean slate.

Much has been made of his epithet 'the Terrible' anyway, because 'terrible' is, apparently, a mistranslation of the Russian word 'grozny'. The Russians gave him his nickname when he seized a place called Kazan during his early reign. A more accurate translation would be 'dreadful' or 'fearsome' because they were alluding to his prowess at ruthless conquest, as opposed to his temperament as a person. In short, Ivan has been dealt a bad press over the years. It would be true to say that he was pretty terrible but not that terrible.

GILLES DE RAIS

For reasons not adequately explained by psychologists, some boys grow into adulthood as paedophiles. That is to say, they identify children as their objects of sexual desire and cannot find sexually mature adults attractive. When Gilles de Rais was alive, in the fifteenth century, the concept of paedophilia as a sexual deviance was something unheard of, and there certainly weren't any words to describe the condition. Nevertheless, a paedophile is most certainly what he was, for he tortured, raped and murdered unknown numbers of children in an attempt to sate his sexual appetite. To some criminologists, he is the first recorded paedophile serial killer.

Gilles seems to have had a fairly uneventful childhood, save for the fact that he was born into a privileged French family and his parents died by the time he was ten or eleven years of age. He was subsequently raised by his godfather. When he was sixteen he moved to the court of Dauphin under Charles the Victorious, who would later become King Charles VII of France. By 1427, he was a commander in the Royal Army. He saw action against the English and Burgundians while under the leadership of Joan of Arc, whose successes led to the coronation of Charles VII in 1429.

Following the wars, Gilles retired from military service and began a more sedentary life. He had inherited a vast fortune but enjoyed a lavish lifestyle, which soon meant that he had squandered most of it. Without any prospect of earning the kind of money he was used to spending, he allegedly began to look for guidance of a supernatural kind. This led him towards the occult under the tutelage of a Florentine sorcerer named Francesco Prelati. The sorcerer promised Gilles that he would regain his fortune if he began sacrificing children to appease the demon who was causing his misfortune.

It appears that Gilles put two and two together to make five. Since he had a predilection for young children, he decided that he may as well begin sacrificing them and get some sexual gratification from it at the same time. Having been given licence to slaughter innocents by the sorcerer, he naturally embarked on his criminal career with the enthusiasm and gusto of a child with a new-found hobby.

In 1440, some five years after his retirement, Gilles made an error of judgement that would lead to his arrest. He kidnapped a clergyman named Jean le Ferron following a dispute at a local church. This prompted the

Bishop of Nantes to investigate the whereabouts of the clergyman. When Gilles' home was searched it was littered with the evidence of his murderous crimes. The Bishop approached the Duke of Brittany, who was moved to allow the rescue of the clergyman. Gilles was simultaneously arrested on suspicion of infanticide along with his two henchmen Henriet and Poitou.

Gilles' fate was now in the hands of both the government and the Church. He was to be tried in two courts of law – one secular the other ecclesiastical. He was indicted for murder and sodomy in the former and heresy in the latter. When Gilles realised that the game was up he opted to admit his crimes to avoid being tortured into a confession, as was the way in those days. Even so, the trials still took place and revealed just what a monster Gilles had become in his pursuit of carnal fulfilment. In fact, much of the transcript of the trials was subsequently destroyed because the judges deemed it too disgusting in detail to survive in documented form. One detail that seems particularly shocking is that Gilles' henchmen were complicit in his crimes, for it was they who acquired the children for him and assisted him in the execution of his despicable wrongdoings.

Surviving testimonies make difficult reading even now, as they describe how so many children were lured to their deaths under false pretences. Gilles had a preference for blonde-haired and blue-eyed boys, who looked something like he did as a child. However, he made do with any boys or girls made available to him. He tortured and raped them, before mutilating them and then ejaculating over their dying bodies. The corpses were then decapitated so that the heads could be displayed as trophies and compared with one another for beauty.

It was a macabre tale by anyone's standards, so the three men were found guilty of their crimes and hanged at Nantes on 26 October 1440. It is perhaps interesting to note that Gilles repented for his sins the day before and wept while expressing his remorse. The Catholic Church rescinded its punishment of excommunication so that Gilles could make his confession. He wasn't afraid of death but he was afraid of the belief that he would be consigned to an eternity of hell and damnation in his afterlife.

As Gilles had a preference for children who were effectively clones of himself as a child, it may be that he had either a narcissistic personality or one of self-loathing, perhaps both. There is a phenomenon known as psychological ontogeny, which is expressed by the subjects inability to see themselves as adult because they have an inner wish to return to childhood – the time when they were happiest. It may be that Gilles's personality was fashioned in that kind of way, so that he had the physical sexual desires of an adult but the affections of a child, so that paedophilia was the outcome.

If you combine that with his embarrassment and anger at past difficulty in performing sexually with a woman – for he was married to a Catherine de Thouars – then you have all the right ingredients in place. This is especially so, given that he committed his acts with an audience. That meant that he couldn't show signs of compassion towards his victims, as he was supposed to be sacrificing them to appease the demons in the eyes of his henchmen. Better then to create the impression that he was emotionally detached from the experience.

However you analyse Gilles de Rais, it doesn't excuse him of his crimes. He was a paedophile and serial killer in much the same mould as Andrei Chikatilo – the Rostov Ripper – who was executed in 1994 in Russia for similar crimes. In Chikatilo's case, he was found guilty of the murders of fifty-two young boys and girls. His modus operandi was to achieve sexual arousal and orgasm while in the act of stabbing and mutilating his victims to death in heavily wooded areas.

Chikatilo blamed his impotence on his childhood in the Ukraine, which was disrupted by World War II. In addition, there had been a severe famine shortly before his birth and he had believed rumours that he had once had an older brother who was killed and eaten in the woods by starving neighbours. His first sexual experience involved him prematurely ejaculating while attempting to force himself upon a girl, thereby causing him to associate sex with violence. Somehow his experiences eventually crossed wires in his head and it seems that Giles de Rais was a similar case.

It can never be known for certain how many children Gilles murdered. Estimates vary greatly from multiples of ten to multiples of a hundred. He can only have been active for two or three years at the most, so it seems that the lower estimate is probably the more likely. He would have had to search increasingly further afield to find suitable children to lure and would have been found out much earlier if he had simply taken every child within the immediate vicinity. That is the only consolation that can be derived from the case, which still resonates now, even with the historical distance of some 600 years.

PETER THE GREAT

Peter the Great ... what? You may ask. Well, his epithet arose from his success at transforming Russia into an empire, it having formerly been only a tsardom or kingdom. So, it meant Peter the Great 'transformer' or 'modernizer'. He achieved his aims by expanding Russia through conquest and by Westernizing its culture. In addition, he happened to be an unusually imposing figure, standing some 2.03m (6ft 8in) tall, which was very unusual in a world when most people were far shorter, on average, than they are today.

However, his height is generally regarded as having been a result of a genetic defect from inbreeding, for he was actually lanky, badly proportioned and physically weak. In addition, he had muscular tics, which indicated a nervous disorder such as absence seizures – a type of epilepsy. Inbreeding has been a problem among royal families for centuries as it promotes genetic mutations which express themselves in all manner of congenital defects and flaws. In short, it isn't the way nature intends genes to be inherited as it has a tendency to amplify any miscodings in the DNA because closely related people are likely to share them and show a match.

Peter was born in Moscow as Peter Alexeyevich Romanov in 1672. He was not heir to the throne, but he was healthier and fitter than his elder half-brother Ivan V, who was sickly in body and mind – another product of inbreeding. So the boyars decided to make Peter the new tsar, as Peter I, in 1682, at the age of ten years. One of his half-sisters then led a bloody rebellion, which saw most of Peter's relatives and friends savagely murdered. It is reckoned, with some justification, that Peter was traumatised by these events at such an impressionable age, so that he learnt to be ruthless in his political dealings from early on.

The rebellion, which became known as the Streltsy Uprising, forced Peter into a stalemate position so that he had to agree to a joint leadership, with both him and Ivan as tsars. Sophia Alekseyevna, the half-sister who had caused the rebellion, then took it upon herself to act as advisor, effectively controlling Peter and Ivan. In fact, she had a hole cut in the back of the double-throne, so that she could control matters of state by passing information to and fro. This is where the term 'puppet ruler' originates, as it was as if she operated them with her arms, like a pair of puppets.

Sophia remained quasi-ruler for seven years, until Peter decided enough was enough. She attempted a second rebellion but the Streltsy (royal armed guards) this time took the side of Peter. Sophia was forced into a convent, where she spent the rest of her days, having relinquished her titles and powers. She was lucky to escape with her life given the way she had treated Peter's family and friends seven years beforehand.

Peter continued to reign alongside the invalided Ivan until 1696, when Ivan died. Peter then became sole ruler in both name and status, for until then his own mother had always had the last word, for she was officially regent. Peter was now twenty-four years of age and he had big plans for Russia. He immediately began implementing reforms in his aim to bring Russia in line with other powerful nations in Europe, the Middle East and Asia.

Of particular interest to Peter were potential places to establish new Russian ports, so that sea trade could be expanded. At the time his only point of access to the world's oceans was the port of Arkhangelsk on the White Sea, which joins the Arctic Ocean above Moscow and is therefore seasonally affected by temperatures. So Peter set his sights on the Black Sea, as he fancied his chances against the Ottomans, as opposed to the Swedes, who controlled the Baltic Sea. In 1697 he managed to seize Azov, on the north coast of the Black Sea, with the use of thirty new ships that were especially built for the task. He subsequently established a navy base at a place called Taganrog nearby, to make certain of his conquest.

Peter now embarked on a tour of Europe. His intention had been to form alliances against the Ottomans, but the European powers had other fish to fry. So Peter became the Renaissance man and used his time in Europe to learn as much as he could about Western cultures, especially their advances in science and technology, which he knew would be a useful knowledge base. He spent about a year on the road, travelling as far as London.

Then the Streltsy formed a rebellion in his absence, but Peter rushed back to Moscow and managed to quell an uprising. This was when he really began to show his mean streak. To make an example, over 1,200 mutineers were tortured and executed. Peter even mucked-in himself to show that he wasn't about to let others do his dirty work for him. It is fair to assume that he was pretty miffed that he'd had his holiday cut short.

Peter had been so impressed by what he had seen abroad that he thought it best to mimic Western ways as a part of the modernisation process, in much the same way that so many countries are influenced by the US culture in these modern times. He ordered all members of court to ditch their traditional garb and begin wearing European clothing, which he viewed as more sophisticated. He also gave the thumbs down to beards and introduced a beard tax for those who just couldn't give up their hirsute ways.

In order to fit in with the world at large, Peter even altered the Russian year and timeframe. He adopted the Julian calendar so that the year began on January 1st instead of September 1st. This also meant that years were counted from the birth of Jesus as dictated by Christianity. As it happened, Europe had taken up the Gregorian calendar in 1582, which was slightly more accurate, but the two were similar enough to be workable and Russia wouldn't bother to change again until 1917, with the takeover of the Communists. Incidentally, it was they who killed off the Romanov lineage, too.

Having taken Azov back in 1697, Peter now managed to negotiate a peace treaty with the Ottomans. This enabled him to focus on the Baltic Sea. Peter made several attempts to oust the Swedes from the shores of the Baltic, but proved no match for the king of Sweden, Charles XII. By 1708, Charles had turned the tables and invaded Russia, but he was deterred from reaching Moscow by Peter managing to diminish the Swedish army's supply of food. In much the same way as Hitler in 1942, Charles XII was forced to retreat his forces, which had become demoralised by lack of food and the cold of the Russian winter.

Eventually, Peter managed to overpower the Swedish army in the Ukraine, sending Charles XII into exile with the Ottomans. This led Peter to make the mistake of attacking the Ottomans. After a disastrous campaign, Peter was forced to capitulate and, in so doing, lost his Black Sea ports. Charles XII was returned to Europe in the peace process and Peter resumed his efforts to take the eastern Baltic coast. Ultimately, Charles died in battle in 1718, enabling northern Europe to agree peace terms with Russia. Peter emerged triumphant, as he had managed to secure a portion of territory from Finland so that Russia had a major port on the Baltic coast at St Petersburg. Peter was so pleased that he made the city his new capital.

The remaining four years of Peter's life were spent as emperor of the newly formed Russian Empire. His official title was 'Peter the Great, Father of His Country, Emperor of All the Russians'. Naturally, just 'Peter the Great' stuck in the public consciousness. This was not least because most European nations refused to recognise him as an emperor anyway, as it implied superiority over the title of king. Peter was only fifty-two years old when he died of necrosis (gangrene) of the bladder in 1725. He had first become infected in 1723 and suffered surgery to release trapped urine, but the infection remained.

Peter the Great, like so many leaders of note, succeeded by cultivating a necessary ruthless streak. He learnt from his formative years that it would be necessary to rule with an iron rod if he expected to see his reforms put in place and to survive. He certainly did order the deaths of many, but always in a way calculated to make sure that his subjects realised that he meant business. Perhaps the most shocking example of this was the torture and execution of his own son Alexei, but this was because he had disobeyed the emperor and opposed official policies. Peter clearly put the future of his empire above all other concerns. Consequently, his memory is revered by some, vilified by others.

PART TWO

TYRANTS AND DESPOTS

POL POT

The story of Pol Pot is what you get when you mix communist ideology with a lack of insight and wisdom. In short, his political ambitions were perhaps honourable, but he was woefully lacking in necessary intellectual calibre to bring his aims to fruition. As a result, he resorted to carnage as his primary means of people management, thereby exhausting his nation of the very people it needed to make his plan work.

Pol Pot's real name was Saloth Sar. He was born in the country now known as Cambodia, but it was named Kampuchea 1976–89. The name 'Pol Pot' was an abbreviation of the French phrase *politique potentielle*, which translates as 'political potential'. He earned the nickname because of his determination as leader of the communist movement in his country. The predominant ethnic group in Cambodia are the Khmer, so the communist movement became known as the Red Khmer, or Khmer Rouge in French, as red is the communist colour.

Saloth Sar was born into a reasonably well-to-do Cambodian family with connections to the royal family. His sister was a concubine to the king, which meant that Saloth had access to the palace and was able to rub shoulders with members of court. This is where Saloth began to cultivate delusions of grandeur, which would eventually manifest themselves in his political ambitions.

He was not blessed with the academic prowess he had hoped for and failed in his university studies in Cambodia. He eventually won a scholarship to study at a technical college in France, by which time his inferiority complex had germinated and taken root. It was at this time that he fell in with people of socialist leanings, who introduced him to the ideals of communism.

Then, in 1950, when Saloth was twenty-five years old, something radical happened in the neighbouring country of Vietnam. The French Communist Party (*Parti Communiste Français* – PCF) took up the cause of the Vietnam government's call for independence from colonial rule by the French. Cambodia was also under the colonial thumb of France and within a year Saloth had become a prominent figure in a communist cell affiliated with the PCF and known as the Marxist Circle (*Cercle Marxiste*).

The PCF was markedly anti-intellectual in its policies, enabling Saloth to quickly make a name for himself and, at the same time, nurture the growing chip on his shoulder about his academic failings. Suitably, he became the first member of the Marxist Circle to return to Cambodia, precisely because he had failed his exams in France and been dropped from college. He was thus able to get an early foothold in the political scene, which led to the independence of Cambodia in 1954.

As soon as Cambodia gained its independence, in-fighting began between political parties left and right of centre. The country effectively became a monarchy, with King Norodom Sihanouk manipulating things, so that politicians had to remain liberalist to stand any chance of enjoying the limelight. Leftists, such as Saloth, were marginalised and realised that they could only ever come to power by illegal means.

By the early 1960s, the king was beginning to active-ly persecute the communists. This led to the arrest and murder of the communist party leader Ton Samouth. As a result Saloth – by now known as Pol Pot – became acting leader by default. Pol Pot now went into hiding, where he forged alliances with Vietnamese guerrillas, whom he persuaded to help in establishing a base camp for the Cambodian communists. Between 1963 and 1967 the Khmer Rouge ideology was developed, and the movement grew in strength as many disaffected Cambodians volunteered to join.

In January 1968, the Khmer Rouge – proper name Communist Party of Kampuchea (CPK) – began its uprising against the existing seat of power. The rebellion saw the Khmer Rouge seize army weaponry and begin to establish its own arsenal. As the Khmer Rouge became increasingly powerful in military terms, so Pol Pot became more powerful within the party. He assumed absolute power, consigning his former power-sharing colleagues to positions below him. Pol Pot had metamorphosed into an omnipotent tyrant – a despot. All others had to defer to his wishes, and it only became possible to communicate with him if he chose to summon someone, but that was not necessarily a good thing.

The year 1969 was spent consolidating his position and then events in Cambodia began to assist Pol Pot in his ambitions. Tensions between the Cambodians and North Vietnamese (Viet Minh) had led to rioting in early 1970 because the Viet Minh wanted control of the peninsula. Insurgents blamed the king and his government for the troubles and demanded that he be removed from power. This gave Pol Pot his opportunity. He sided with the Vietnamese, who invaded much of Cambodia in the same year.

Warring between the Viet Minh–Khmer Rouge and the Cambodian government continued for five years. The communists were heavily funded by the communist

Chinese government, which was naturally anti-imperialist. Gradually, the Khmer Rouge grew into a formidable communist army and Pol Pot became increasingly extremist in his leftist leanings. The true nature of the man's insecurities revealed themselves as he banned students and the middle class from joining the ranks of the Khmer Rouge. Only those who came from the peasantry were allowed in, even though he himself had come from a privileged background.

Things began to get unsavoury in 1973, when Pol Pot introduced the torture and summary execution of anyone who stood against the Khmer Rouge. He also began ordering the populations of cities and towns to move away from their urban environments to work in the fields. The logic behind this policy was that a rural life would cause them to forget about their former capitalist ways. By 1974, Pol Pot had also planned to phase out the use of money so that people traded by barter as the ultimate two-fingered salute to capitalism.

The Khmer Rouge seized total control of Cambodia in April 1975. Then all hell let loose on the population. Pol Pot put to death all members of former government. He then began the systematic process of torturing and murdering anyone deemed to be unsuitable for his regime's purposes. This meant anyone who was educated or privileged in any way. The Khmer Rouge used a proverb in summing up their attitude: 'To keep you is no benefit, to destroy you is no loss.' That chilling sentence justified the extermination of perhaps two million people who were simply seen as surplus to requirements. They were known collectively as 'depositees'.

Death camps and killing fields were used in this wholesale slaughter and burial of human life. Inevitably, in their desire to thin out the population, those who lost their lives to the Khmer Rouge also included people from ethnic and racial minorities, those with physical and mental disabilities, and anyone who even appeared to be more intelligent than they needed to be, such as those who wore glasses. The infamous S-21 camp was the sinister heart of the purging machine. It was where thousands were tortured into confessions before dying. Pol Pot justified these acts by claiming that the gleaned information provided useful intelligence for his government. In truth, it was a sadistic way of getting his own back on the memory of all those who had ever belittled him, either intellectually or aristocratically.

Ultimately, the Khmer Rouge shot itself in the foot and failed in its aims. With the deaths of so many able-bodied people, the Cambodian population might have been described as a body without a head. Pol Pot's ideas failed to take account of the fact that intelligent and educated people are needed for any infrastructure to remain functional, whether communist in principle or otherwise. His lack of cognitive ability had let him down in a catastrophic way, seeing widespread famine and associated disease take a grip on his nation. To make matters worse, the Khmer Rouge rejected outside humanitarian aid when the world outside realised what was going on.

Despite these disastrous internal affairs, Pol Pot now chose to wage war on the Vietnamese, who had formerly been his ally. One thing led to another and eventually the Viet Minh decided enough was enough. In late 1978, they invaded Cambodia to overthrow the Khmer Rouge, which they achieved very quickly. Pol Pot went into hiding at the border with Thailand. He, and a hardcore Khmer Rouge following, remained there through 1979. They were not pursued because the Vietnamese justified their occupation of Cambodia by the continued existence of the Khmer Rouge.

Over the next ten years there existed a shifting power struggle between the Vietnamese controlled governments and the Khmer Rouge. During this period, Pol Pot contracted cancer. He resigned in 1985 and became de facto leader, due to the loyalty of his following. In 1997, he was arrested and put under house arrest for the murder of a colleague who had attempted to broker a peace deal between the Khmer Rouge and the government. He died from natural causes six months later at the age of seventy-three.

Pol Pot clearly had ideas above his station. As with many tyrants, the 'perfect wave' theory allows them to rise to positions of power and influence that do not suit their intellect. They then find themselves wholly inadequate for the task in hand and resort to simplistic measures in an attempt to resolve problems, only to create more. In Pol Pot's case, he had only a rudimentary understanding of communist ideology and ended up killing off the very people who could have made it work for him. What he failed to grasp is that you need intelligent and educated leftists to build a successful communist state, and even then it doesn't work very well because human nature is fundamentally one of selfishness, which leads to corruption.

JOSEPH STALIN

It would be fair to say that Joseph Stalin was a man who let power go to his head. In so doing he grew increasingly paranoid that people were out to get him. His way of dealing with his suspicions was to have countless people murdered or sent to labour camps. He then found himself in a vicious cycle, as he then had good reason to think that he had enemies. So his obsession with guarding his own back turned him into a maniacal tyrant. In the end, his ideology had very little to do with communism, for he had established an administration structured with the very worst kind of hierarchy.

Stalin had played a key role in the February Revolution in Russia in 1917. The Russian population had had enough of imperialist rule, because the tsar and his court displayed a blatant disregard for the welfare of the common man. The Bolsheviks and Mensheviks formed an uprising with the aim of turning Russia into a communist state. The royal family were placed under house arrest and then executed to prevent a monarchist reprisal. So the Romanov royal lineage came to an abrupt end and Russia became a brave new world.

From February to October 1917 there was a provisional communist government in Russia, but the October (Bolshevik) Revolution saw the Bolsheviks take control. Vladimir Lenin became leader of the Soviet Communist Party from that time until his death in 1924. There then came a power struggle between Joseph Stalin, another Bolshevik, and Leon Trotsky, a Menshevik. Stalin ultimately won the fight and so began a twenty-nine-year run as leader. Trotsky was expelled from the Soviet Communist party in 1927 and exiled from Russia in 1929. He died in Mexico in 1937, having been killed by a Stalinist assassin.

Trotsky's death was part of a depressing period in Soviet history known as the Great Purge or Great Terror: 1937–38. In the late 1930s, Stalin began a systematic campaign of political repression and persecution against anyone who he deemed a potential threat to his omnipotence. All kinds of trumped-up charges were used to arrest, incarcerate, torture and murder people. Ever-present police surveillance was used to 'find' reasons to bring people down for 'counter-revolutionary activities'.

A great many victims were sent to Siberian labour camps known as GULAG, which is an acronym formed from the Russian for 'The Administration of Corrective Labour Camps and Colonies.' The notion that they served as corrective institutions was misleading though, as the combination of forced labour, extreme cold, poor clothing, insufficient food and rudimentary accommodation meant that vast numbers died from sheer exhaustion.

In addition to this proactive victimisation, Stalin indirectly killed millions of Soviets through intentional neglect. Under his administration, the infrastructure had become hierarchical to such an extent that those at the bottom of the pyramid suffered from extreme poverty and starvation. Waves of famine swept through the Soviet Union, taking untold numbers of peasants to their graves. Stalin displayed blatant disregard for their fate. In fact, he decided it was a good thing as it was a natural way of thinning out the population so that only necessary people would survive to build the Soviet future.

He lived to regret this point of view in the early 1940s however. In June 1941, Adolf Hitler broke a pact with the Soviet Union and began an invasion eastward towards Moscow. Stalin had inadvertently shown Hitler how weak his infrastructure was by the Red Army's struggle to overpower the Finnish army during the Winter War (1939–40). Seeing his opportunity, Hitler sent his army rampaging its way across the sub-Baltic belt and into Russia itself.

Despite the colossal size of the Red Army, it was so ill-equipped and supplied that the Soviet troops dropped like flies. By December 1941, the Germans were just 16 km (10 miles) from Moscow and things were looking very bad. It was only thanks to the Russian winter that the Germans failed to take Moscow and were eventually forced into retreat. The Red Army then took advantage of their forward momentum and managed to push the Germans all the way back to Berlin by 1945. They paid a heavy price though.

Approximately thirty million Soviets (twenty million civilians, ten million soldiers) died in World War II. At least half might have survived had Stalin paid more attention to his infrastructure before the war. Indeed, Hitler may not have even reneged on his pact with the Soviet Union in the first place if he had seen that its vital functions were healthy. He only went in for the kill because he perceived the Soviet Union to be a weak target. He was right, but ultimately lost the fight only because Stalin had such a large population to throw into the war effort.

To add insult to injury, Stalin treated all troops who had been imprisoned during the war as traitors and deserters. Instead of being returned to their homes, they were sent to special concentration camps for interrogation. Only fifteen per cent or so were released. The

remainder were either sentenced to death or condemned to GULAG punishment for between five- and
twenty-five-year terms. Of course, many perished before
their terms were up.

In the post-war era, the Soviet Union grew con-
siderably in size, due to the addition of Eastern
European countries as spoils of war. They included
Poland, Hungary, Czechoslovakia, Romania, Bulgaria
and East Germany. They became dubbed the
'Communist Block.' Stalin had become a hero of the
Soviet people for winning the war, despite the loss of
life. The political machine was such that the common
man was beguiled by propaganda anyway, and Stalin's
atrocities were either brushed under the carpet or
explained away as necessary acts for the greater good.

By the early 1950s, Stalin had become increasingly
isolated on a personal level. He had become so wary of
other people that even members of his own family fell
under suspicion. Many disappeared or died under
mysterious circumstances, such was his fear of
assassination. He had, by then, honed his behaviour to
the point where former friends and family were erased
from memory. This process even included the
retouching of photographs, so that Stalin could still
admire his own image but, in the absence of people he
viewed as apostates. His motivation was presumably a

combination of denial as well as resentment, for he must have known deep down that simply removing people with opposed views was not an honourable solution to anything as it denies a balance of opinion.

Stalin met his maker as the result of a stroke in 1953, at the age of seventy-four. He had forged such a baleful reputation for himself by then that he was even regarded with caution on his deathbed. His own daughter was convinced that he had put a curse over all those in the room as he approached death. He apparently opened his left eye and then raised his left arm into the air before uttering something incomprehensible as he stared and pointed at everyone. He was evidently convinced that he had been poisoned. So, Stalin died alone even though he was surrounded by people who might have shown him some compassion if not affection. It was a fitting end to a man who trusted no one but himself.

KIM IL-SUNG

North Korea, officially known as The Democratic People's Republic of Korea, is infamous as the only surviving bastion of hard-line communism. What makes it intriguing as a nation though, isn't it's political ideology but the fact that it has become culturally isolated from the rest of the world. In fact, the introspection of North Korea has become something of a worry in the modern political climate, because it apparently also lacks a sense of global community responsibility. This has been expressed most clearly in its development and testing of nuclear weapons without notifying the world beyond its own borders.

It doesn't harbour territorial ambitions however, but rather is deeply suspicious of the intentions of other nations. The untrusting and paranoid mindset of North Korea is largely due to the leadership of Kim Il-Sung, who was instrumental in turning the country into the closed system it is today. As well as adhering to hard-line communist ideology, Kim also introduced the ethos of Juche, which translates as 'self-reliance.' This meant that North Korea would have no need for trade with any other nation, as if it were an island in total isolation.

The intrinsic problem with communism is that it largely goes against human nature. The human condition is such people tend to thrive when given life elements that communism doesn't offer them. Those elements include freedom of speech, the freedom to make choices, a social ladder to climb, fulfilment of ambition, psychological independence and so on. When people impose communism upon a nation they, themselves, are the only ones allowed to enjoy those elements, while the rest of the population are expected to become conditioned clones, like worker ants in a nest.

Some readily comply with the communist directive, but many do not, simply because their imaginations generate dreams and ambitions for a better life. The result is a need for a heavy-handed approach to governing them. In short, a controlling regime is required to keep the minions in their place. Inevitably, the situation then escalates so that active persecution and oppression become the tools of control.

Therein lies the advantage of Juche, as it means that the population is never exposed to other ways of doing things and other ways of thinking. So, without outside influence, the North Korean population was, and still is, that much more malleable in the hands of the ruling elite. At the same time, it has the propaganda value of making the population feel self-important – not needing to rely on outside help in any way, shape or form. It is the perfect ruse for effectively manipulating a population into doing what you want it to do. It is a form of self-policing as the North Korean population 'believes' that total autonomy is right and proper, so it readily submits to orders from above.

Nevertheless, it was still necessary for Kim Il-Sung to rule North Korea with a rod of iron, which he has earned an entry in this book. You see, North Korea has the worst human rights record of all the world's nations. Restrictions on political and economic freedoms are so severe that Amnesty International and HRW (Human Rights Watch) have actively campaigned to address the problem. When one considers that the whole point of communism is to create a utopia of egalitarianism, then it is only possible to conclude that Kim Il-Sung's efforts have resulted in catastrophic failure of duty to his nation.

Defectors and exiles from North Korea have made a litany of complaints about the remand, trial and punishment system of their former country. More often than not they describe trumped up charges, summary trials and corporal punishments that include forced labour, starvation, torture, rape, murder and execution. Perhaps twenty-five per cent of those who enter the prison system die as a result of maltreatment. Needless to say, the other seventy-five per cent are permanently scarred by the experience, both physically and mentally.

There have also been reports of routine show executions to remind people of the dangers of breaking the rules. In addition, it is reckoned that military weapons are tested on prisoners for their efficiency at killing. Also, it has been said that any women prisoners found to be pregnant are forced to abort or have their new born babies killed to avoid the problem of having to provide for their maternity needs.

It has been estimated that about two million North Korean civilians have been exterminated so far. It seems to be business as usual too, as the government still refuse to allow independent human rights observers into the country, suggesting that there is a great deal worth hiding from the rest of the world. It also seems likely that punishments for dissidence extend beyond the borders, because some whistle-blowers have been murdered in neighbouring territories.

Kim Il-Sung became leader of North Korea in 1946, following World War II. He was placed in power by the Soviets, under Joseph Stalin, when it became apparent that the Korean peninsula would need to be divided in two, due to ideological differences. The Korean War (1950–53) saw Kim assert his authority as leader of

North Korea and establish the armistice or ceasefire line that now forms the territorial divide between North and South Korea.

From 1953 onwards, Kim Il-Sung propagated the North Korean version of communism. When a few high-ranking politicians voiced their opposition to it in 1956, they found themselves the victims of a Stalin-like purge. Many were put to death, while others were exiled from their homeland. By 1966, Kim had let the power get the better of him. He ordered that he should now be addressed as the Great Leader and introduced the ethos of Juche.

Kim used the media to develop a phenomenon now known generically as the personality cult. He created a larger-than-life personality for himself by displaying his image ubiquitously, so that people were brainwashed into revering him as the Great Leader. The use of public displays of flattery and praise also did much to cement the idea that he was some kind of god-like figure who rewarded the good and punished the bad. It would have been true but for the fact that his definitions of good and bad were not especially godly.

In 1972, Kim became president of North Korea rather than just 'leader' or 'prime minister'. This allowed him to add nepotism to his list of wrongdoings, by designating his son Kim Jong-il as his successor in waiting.

State duties were gradually shifted onto his son's shoulders over the next two decades, while Kim enjoyed the high life. His personality cult reached a point where he was purported to have supernatural powers and he took full advantage of the myth. Anyone who so much as voiced their disapproval of his behaviour was either executed or sent to a GULAG-like labour camp.

By the time Kim Il-Sung died, in 1994 at the age of eighty-two, he had left North Korea in economic ruin. He had spent so much money on military defence that the infrastructure had collapsed, causing poverty and starvation for millions. Despite this legacy a three-year period of mourning was declared after his death so that people might still be punished if they failed to express sufficient grief for the loss of the Great Leader. Kim Il-Sung turned out to be another one of those leaders who had set out with good intentions but evolved into a tyrant to compensate for his inadequacies in office.

ADOLF HITLER

Some people are turned, by circumstance, away from the path prepared for them. Adolf Hitler is a good case in point. He had a rather unhappy childhood that led him to leave school with no qualifications, despite his evident intelligence. He happened to possess a raw talent at drawing and painting, so he decided that he would become an artist. To achieve his ambition he relocated from his home town in Austria to the capital city, Vienna, where he attempted to win a place at the Academy of Fine Arts. However, his lack of formal training and entry requirements meant that he was twice turned away, in 1907 and 1908.

He produced as many as 2,000 workmanlike drawings and paintings to sell on the streets but ended up destitute and living in a homeless shelter. During this period of hardship, the impressionable young Hitler began to germinate anti-Semitic ideas in his mind, because he saw wealthy Jews around him who showed little empathy for him and others like him. In marked contrast, he was shown compassion by people of his own stock, so that he began to view society in a very black and white manner.

Hitler readily volunteered to join the German army when World War I broke out in 1914. He had always admired the Germans, so it gave him a chance to become Teutonic by proxy. During the war he performed duties as a messenger, which was dangerous work as it involved leaving the relative safety of the trenches and racing across exposed terrain. Over the course of the war he was shot in the leg and suffered a poison gas attack, but was noted for never complaining. His bravery won him the Iron Cross, second and first class, which was highly unusual for a private. He wasn't promoted to officer, apparently because he lacked German citizenship.

Hitler was shocked and angered by Germany's capitulation to the enemy in 1918, especially as the Germans weren't in retreat and still held foreign territory. To him it was a sign of cowardice and it marked a radical change in his thinking. He decided that his purpose in life was to avenge and save the German people. He also decided that communist ideology was to blame for the surrender, so communists joined his list of hate figures. In addition, he decided that to fight until the last man is standing was a better approach to warfare. All of those notions propagated in his mind, and so began his road into politics.

Following the war Hitler remained in the army, not least to earn a wage. Within a year he had become a military police spy and was assigned duties involving the procurement of evidence against Jews and communists in the government, whom the National Defence Force wanted to blame, as scapegoats, for the way the war had ended. Hitler's espionage led him to investigate the German Workers Party, where he met Anton Drexler and Dietrich Eckart, both of whom greatly influenced his politics. Before long he had left the army and joined the party, where he quickly established himself as a charismatic and powerful orator. By July 1921 he had become leader and renamed the party to National Socialist German Workers Party – the Nazi Party.

In the mid-1920s Hitler attempted to take control of the German Republic by coup, but failed and ended up in jail for a year. He then set about earning power and influence by legal means. His winning formula was to keep reminding the German people of the economically disastrous state the nation had been left in by those who had lost the war. Bit by bit he won the nation over by means of this propaganda, because he appealed to people's sense of wounded pride and their desire to stand proud on the world stage once more.

By 1933, Hitler had climbed to the position of chancellor of a coalition government. Then in 1934,

President Hindenburg died. Hitler's Nazi cabinet muscled in to make him both leader and chancellor of Germany. By this move, Hitler also assumed the role of supreme commander of the military. He now described himself as Fuhrer (Absolute Ruler) of the Third Reich (Third Empire). A year later he broke the Treaty of Versailles – the terms of German surrender – and introduced army conscription, so that he could begin rebuilding the German war machine. A worried Europe looked on.

Ultimately, of course, Hitler took Germany to war once again. World War II lasted for six years, from 1939 to 1945. Hitler, although skilled at taking the lead, proved fundamentally flawed once ensconced as a leader. He quite simply bit off more than he could chew in military terms, so that he spread his armies too thinly in all directions. An impressive initial push saw him take most of Europe – from the Pyrenees in the west to Moscow in the East, Norway in the north to North Africa in the south. But, he ended up taking his own life, trapped in a bunker in Berlin, while enemy shells rained down over the city.

It is estimated that around 60 million people lost their lives during the war. Arguably, Adolf Hitler was responsible for a sizeable proportion of those, remembering that Austria, Italy and Japan were involved, too. However,

Hitler's legacy as a killer has more to do with his policies of extermination, as opposed to his ambitions in the field of battle. The word that sums up the reign of terror he meted out on his victims is 'holocaust', which is derived from the Latin 'holos-kaustos' – 'whole-burn.' Because Hitler and his cronies wanted to burn, to erase, all undesirables from their world.

Those undesirables came in all shapes and sizes. The primary target was the community of European Jews, whom the Nazis rounded up into ghettos, concentration camps and death camps and systematically exterminated by all manner of despicable means, including starvation, gasing, shooting and experimentation. By the close of the war, some six million Jews had perished.

The Jews, however, were by no means the only target of the holocaust. Hitler's basic ethos was centred on developing a master race of Aryans. They are a mythical race of people who were supposed to be tall and muscular, with blond hair and blue eyes. Hitler therefore suggested that all those who didn't fit the bill were inferior specimens and should be treated as such. Not being an Aryan type himself, he categorized people in a descending order of perfection, so that he and other Caucasians belonged to the group immediately below.

All other racial and ethnic groups were at risk of extermination, as well as all those who had physical and mental disabilities. It meant that millions more died from general persecution by the German army and the SS – the Nazi special police force that administered the Holocaust. The most feared body of the SS was the Gestapo – the German secret police. Under Heinrich Himmler, the Gestapo officers did all of Hitler's evil and dirty work. They infiltrated all echelons of society to weed out anyone who attempted to escape what Hitler described as the 'Final Solution'.

A key part of Hitler's strategy was to begin indoctrinating or brainwashing Germans at an early age, so that they grew up accepting a belief system as a given truth. This process forced people into believing completely in things that have their origin entirely in the human imagination. It was therefore a very potent weapon in building a devoted following. From 1922 until 1945, there existed a paramilitary organisation called the Hitler Youth, which was used for just this purpose.

Germany's teenagers were conditioned to believe that they were superior, in every way, to other human beings. To such an extent, in fact, that they viewed other races as sub-human. This meant that they would think nothing of killing them. To help in this process, victims were stripped of their clothing and belongings and had their heads shaven, so that they resembled one another, just like farm animals. It removed their individual human identities and personalities so that the Nazis felt no human connection with them and could more easily commit their atrocities.

Adolf Hitler is something of an anomaly to historians. He is viewed as something like a real-life Hannibal Lecter. That is to say, that his achievements in rising to power and leading Germany are regarded as rather impressive, especially to those who are insecure and have a fundamental need to feel racially superior. On the other hand, the atrocities committed in his name cast such a dark shadow that those same people wish it wasn't true. Their way of justifying their admiration for Hitler is to deny that the Holocaust happened, despite the evidence. Ironically, in so doing they have simply indoctrinated themselves with another belief system.

MAO ZEDONG

The German philosopher Karl Marx has a lot to answer for. In 1836, a movement called the League of the Just was founded by German workers based in Paris. They were the first people to describe themselves as communists and changed their name to the Communist League in 1847. A year later they published their Communist Manifesto, which was written by Karl Marx and Friedrich Engels. The ideology expounded by the book became known as Marxism. It suggested a course of action that involved the pursuit of a classless society by using the working class (proletariat) to overthrow the ruling classes (bourgeoisie).

At that time in Europe, the Industrial Revolution had transformed the socioeconomic landscape, leaving millions of working-class people downtrodden and disadvantaged by the class structure, so Marxism was a very appealing idea. As capitalism and imperialism continued their stranglehold, so Marxism developed a cult following as workers dreamt of the utopia it suggested. Ultimately, the plan was put into action for the first time in Russia in 1917. The Communist Revolution saw the royal family overthrown and a communist government take control of the country. Meanwhile, the rest of the world looked on. Some nations were dismayed by the events, others were inspired.

In China in 1911, there had already been a revolution, but it had been executed by a republican movement, which had overthrown the Qing Dynasty of the Manchu Royal Clan. However, in 1921 the Communist Party of China (CPC) was founded and it began to grow in membership very quickly, inspired by events in Russia. Mao Zedong, also known as Mao Tse-tung, joined the CPC in the first year, and by 1927 he had established a sufficient power base to take action against the republican government. He formed the Revolutionary Army of Workers and Peasants and initiated an uprising in Hunan Province. It failed in its aim but established Mao as a leader to be reckoned with.

Mao first demonstrated his ability to kill in cold blood when challenged, not by republican enemies, but by fellow communists with a different take on Marxist ideology. In order to establish his supremacy, he ordered the torture and deaths of those who presented a threat. An estimated 180,000 plus died in what became dubbed Revolutionary, or Red, Terrorism. Mao justified the deaths as being a necessary evil in pursuit of the greater good for the Chinese nation.

Republican persecution of the communists in 1934 led to an escape called the Long March. The CPC marched almost 9,660 km (6,000 miles) from their former stronghold of Jiangxi in the south-east of China to Shaanxi in the north-west. During the march, Mao Zedong left no doubt in people's minds that he was the natural leader of the CPC. He even ordered his wife to leave their baby by the roadside so that they wouldn't be burdened by the infant's needs. His wife later went insane through her sense of guilt at this act of cruelty.

In the years leading up to and through World War II, Mao demonstrated his abilities as a military tactician by fending off attacks by the Japanese, who regarded the Chinese as a sub-human race in a similar vein to the Nazis' view of the Jews and Slavs. By the close of World War II, there was a marked anti-communist feeling in the West, and the USA began to support the Chinese republican government under Chiang Kai-shek. This catalysed a full-blown Chinese civil war, as the Soviets responded by supporting Mao. In 1949, the CPC succeeded in seizing total control and the People's Republic of China (PRC) was established. Mao was fifty-six years of age and battle worn. His direct leadership of China continued until 1959 when it became clear that he was not quite so good at running the domestic affairs as he was at leading his party to power in the first place.

The years of his leadership had seen vast numbers of people summarily executed due to a policy of removing any individuals who were perceived as anti-communist. Victims included political rivals, capitalists, suspect intellectuals and rural gentry who owned land to be given back to the peasants. We can never know for certain how many people died during Mao's purge, but a conservative estimate puts it at a million plus, and all in the name of a supposed communist utopia.

Mao's leadership style was characterised by two Five Year Plans (1953–58 and 1959–64) and a cult of personality to generate a god-like reverence for his public image. The 'plans' involved the instigation of reforms such as the introduction of the principle collectivization. This is true to the notion of communal life, where peasants collectively own and operate farms, so that they share in all aspects. It's a nice idea on paper but, as with all communist ideals, it falls apart somewhat when put into practise due to that age old problem – human nature.

Put in simple terms, people are at their happiest when they are progressing relative to others, so forcing them into a totally egalitarian lifestyle is fraught with pitfalls. This leads to people falling out and crimes being committed, so that communist governments resort to heavy-handed policing to repress unlawful behaviour. That, in turn, leads to a sense of oppression and a disaffected population. Communism doesn't work.

Mao pulled a fast one in 1956 by announcing a more liberal CPC policy, which became known as the Hundred Flowers Campaign, or Movement. The CPC openly encouraged people to express any opinions that countered or opposed the hard line Marxist line. Mao indicated that he was of an open mind and that he might even consider incorporating such ideas into the CPC doctrine. It proved to be a confidence trick. A clampdown in 1957 led to the persecution of millions who had been beguiled into revealing their innermost thoughts, which were interpreted as anti-communist. Trickery had been added to Mao's political portfolio.

His downfall came in 1959 when Mao's mismanagement of China's infrastructure caused the worst famine in modern history. Millions of peasants starved to death. Mao had diverted so much labour into the industrial development of the nation – the Great Leap Forward – that there weren't enough people to produce food. It only took droughts in some areas and floods in others to upset the balance and send the entire population into a crisis. It is believed as many as seventy million men, women and children perished through

Mao's neglect 1959–61, and he was removed from his presidency. The exact figures will never be known, because the CPC did their utmost to hide the truth from the world at large.

Even so, Mao remained the figurehead of the People's Republic of China until his death in 1976, such was the potency of the personality cult that surrounded him. In 1966, Mao reacted to his fall from grace by initiating the Cultural Revolution. He circumvented the CPC and handed power to a movement known as the Red Guard. They were Mao loyalists who effectively continued his 'good' work. The Red Guard were very much like Pol Pot's Khmer Rouge. Under Mao's instruction they closed schools and forced city folk out into the countryside to work the land. This last ditch attempt at creating a communist utopia ended three years later, having severely disrupted the lives of countless more millions of people.

Perhaps not surprisingly, Mao's legacy is a contentious issue. As with all leaders who take up the communist banner, he undoubtedly believed that his was a cause for the good. But, while he may have been an effective guerrilla leader and visionary, he was woefully lacking in the qualities that were needed to run the nation once the People's Republic of China had been set up. He was, by turns, both an inspiring personality and an uncompassionate human being. Having left so many people dead or emotionally scarred it is difficult to see that he benefited his people at all in the long term. If the current growth in the Chinese economy is anything to go by, then it shows that communism just doesn't suit the human condition.

SADDAM HUSSEIN

Like that of so many tyrants, Saddam Hussein's story is one of rags to riches. Saddam was born into a shepherd family near the town of Tikrit. His father was absent and his mother remarried. His stepfather turned out to be something of a child beater, so he fled to Baghdad, at the age of ten, to live with an uncle. In 1957, at the age of twenty, Saddam dropped out of university to pursue a political career in the Ba'ath Party, a pan-Arab organisation. A year later, King Faisal II was murdered in a coup d'état and Iraq became a republic under the rule of Abd al-Karim Qasim, who's government the Ba'ath Party opposed, but it left the way open for Saddam's eventual rise to power.

In 1963, The Ba'ath Party overthrew Qasim's government and assumed power under Abdul Salam Arif, but he then withdrew from the Ba'ath Party. Saddam eventually tasted power as deputy under president Ahmad Hassan al-Bakr, when they again took power from Arif's son in 1967. Although Saddam was deputy, he played a strong hand behind the scenes, so that al-Bakr was more-or-less a puppet president by 1969. At that period, Saddam's primary concern was to unify the opposed factions within the Ba'ath Party, as he knew it would be the key to continued power in Iraq.

As well as the Ba'ath Party infighting there were, and still are, other domestic divisions in Iraq. Although an entirely Muslim country, the population is fragmented by subtle religious and ethnic differences. There are two types of Muslim for starters – Sunni and Shi'ite – who both detest one another. Saddam was among the Sunni, who make up only twenty per cent of the Iraqi population but are the largest denomination in the Arab World. In addition, there is a non-Arab population in Iraq – the Kurds – who happen to be Sunni also. So, the situation was a complex one and took some governing.

A Revolutionary Command Council was formed and Saddam instigated a modernisation programme for Iraq. It turned out to be a visionary and progressive move on Saddam's part. The programme introduced social services for the first time anywhere in the Middle East, including free hospitals, state schooling and a campaign to make all Iraqi citizens literate. It was so effective that UNESCO (United Nations Educational, Scientific and Cultural Organisation) presented Saddam with an award for his achievements. At the same time, the economy of

Iraq underwent a marked improvement due to the worldwide increase in crude oil prices. Things were looking good for Saddam who, perhaps not surprisingly, saw himself as the saviour of the Arab world.

In July 1979, Saddam was forced to seize power in Iraq because al-Bakr had proposed an Iraq–Syria unification, which would have left Saddam out in the cold. This led to the first truly ugly episode in Saddam's political career. An assembly of the Ba'ath Party leadership was used to identify and arrest dissenting voices, and sixty-eight people were arrested and tried on charges of treason. All were imprisoned and tortured, and twenty-two were found guilty and executed for their crimes against the nation.

Saddam evidently felt that an example needed to be made of them, not least because the Iranian Revolution had just taken place. This was significant because Saddam's regime was essentially of a secular doctrine, while the new government in Iran was conservatively Muslim and Shi'ite, so Saddam feared a Shi'ite uprising. Tensions between the two countries began over claims to ownership of a waterway that geographically divided the two nations. By 1980 all out war had erupted. However, both sides were evenly matched and the war dragged on for eight bloody years.

The Iran–Iraq War was finally brought to an end in

1988, with neither side having benefited. Iraq had been assisted financially by the USA, ironically enough, but the infrastructure had been wrecked, so that Saddam had no prospect of paying the Americans back in the near future. Part of his solution was to ask neighbouring Kuwait to waver his debt to them, arguing that the war had been fought in their name too. The Kuwaitis disagreed, so Saddam decided to invade and annex their country in 1990. It would teach them a lesson and give Iraq access to ten per cent of the world's oil, to add to the ten per cent they already owned.

The USA, which had previously supported Saddam, had to take exception to this move for political reasons and initiated the Gulf War. They, and a number of allied nations, forced Saddam out of Kuwait in early 1991. In so doing, they had made an enemy of Iraq and lost access to its ten per cent of the world's oil, which was why they had supported Iraq against Iran in the first place. That left unfinished business to be taken care of and so began the gradual process of demonizing Saddam in the eyes of the Western world, so that the USA might one day find a reason to return.

That day came on September 11, 2001, with the event known as 9/11. The terrorist attack on the World Trade Center and the Pentagon by extremist Shi'ite Muslims was just the ticket the USA needed. The attack presented itself as the perfect excuse for waging a crusade – quite literally – against the Arab world.

Having failed in their initial attempt to locate and destroy Osama bin Laden, a Saudi Arabian guerilla leader and the brains behind 9/11, the USA turned once more to Iraq. Waging war on Saddam would give them the ideal opportunity to flex a bit of military muscle on the world stage and end up with a high percentage of the valuable oil back in their control. All they had to do was find their excuse, and Saddam played right into their hands. They began by insinuating that there was a link between bin Laden and Saddam. They then suggested that Saddam was building weapons of mass destruction. Naturally, Sadam saw it all as the political game that it was and played along, not least because it made him look good in the eyes of the Arab world.

Then, in March 2003, the game backfired on Saddam. The US army, supported by UN allies, entered Iraq intent on toppling Sadam from power. As it turned out, it only took three months because Saddam was only powerful within his own borders. The military might that the USA imagined Saddam had, turned out to be exactly that – imagined. His army was ill-equipped with outdated weapons and poorly trained. As for the weapons of mass destruction – not so much as a cardboard decoy was found. Still, the USA had got what they came for – the kudos of finishing their business with Sadam and the oil.

In the years to come, Saddam was tried and executed for atrocities against the Iraqi people. But the Iraqi people themselves were left in total disarray. The regime that served to quell factional problems in Iraq had been removed by Western nations who were naive enough to think that the population would thank them and play by their democratic rules. Instead, they ended up policing a civil war, having given Sunnis and Shi'ites free reign to begin slaughtering one another in the name of Allah. It turned out that Saddam's way of governing Iraq was entirely necessary, as despotic as it was, simply because it was the lesser of two evils.

Although Saddam was hanged in 2006 the jury is still out, among historians that is, as to whether he was really such a force for bad. The atrocity for which he was executed was the massacre of thousands of innocent Kurdish civilians, so it is understandable that people would remember in such a negative way. However, the event was apparently part of the Iran-Iraq war, and Saddam saw this war as a way of saving Kuwait from the imminent threat of Iranian domination. But it is hard to ignore the horrific atrocities committed by Saddam Hussein especially when he ordered a retaliatory massacre in the Shi'ite village of Dujail following an attempt on his own life in 1982. Saddam viewed these atrocities as necessary gestures but regardless of anyone's political views it is hard to forget how many innocent people have lost their lives as a result of his actions. His brutal approach to keeping law and order, often torturing confessions from victims and then murdering them for good measure, just confirms that his reign was most definitely one of pure evil. Saddam died a broken man with obvious signs of fear in his face, perhaps that was a fitting end for a someone who seemed to like to see pain on the faces of others.

AUGUSTO
PINOCHET

It would be true to say that Augusto Pinochet is one of those figures who polarizes opinion, because the equation is so finely balanced. He took control of Chile by coup d'état, forcing a democratically elected president out of office and establishing a military regime. His motivation for doing so however, was that Chile was on the verge of becoming a communist state, for ousted President Salvador Allende was a hard-line socialist.

In 1973, when the uprising took place, communism had had its day on the world stage and people were beginning to realise that it doesn't work in practice, even if it's a nice idea in theory. So, to that extent Pinochet had saved the Chilean people from beguiling themselves into thinking that communism offered some kind of utopia for them. Nevertheless, Pinochet proved to be a tyrant, so life was certainly no better for many under his rule than it would have been otherwise.

Pinochet enjoyed a steady rise through the ranks of

the Chilean army between 1933 and 1973. He was Army Commander and Chief when he removed Allende from office for violating the constitution. Allende committed suicide before troops entered his room, prompted by the fact that the coup was a violent one and so he probably expected execution. Following the coup a military junta was set up with power shared between the heads of the army, navy, air force and national police force.

Pinochet became president because the army was the oldest institution of the four. He looked something like a Mafioso, with slicked back hair, dark glasses and a low trimmed moustache. It reflected his mindset, for he quickly made it clear that he was the boss. Anyone who voiced their opposition to him was quickly removed from power or forced to retire. So, the junta soon evolved into a regime with Pinochet omnipotent.

One of Pinochet's aims was to encourage ambitious thinking in the Chilean people. As opposed to the communist ideal of their being an empowered proletariat, he had a vision of the lower classes becoming proprietorial – owning their own homes and businesses. It wasn't a bad thing, on the face of it, as it gave the opportunity of prosperity to individuals and the nation. But, it was all too much too quick. Pinochet used a group of US trained economists called the Chicago Boys to control his reform policies. By 1983, the country's economy was in serious trouble. Over one-third of the population was unemployed and poverty had actually increased. Too few people had got rich and too many had lost out.

Underpinning Pinochet's failings as a politician were his draconian ways of dealing with political adversaries. Like all incompetent leaders, he resorted to the annihilation of political opponents rather than see that they are a necessary part of society and a part that should be dealt with by diplomatic means, even if only to remain an honourable human being.

His first shameful conduct came following the coup in 1973. Allende's political party had been the PU (Popular Unity) and many dissident PU members were still at liberty. Pinochet offered them sanctuary in a number of military prisons, so many gave themselves up to avoid persecution while the country was in turmoil. Pinochet then ordered a group of army officers to visit the prisons by helicopter and execute the PU members. Some seventy-one people were summarily executed simply for having socialist leanings. The event became known as the Caravan of Death due to the methodical and whistle-stop nature of the execution tour.

Over the next seventeen years, Pinochet continued in a similar vein. Anyone who so much as voiced an opinion that countered the government was dealt with.

Tens of thousands were taken in for questioning and imprisoned and tortured. Around 3,000 disappeared, never to be seen again. It eventually emerged that those who were deemed to pose a significant threat to Pinochet's presidency were murdered in cold blood. It has been reported that they were dealt with in a particularly gruesome manner. They were flown out to sea and dumped into the ocean, having had their stomachs slashed open so that sharks would devour them alive.

Pinochet's fall from power came in a surprisingly capitulatory way. In 1988, he lost a referendum that would have kept him president for another eight years. Then in 1990 an open candidate presidential election was held, so that his successor – Patricio Aylwin – was, like Allende, a democratically elected leader. Pinochet was careful to protect his back though by being sworn in as a senator-for-life, which meant that he was afforded considerable protection against indictment for his crimes.

In fact, Pinochet remained immune from prosecution until he travelled to the UK for medical treatment in 1998. He had been the only South American leader not to side with the Argentineans during the Falklands– Malvinas War in 1982, so Margaret Thatcher viewed him as a political ally and gave him an open invitation to come.

Five days into his visit he was issued with an arrest warrant from a Spanish court and charged with human rights abuses – the torture, murder, illegal detention and disappearance of Chilean citizens. He returned to his home country but, unfortunately for the prosecution and his victims, he was declared too unwell mentally to stand trial, so he was placed under house arrest, which did nothing to make him suffer for his wrongdoings as he was too senile to leave the premises. In 2006, he finally issued a statement admitting full responsibility for his crimes. Evidently, his Catholic guilt had finally got the better of him. He died in December of that same year.

What is so heinous about Pinochet's crimes is that people lost their liberty and their lives simply because they had different ideas about the best way to run a country. What's more, had they been in power they wouldn't have resorted to such underhand behaviour themselves. That is the whole point about modern democracy – it allows for the fact that people are different from one another but that they all have an equal voice. What is more, some of those who died might simply have been voicing socialist rhetoric merely to be seen to be anti-establishment, such as the young and impressionable are want to do.

The message should be clear; that regimes are outmoded and outdated in a modern world where civilisation demands freedom of speech. What makes humanity so special is the fact that all forms of society are works in progress, because they are all invented ways of living together in an increasingly populated world. So far, democracies have shown themselves to be the means by which most people are happy most of the time. Furthermore, anyone who has a grievance is free to let it be known, so that things remain in a constant state of flux and administration adjusts accordingly. For anyone to remove that possibility, be they communist, capitalist or extremist, it is always a cancer on the body of the human condition.

HIDEKI TOJO

When people think back to the Axis Powers or enemies of the Allied nations during World War II, they tend to think of the key nations involved and their leaders at the time. In Europe, Hitler was leader of the Germans and Austrians, while Mussolini was leader of the Italians, but who was leader of the Japanese in the Asian-Pacific part of the war? Well, in Japan it was more complicated, as they effectively had three leaders – Emperor Hirohito (Emperor Showa officially) and his prime ministers Fumimaro Konoe and Hideki Tojo.

As befitted the Japanese mindset of that era, the emperor was treated as something of a godlike figure, so he had the last word when it came to decisions over the war. It was an odd relationship though between emperor and government, because the emperor lived in a palatial world separated from his people, both physically and psychologically. This meant that he could make decisions without fully understanding the consequences of his actions. On the other hand, it meant that he could be manipulated into making decisions by being fed selected information. He was a puppet ruler and the politicians pulled the strings.

Central to the Japanese doctrine was a notion of racial superiority over their neighbours, which was something they had in common with the Nazis in Europe. In the case of the Japanese their target of hatred was the Chinese, whom they regarded as subhuman and so treated them with utter contempt. From 1937 to 1941 the Japanese had waged war on China under the premiership of Konoe, committing any number of atrocities in the name of their emperor, who had readily authorised the use of unethical means, such as chemical weapons, to exterminate the enemy.

By 1941 the Japanese were ready to join the world war, which had begun in 1939, seeing that the Nazis had weakened the position of Britain and the Netherlands with regard to their colonies in the Far East, which the Japanese fancied for themselves. By then the USA was in their sights, too, as the Japanese wanted control of the Pacific Ocean islands, so Japan declared war on the United States, Great Britain and the Netherlands.

Japan went to war under the premiership of Hideki Tojo. He took office on October 18, 1941. The Japanese attack on Pearl Harbor, Hawaii, took place on December 7. It marked the beginning of the Japanese offensive. Hideki had laid plans for attack as war minister in August of the same year. Initially, the emperor was reluctant to go along with his ambitions as he held the British Empire in high esteem, but he was swayed by the success of the Nazis in Europe.

The Japanese war plan was to take control of as many territorial possessions from the Western nations as possible. They included lands that belonged to France and Portugal, as well as the USA, Great Britain and the Netherlands. In addition, they planned to move in a north-westerly direction to take communist-held territories.

Like the Nazis in Europe, the Japanese initially did well with their invasions, but they too spread themselves too thinly, so that inevitably the scales tipped in the favour of the Allied Powers. The Japanese forces began to lose ground and were slowly but surely pushed back towards their place of origin. By early 1945 the USA had developed the atomic bomb and opted to use it to end the war. They reasoned that it would save hundreds of thousands of lives that would otherwise be lost in a continued military push to force the Japanese to capitulate.

In addition, the US knew, from intelligence reports, that Japan and Germany had been working on nuclear weapons, so they didn't want to give the Japanese any more time, just in case they too managed to reach nuclear capability. In August 1945, the Japanese cities of Hiroshima and Nagasaki were hit by nuclear explosions.

They had such a devastating effect that Hideki and Hirohito had no choice but to give in to the demands of the Allies. The bombs fell on August 6 and 9, Japan surrendered within a week and the hostilities of World War II had been truncated by several months, if not years.

Following the war it quickly emerged that the Japanese had behaved atrociously towards their captives. Hundreds of thousands had died unnecessarily due to the most appalling treatment in prison camps, at construction sites and on forced marches. The Japanese had displayed a blatant disregard for peoples of all other nations, creeds and races. Many millions more civilians had been summarily executed on the Japanese trail of conquest as though it were too great an inconvenience to deal with them alive. In many ways they had been even worse than the Nazis, because their callousness was a cultural phenomenon that had infused the entire Japanese population due to centuries of isolation. Consequently they genuinely regarded themselves as a divine people, above all others. For example, at school they famously compared the Chinese with domestic swine.

In September 1945, the Allies began rounding up those military officers and politicians who had not already committed honourable suicide – *hara-kiri* or *seppuku*. On September 8 they caught up with Hideki Tojo, but he had managed to shoot himself in the chest only minutes beforehand. Hideki had missed his heart, however, and recovered from his injuries to stand trial for war crimes. In May 1946, the Tokyo War Crimes Tribunal was convened. Hideki was one of twenty-eight defendants tried for a number of different crimes. He was found guilty and sentenced to death by hanging in 1948. His execution was carried out in December of that year.

In many ways Hideki Tojo is seen as having taken the rap for Emperor Hirohito, who was granted immunity from prosecution. Before his hanging, he repented and admitted ultimate responsibility for all of the atrocities committed by the Japanese military during the war, because he insisted that the buck stopped with him. In so doing he saved the emperor from disgrace in the eyes of the Japanese people in their hour of need. In the postwar years they benefited from having their figurehead still in place – it gave them something to remain proud of to counter the humiliation of losing the war.

It is undoubtedly true that Hideki was a political aggressor, so it shouldn't be thought that he lacked responsibility by any means, but in truth the buck stopped at the door of the emperor's palace. Although he had little direct involvement with operations the emperor certainly had the power to control Hideki and other military and political leaders, but he seems to have not exercised that power. At best he neglected his humanitarian duty in this respect, at worst he went along with their views and even encouraged them to continue doing as they pleased. He had been conditioned to believe that he was divine after all.

Some historians refer to the Japanese war crimes as the Asian Holocaust to afford them the same level of abhorrence as the Nazi Holocaust in Europe. The Japanese were not so systematic in their actions because they were not actively trying to eradicate types of people. In that respect they didn't practise genocide, as such, but they certainly slaughtered a great many people as part of their process of warfare.

Perhaps the very worst Japanese atrocities on record are their acts of cannibalism. There are many accounts of prisoners being treated as livestock to be killed and eaten as a necessary way of coping with limited supplies. Much of the territory conquered by the Japanese was geographically fragmented so that supply routes were difficult to maintain. This led them to devour human flesh in a seemingly matter-of-fact way, and it only served to highlight their view of other peoples as being subhuman.

It doesn't seem to have repulsed them in any way either, which says something about their cultural foundation. For one thing, the traditional and state religion of Japan at the time – Shinto – was and still is an animistic religion, so that the Japanese soldiers didn't hold with any notion that humans have souls. In addition, Shinto has no doctrine or fixed ethical system so that there is no sense of behavioural rightness or wrongness to the Western way of thinking. Secondly, there was something of a tradition in culinary experimentation, as the Japanese historically had had to learn to be self-sufficient as an isolated island nation.

It has been argued that cannibalism gives the perpetrators a sense of empowerment over their enemies, because it provides a sense of having somehow absorbed their energy and so gained their strength. That may have been true of the Aztecs, for whom cannibalism was an intrinsic cultural component of their spirituality, but in the case of the Japanese it seems to have simply been a practical solution to remaining healthy and fighting fit, quite literally, in the theatre of battle. Their ethos seems to have been – Why waste perfectly good meat, when rations were getting a bit low and stale?

Since that time Shinto has been largely replaced by Christianity and Buddhism, although Japan has essentially become a secular state in the Western mould. Many of the Japanese military converted to Christianity after the war as it seemed to offer a way of assuaging their sense of guilt about certain events.

HO CHI MINH

Many people will be familiar with the term 'Viet Cong' or 'VC'. It was an abbreviation for 'Viet Nam Cong San', which was the name of the Vietnamese communists who fought for the independence of South Vietnam against the USA and others during the Vietnam War 1959–75. Before the Viet Cong there were the Viet Minh. They were the League for the Independence of Vietnam, formed by Ho Chi Minh in 1941. At that time Vietnam was a colony of France and was shortly after invaded by Japan as a development of World War II. On September 2, 1945, immediately following Japan's surrender to the Allied Powers, Ho Chi Minh seized the day by proclaiming his country to be the Democratic Republic of Vietnam.

Things were not to be that simple though, for other nations had vested interests in the Vietnam– Cambodia peninsula. For a start, the French still laid claim to ownership of the territory, so they were not about to give it up just like that. In addition, the Soviets and

Chinese wanted a slice of the proprietorial action. Following 1945, the French did their utmost to suppress Ho Chi Minh. Between 1946 and 1954 the First Indochina War was fought between the French and the Ho Chi Minh's forces. Ultimately the French were defeated fairly and squarely at the Battle of Dien Bien Phu, which saw Vietnam divided in two along a line of latitude known as the 17th parallel. Some 400,000 soldiers and civilians lost their lives.

To the north of the line was the Democratic Republic of Vietnam (North Vietnam), controlled by Ho Chi Minh. To the south of the line was the Republic of Vietnam (South Vietnam) controlled by Ngo Dinh Diem. North Vietnam was backed by the Soviet and Chinese communists while South Vietnam was backed by the anti-communist United States of America. It was a recipe for continued trouble and strife, which eventually erupted into the Vietnam War (Second Indochina War) in 1959. Between 1955 and 1959 tensions steadily rose between North and South because the territorial divide was not secure, so that in essence a civil war was on the cards.

For the first four years of the war, 1959–63, it was fundamentally that – a civil war between the Vietnamese factions. But then Ngo Dinh Diem was overthrown in a military *coup d'état* and assassinated. The military had seen Diem's government as a failing one and decided to take control. This escalated the war so that US troops began arriving in 1964 to support the South Vietnam army. Diem had been so unpopular that a Buddhist monk, named Thich Quang Duc, had self-immolated (set fire to) himself in the middle of Saigon, which led to images of his burning to death being broadcast worldwide. It served to heighten awareness of the tensions unfolding in Vietnam and encouraged the US to offer support.

From 1964 onwards the Vietnam War proper raged between North and South Vietnam. The Viet Cong, under Ho Chi Minh, waged a war that proved highly effective, so that the US–SV army struggled against them and lost more lives than expected. By 1969 the USA had over half a million troops in Vietnam, yet they could do nothing to overpower the Viet Cong. The trouble was that the Viet Cong were far more efficient at jungle warfare than the US troops. They secreted themselves in underground camps and used guerrilla tactics to ambush the enemy. The USA resorted to blanket bombing with incendiaries and napalm in an effort to smoke the Viet Cong out from their foxholes, but to no avail. Eventually US public opinion, which had initially been in favour of intervention, swayed the other way due to the number of soldiers returning in body bags. The USA had never lost a war before, so there was a sense of defeatism that led to the withdrawal of troops.

The Viet Cong eventually won the war outright and declared the whole country to be the Socialist Republic of Vietnam in 1976, having captured Saigon in the far south in 1975. It has remained a single party nation until the present day, although it gave up the communist ideology in 1986, allowing a transformation to democracy and capitalism.

As for Ho Chi Minh; he died in 1969 at the very apex of the Vietnam War. He was seventy-nine years of age and died of heart failure. Even though he didn't live to see Vietnam become the communist state he dreamt of, his successors continued in his name, such was the influence he had over his people. His embalmed body is held in a mausoleum in the northern city of Hanoi. His memory has become so revered by the Vietnamese that he is referred to as 'Uncle Ho' and Saigon has been known as Ho Chi Minh City since 1975.

Although Ho Chi Minh played a part in the deaths of many people during his lifetime he was not a tyrant in the same mould as other rulers, such as Pol Pot in neighbouring Cambodia. He was a political activist who pursued the communist ideology because he felt that communism offered a better future than continued rule by the French and a better future than the capitalist ideology adopted by South Vietnam. Unlike Pol Pot, he was a highly intellectual person who didn't have a chip on his shoulder about his place in society. He was noted for being polylingual – speaking Vietnamese, Chinese, Thai, English, Spanish, German and Russian. On his 100th anniversary – May 19, 1990 – he was recognised as a 'great man of culture' by UNESCO (United Nations Educational, Scientific and Cultural Organization) for his humanitarian achievements.

Ho Chi Minh is one of those historical figures who is the victim of propaganda. The success of the Viet Cong against the US army inevitably earned him a reputation for being yet another 'Dirty Red' in the eyes of the Western world, such was the anti-communist feeling of that era. Since then, however, the world has realised that his motives were sincere and that he didn't actively practise cruel methods in the name of a communist utopia.

With regard to atrocities committed during the Vietnam War, it has become clear that it was a two-way street. That is to say, the US army carried out a number of massacres during their campaign, which overshadow any attempts to accuse the Viet Cong of playing unfairly. Due to the guerrilla modus operandi of the Viet Cong the USA were always at odds with them in terms of what is proper warfare etiquette and what is not. This in itself led to the US massacres, because the US troops were always on edge when they searched settlements for signs of enemy presence. The slightest disturbance could result in soldiers opening fire through paranoia at the thought of being trapped. Panic could easily lead to the slaughter of innocent civilians in order to be better safe than sorry.

JOSIP BROZ 'TITO'

Some people might be described as killers in a good way, perhaps! Josip Broz 'Tito' falls into that category, because his enemies were primarily the Axis Powers during World War II. He was regarded, by the Allied Powers, as an important resistance leader in the Balkans area of Europe during that period.

He was born Josip Broz in a place that is now in Croatia, but was then in a country known as Austria-Hungary, which has since been dissolved. In 1913, at the age of twenty-one, Josip was enlisted into the Austro-Hungarian army, prior to the hostilities of World War I. At the outbreak of war he ended up fighting on the Eastern Front against the Russians, where he was caught and imprisoned as a POW in 1915. He managed to escape in 1917 and hide out with a Russian family until 1918. By then he had been influenced by the communist ideology of the Bolsheviks and returned to his homeland with new political ideas.

When Josip returned to his stamping ground Austria-Hungary no longer existed, because his side had lost the war. Instead, various regions had formed a new union known as the Kingdom of Serbs, Croats and Slovenes – later to become the Kingdom of Yugoslavia (First Yugoslavia), which comprised Kosovo, Macedonia, Montenegro, Serbia, Bosnia-Herzegovina, Croatia, Slovenia and Vojvodina. Josip joined the outlawed Communist Party of Yugoslavia (CPY) and became politically active.

Josip spent the next decade working as a machinist and being generally oppressed by the Yugoslav government, which was anti-communist. In 1934 he adopted the moniker 'Tito' as a codename and the following year moved to Russia once more, where he was actively involved with the Stalinist regime. All communist parties belonged to an international umbrella organisation known as the Comintern, which Stalin orchestrated. In 1936 they sent him back to Yugoslavia to purge the CPY of anyone Stalin considered suspect. It led to the murder of the CPY Secretary-General in Moscow in 1937, so that Tito took his place.

The CPY was still an illegal organisation at that time, but it was gaining in strength due to the turmoil in Europe that would erupt into World War II. Tito was defiant and openly voiced his criticism of both the fascists, who would form the Axis Powers, and the democrats, who would form the Allied Powers.

Consequently the CPY became a partisan guerrilla force and hostilities began in 1939. Yugoslavia itself wasn't invaded until April 1941, by the Axis Powers of Germany, Italy, Hungary and Bulgaria.

In July Tito called an emergency meeting of the CPY. He had held back from attacking the fascists until then because Stalin had signed a treaty with Hitler, but then Hitler turned on his word and invaded Russia. Seeing his opportunity, Tito made himself military commander of the CPY and announced plans to attack the occupying forces with the aim of catalysing a communist revolution in Yugoslavia. When the Germans realised what was afoot they introduced retaliatory measures to check the activities of the partisans. They announced that 100 civilians would die for every one German soldier killed, or fifty civilians executed for each soldier injured.

Despite these measures, which the Germans readily carried out, by the close of 1942 Tito had managed to liberate enough territory to form a governing body, known as the Anti-Fascist Council of National Liberation of Yugoslavia, of which Tito was named president. Initially the Allied Powers were reluctant to support Tito, as they had vested interests in returning the government exiled at the outbreak of war. However, Tito was so effective at resisting fierce attacks by the Nazis that Churchill and Stalin gave him the recognition he deserved. With Allied support he continued his war of attrition against Hitler's forces, managing to evade capture on a number of occasions. Ultimately he allowed Soviet troops to enter Yugoslavia in their push westward, driving the Nazis back into Germany to end the war in 1945.

Following the war, the Yugoslav peoples had a collective election. The CPY won the election, with Tito as premier. Although the various Yugoslav peoples had nationalist sentiments, Tito's government suppressed divisive ideas in favour of maintaining Yugoslav unity. Tito was unrelenting in his aims. He imprisoned an archbishop for collaborating with the Nazis, and thereby found himself excommunicated from the Catholic Church by the pope.

In 1948, Tito severed ties with the Cominform (the new version of the Comintern) and made an enemy of Stalin. When Stalin attempted to have him assassinated he simply responded by letting Stalin know that he would be assassinated, too. Remarkably, Stalin backed off, although it led to the deaths of many communists who were seen as Tito sympathisers and could conceivably be bringers of death to Stalin's door. Relations improved between Yugoslavia and Russia in 1953 when Stalin died of a stoke, but tensions would rise again in the late 1960s.

In 1963, Tito renamed his country the Socialist Federal Republic of Yugoslavia and introduced some reforms to relax the communist hold. He allowed private enterprise and gave people the freedom of speech and religious expression, effectively making Yugoslavia an evolving democracy, much to the chagrin of the Soviets. Then, in 1967, Tito opened the borders of Yugoslavia to all foreigners. Despite these seemingly uncommunist moves, the Soviet block found a way to tolerate Tito, because he was a popular and well-respected politician on the world stage.

A new Yugoslav constitution was passed in 1974, which saw Tito named President for Life. He lived for six more years, in which time he made sure that Yugoslavia maintained a neutral stance with regard to the Cold War between West and East. He died in 1980 at the age of eighty-eight. By then he had become such a humanitarian figure that his funeral is recorded as the largest in history, attended by statesmen from all four corners of the world.

If anything, Tito became the exact opposite of a killer, because his leadership maintained an equilibrium among the Yugoslav peoples, so averting bloodshed. Inevitably, following his death instabilities developed so that a decade later a series of Yugoslav 'civil' wars were fought, leading to the disintegration of Yugoslavia. There are now nine separate countries: Slovenia, Macedonia, Central Serbia, Serbia (Vojvodina), Kosovo, Montenegro, Croatia, Federation of Bosnia-Herzegovina and the Republic of Srpska.

Clearly Tito had had his work cut out managing to keep so many different populations happy under one roof. Fittingly, it is said that his nickname 'Tito' was the marriage of the two Serbo-Croatian words *ti to* (you-that), which he used to use as a phrase to order people about: i.e. 'you do that'. Others think it may have been a reference to the Roman emperor Titus. Either way, it was a sobriquet that fitted the man.

PART THREE

COLD-BLOODED WOMEN

ELIZABETH BATHORY

Belief systems are peculiar and dangerous things. Humans have minds that rationalise the world around them by processing information and constructing interpretations of reality based on their ability for common sense and the level of their self- education. Alas, more often than not this leads to people believing in things that stem entirely from their own imaginations, as in the case of Elizabeth Bathory. She became so obsessed with ideas of the occult, that it led her to believe that bathing in the blood of young virgin girls would halt the ageing process in her skin. She also drank their blood because her belief system naturally concluded that it would prevent her ageing from within, too. Consequently her beauty regimen made her perhaps the most prolific female serial killer in history. Women preyed upon by other women are rather rare, but Bathory made up the numbers nicely and she got away with it for good measure.

There are comparisons to be drawn between Elizabeth Bathory (1560–1614) and Gilles de Rais (1404–40). Both were wealthy nobility of the European Renaissance period, who developed interests in the worship of mystical powers and lured hundreds of innocents to their deaths to fulfil the carnal demands of their demons. It appears that they both must have also 'got off' sexually from delivering pain and suffering to their victims and were in the perfect position to satisfy their sadistic appetites.

They both lived in castles and used their social advantage to entice their young victims with the promise of work. Both also had accomplices in their employ and managed to evade detection until they had killed a great many victims. Gilles de Rais ended up being hanged for his evil deeds, but Elizabeth Bathory escaped execution because she was so well connected that the authorities thought it better to place her under house arrest and convict her accomplices instead. Despite her attempts at rejuvenation, she continued to age and eventually died of natural causes, albeit at the relatively young age of fifty-four.

Elizabeth Bathory was a Hungarian countess who resided in an area that is part of Slovakia in modern times. To be fair, like Gilles de Rais, it is impossible to know just how many people she killed. For one thing there was no forensic investigation as there would be now. In fact, there was virtually no investigation, as the trial of her collaborators was based around the accounts of witnesses who had lost children and the fact that a few victims were found dead and alive within the confines of her castle. The testimonies of her accomplices and those of other witnesses led to a great deal of conjecture and hearsay, as one might expect.

Consequently, rumours, legends and myths were generated that probably distorted and exaggerated whatever the truth may have been. For this reason the number of reported victims varies between several dozen and several hundred. In addition, the motives vary also, from pure sadism to a genuine desire for immortality, or a combination of both. One thing is for sure, Elizabeth Bathory was only prevented from continuing with her murderous activities for the final three years of her life. Also, her husband was frequently away on campaigns of war during their marriage and he died around 1600, so it seems likely that she was able to carry out her evil deeds for at least thirty years, more or less uninterrupted. So, even a conservative estimate of one a month puts the figure at 360. One account puts the figure at 650, based on a diary that was supposedly kept by Elizabeth Bathory, although there was no official record of its existence during the trial.

It is only possible to speculate about the behaviour of Elizabeth Bathory, but she seems to have been a pathological sadist. That is to say, she acquired and developed a taste for torturing her victims because it satisfied a maladjusted mind. Some people have naturally dulled senses, so that they can only reach sexual arousal with the heightened stimulation that comes from witnessing the death throes of unfortunate souls. All of the senses are supplied with sensations that do not come from everyday life with the result that the person enters a frenzied state of excitement. In turn, endorphins are released by the brain that activate opiate receptors to achieve analgesia. In simple terms, this means that the experience becomes addictive and the sadist craves for the experience to be repeated time and time again.

For Elizabeth Bathory the bringing together of her sadism with the occult must have seemed like a natural marriage. It would have legitimised her behaviour in her own mind and those around her. She would have had licence to torture and kill in the name of sacrifice to the demons she worshipped. Similarly, it would have been only a short step to begin developing ideas of attaining immortality and perpetual youth. She wasn't an attractive woman to begin with, judging by contemporaneous portraits, so she probably felt the impact of ageing all the more for that reason. It is said that she convinced herself that bloodied areas of her skin seemed more supple and pure, so she took to bathing her entire body in blood as a matter of routine.

Having consulted with her occult shamans she developed a method to get the most from her victims. She would have them strung up by the legs above her bathtub and then climb in below. The victims would then have their throats cut so that their warm blood poured directly into the bath, where she performed her abhorrent ablutions. She would also drink blood from the streams coming from the victims as their lives slowly drained from their bodies. Inside her castle, Elizabeth had a gynaeceum. This is a part of the castle where only females are allowed. In the gynaeceum she had dungeons and torture chambers, with all manner of gruesome devices at hand to carry out her work. She always had a stock of new victims imprisoned so that she could satisfy herself whenever she had the slightest whim.

A woman named Anna Darvulia was Elizabeth's principal collaborator in the early years of her criminal career, but she died young, so Elizabeth relied on the loyalty of the maids in her employ. Three of them were executed on January 7, 1611. Two had their fingers cut off before being thrown into a fire. The other was beheaded before being thrown in, as she had apparently been less involved. A fourth escaped with her life, because she had been bullied into collaborating by the others. As for Elizabeth Bathory, she escaped justice and continued to live in her castle under house arrest, where she died only three years later.

It seems fair to say that Elizabeth Bathory's inhumanity to humanity was as much to do with circumstance as anything else. Had she not been born into the nobility she may have had a more socialising experience as a girl and not developed her sadistic tendencies. Indeed, even if she had shown such tendencies, society would have put a stop to them much earlier on. Of course, there is also the possibility that she suffered from a mental disorder due to the effects of inbreeding, which had long been a problem in high society, simply because the accepted gene pool for pairing was so restricted in size that people married their cousins, or worse.

MARY ANN
COTTON

Some people like to move on whenever they get bored with their lives. Mary Ann Cotton always made sure that she removed all ties with the past by killing so-called 'loved ones' with poison. She lived in the north-east of England during the Victorian era but never stayed in the same place for more than a few years. It is unlikely that she would have gone undetected even once in the modern age, with meticulous post-mortems or autopsies being carried out as matters of routine and with state-of-the-art forensic science, but Cotton had murdered three legal husbands, an illegal husband, a lover, a friend, a mother and thirteen children by the time she was convicted. That's twenty victims, although some may have died of natural causes, given that life expectancy was very low at that time due to contagious diseases and the lack of medical treatments.

She was born Mary Ann Robson in 1832, at Murton, County Durham. Mary's father was deeply religious and a fierce disciplinarian to boot, and Mary lived in fear of his harsh punishments. He worked long hours as a pitman to try and make his family as comfortable as possible, but the harsh conditions took their toll and he died shortly after Mary's fourteenth birthday. Life was extremely hard for a working-class family in nineteenth-century England, and especially as Mary and her younger brother Robert, now had to be raised by their widowed mother. Mary was petrified of being sent to the workhouse, but was saved from this fate when her mother remarried. However, Mary did not like her new stepfather and the feeling was mutual, so she started to look for a way to escape her unhappy home life.

Mary eventually left home at the age of sixteen to work as a servant to a well-to-do family in South Hetton. Although the family had no complaints regarding Mary's work, rumours reached the head of the household that their servant had been seen in the company of a local churchman on more than one occasion. However, when questioned by her employers, Mary denied any such illicit liaisons.

After three years of working for the family Mary decided to take up an apprenticeship to be a dressmaker. Around the same time she met a miner by the name of William Mowbray, by whom she became pregnant. Mowbray did the rightful thing and married his lover in

July 1852 and for the next few years Mary moved round the country as her husband took employment wherever he could. Within the first four years, Mary gave birth to five children, but only one survived past early infancy. Although infant mortality was quite common at the time, it would be fair to say that this number of deaths in one family was quite exceptional.

William and Mary argued frequently and she drove her husband to work longer and longer hours dreading the thought that they should have to live in poverty. William, who was tired of the constant fighting, decided to take a job on a steamer which meant he spent many days away from home. The family set up home in Sunderland and the number of children dying from unexplainable illnesses continued in abnormally high numbers.

In January 1865 William was forced to spend some time at home because he had suffered an injury to his foot. Mary became his nursemaid but as his foot got better his general state of health went downhill. He died from an intestinal disorder which the doctor found hard to understand as his patient had shown no signs of illness prior to his spell under Mary's care. The doctor decided to pay the grieving widow a visit fearing that she would be in a state of depression having lost so many of her children and now her husband as well. What he hadn't expected, was to find Mary dancing around the sitting room in a new dress which she had bought using the money from William's life insurance.

After William's death, Mary decided it was time to move her family once again, and they settled in Seaham Harbour. She wasted no time in forming a new friendship with a local man named Joseph Nattrass, despite the fact that he was already betrothed to another. Despite Mary's pleas, Joseph told her he planned to go ahead with the wedding and Mary left Seaham Harbour downhearted with her one remaining child.

Mary returned to an area that she knew and found a home and employment in Sunderland. She was taken on at the Sunderland Infirmary and because of the long hours, Mary's daughter, Isabella, was sent to live with her maternal grandmother. Mary kept the wards at the infirmary spotlessly clean and her employers commented on her diligence and friendly manner. She was particularly friendly with one of the patients, George Ward, and the couple married as soon as he was well enough to leave. However, shortly after the wedding, George became ill and died in October 1866. The doctors were puzzled by his condition which included paralysis and violent stomach cramps, neither of which responded to regular treatment.

After George's death, Mary decided to move on again, after all she didn't want the finger of suspicion pointing at her. On her own again, Mary needed to find employment once again and managed to get a job as a housekeeper to shipwright James Robinson. He had recently lost his wife and needed someone to look after his children. Mary had excellent references and James decided to employ her in November 1866.

True to form, tragedy followed Mary wherever she went and just two days before Christmas, James's youngest child died following a bout of gastric fever. Still grief-stricken over the loss of his wife, James turned to Mary for comfort which resulted in her becoming pregnant. Although a new marriage was now on the cards it had to be postponed when Mary was needed to go and nurse her mother following a sudden illness in March 1867.

Although her mother was showing signs of making a full recovery by the time Mary arrived, within days she started to complain of stomach pains which had not previously been a symptom of her illness. Nine days after Mary's arrival, her mother was dead. Before returning to the Robinson house, Mary decided to go and fetch her daughter Isabella, who had enjoyed her life with her maternal grandmother. Within three weeks of returning to James Robinson, not only was her own daughter dead, but a further two of the Robinson children. Amazingly James did not suspect that his sweet Mary

Ann was in any way connected with the deaths and they mourned their losses together. The couple got married in early August and their first child, Mary Isabella, was born in late November. However, by March the new baby had also died from a gastric disorder and now James Robinson was starting to have doubts. Not only had there been so many deaths since Mary had arrived in his house but she also constantly pressed him for money and was also pressurising him into taking out an insurance on his life.

James Robinson had always been very good at handling money so you can imagine his shock when he started hearing rumours that Mary had run up vast debts without his knowledge. When he questioned his remaining children, he learned from them that Mary had coerced them into pawning valuables and giving her the money. James was fuming and after a violent argument he threw Mary out of the house and she left, taking their baby daughter with her.

Mary had always dreaded living in poverty and for once in her life she was forced to wander the streets. Desperate and alone she visited an old friend and asked the woman to look after her baby while she went to post a letter. Needless to say, Mary never returned and Mary Isabella was returned to her father on January 1, 1870, a move which undoubtedly saved the young child's life.

Mary was soon back on her feet and dating a recent widower Frederick Cotton, having been introduced by his sister Margaret, a friend of Mary's. Like James he was a recent widower and had lost two of his four children in infancy. Margaret had been left to raise the family but, as I am sure you have already guessed, she died from an undetermined stomach complaint shortly after Mary started seeing her brother. This left the way open for Mary to console Frederick and once again she soon became pregnant with his child. They were married in September 1870, despite the fact that she was still legally married to James Robinson. However, compared to her other crimes, bigamy seemed of little importance.

Mary wasted no time in insuring the lives of Frederick and his two surviving sons. Mary gave birth to baby Robert in 1871 and a couple of months later learned that her former lover, Joseph Nattrass, had never gone ahead with his planned wedding and was living in West Aukland. Suddenly, Mary lost all interest in her husband and moved to West Aukland to rekindle her old passion.

Frederick Cotton died of gastric fever in December 1871, and as soon as the coast was clear Mary asked Joseph to move into the house. However, quickly realising that Joseph was never going to keep her in the lifestyle she had become accustomed to, she decided to get a job working as a nurse to an excise officer called

John Quick-Manning. John was recovering from a bout of smallpox and Mary realised that he was a far better prospect than Joseph Nattrass. She soon became pregnant by her new paramour, but there were just too many obstacles standing in the way of another marriage.

Undaunted by this fact, Mary worked quickly. Frederick Jr died in March 1872 and baby Robert shortly afterwards. Joseph became ill several days later but not before revising his will and leaving everything to Mary. Young Charles Cotton was still a problem, however, and in spring 1872, she sent him to the local pharmacy to buy a small quantity of arsenic. The chemist would not sell to Charles as it was illegal to sell toxic substances to anyone under the age of twenty-one, but Mary was undeterred and sent a neighbour instead. By July Charles had died of gastric fever. Mary started to panic and realised she had been living in one area for far too long, particularly as there were already some malicious rumours going round the neighbourhood.

The only person Mary had talked to about Charles's death was a government official by the name of Thomas Riley, whom she had originally approached to see if she could get Charles into a workhouse. When Riley had seen the boy he had been a healthy young lad and he was quite shocked to learn that he had died so quickly. He took his suspicions to the police, who questioned the physician who had attended Charles. The physician was also surprised to learn of his death and Riley managed to talk him into delaying writing a death certificate until the boy's death had been investigated.

Mary made a big mistake following the death of Charles. Instead of calling for the doctor, she had gone straight to the insurance office and collected on his life insurance. However, she learned that they would not give her the money until she was in receipt of a death certificate and Mary went visibly pale when she learned that there was to be a formal inquest.

However, the brief inquest did not show that Charles had died from unnatural causes, which is not surprising because arsenic poisoning was very hard to trace and its symptoms were similar to those of natural illness. Mary was angry at Riley and told him in no uncertain terms that he could pay the costs of Charles's burial.

This could very well have been the end of the matter, leaving Mary free to kill again and again, had the press not got hold of the story which set a spark to the gossip that was already rife in West Aukland. Quick-Manning was appalled when he heard the gossip and quickly severed his ties with Mary.

Mary decided it was time to leave, unaware that the net was closing in around her. A doctor who had taken part in the initial inquiry into Charles's death had kept some samples from the contents of his stomach. He was unconvinced that his death was natural and when he carried out further tests, his suspicions proved founded when he discovered large quantities of arsenic. The doctor went straight to the police and Mary was arrested before she could run from the hands of the law.

Mary Ann Cotton was forty when she went to court in March 1873 and she looked like a haggardly old woman. The trial had to be delayed while Mary gave birth to the daughter fathered by Quick-Manning. Her defence was that her most recent victim had inhaled arsenic vapours from wallpaper, as arsenic-based paints were often used in those days. However, a local newspaper had revealed the trail of death behind her movements, so the jury only took ninety minutes to find her guilty of murder.

As she seemed an outwardly pleasant and affable person, a number of petitions were presented to the home secretary in an effort to have her death sentence commuted to life imprisonment, but to no avail. Even her pleading letters to James Robinson fell on stony ground. She wrote:

. . . If you have one spark of kindness in you – get my life spared . . . you know yourself there has been . . . most dreadful lies told about me. I must tell you, you are the

cause of all my trouble. If you had not abandoned me, I was was left to wander the streets with my baby in my arms . . . no place to lay my head.

Mary was led to the gallows on the morning of March 24, 1873, at Durham County jail. It may have been deliberate or perhaps just an error of judgement, but the executioner made Mary's rope too short. Her neck failed to break and she died slowly but surely from strangulation.

Although no one is certain exactly how many people died as a result of Mary's toxic potions, it has been estimated that it could have been as many as twenty-one – ten of her children by various husbands, three husbands, five stepchildren, her mother Margaret Cotton and her lover Nattrass. Mary Ann Cotton, however, maintained her innocence right up to the end.

LIZZIE BORDEN

Lizzie Borden will be forever immortalised by the Victorian playground rhyme:

Lizzie Borden took an axe and gave her mother forty whacks, when she saw what she had done she gave her father forty-one.

In fact Borden wasn't convicted for the crime, but it was one of those cases where likelihood convicted her in the eyes of the public, despite the lack of evidence in court. The rhyme itself was composed by a newspaper journalist shortly after the double murder and was actually inaccurate, even though it stuck in the public consciousness. Apart from the fact that Borden's guilt could not be proved, she actually gave her stepmother eighteen whacks and her father nineteen.

Had the crime occurred in the modern era Borden would undoubtedly have been convicted through forensic evidence, but she committed the heinous act back in the day when forensics meant obvious proof, such as blood stains – hence the phrase 'caught red-handed'. As there were no witnesses and Borden had had plenty of time to clean herself up, she was effectively in the clear before the police had even arrived on the scene.

In the present day, police work by the principle that 'every contact leaves a trace', a motto coined by Edmund Locard (1877–1966) who was a leading French criminologist. Even he didn't live to see the time when it would be possible to detect the tiniest trace of DNA, chemical or fibre that could incriminate a suspect, but he set the benchmark that forensic scientists continue to aspire to achieve. Very few people are found not guilty of indictment in modern times if forensic evidence seems to place them fairly and squarely in the frame.

Lizzie Borden's stepmother and father were found with their heads bludgeoned by a blunt instrument on August 4, 1892 in Massachusetts, USA. Andrew and Abby Borden were apparently 'found' by Lizzie Borden, who summoned the help of the family maid Bridget Sullivan, who had been cleaning windows outside at the time of the slayings. In fact, Lizzie only reported the death of her father at first, whose body was found on the couch. Her stepmother's corpse lay in a room upstairs and was 'discovered' afterwards.

It would be no exaggeration to say that the police investigation and court case left something to be desired by contemporary standards. An axe-head and shaft were found in the basement, but officers argued about whether Borden would have had time to clean them, so they were dismissed as the murder weapon. The police also found a number of bloodstained rags, but they were dismissed as evidence too, simply because Borden had stated that she was menstruating at the time and that she had used the rags as sanitary towels.

The police failed to discover any bloodstained clothing when they first searched the house, but Borden was seen burning a dress only a few days after the murders. Unbelievably, the jury believed her when she told them that she had disposed of the dress because she had ruined it with paint. The twelve good men and true deliberated for only an hour and acquitted her, because they had been presented with no hard evidence as absolute proof of guilt.

Borden became something of a *cause célèbre* following the murders, not least because she was the subject of trial by media. She was ostracised by family, friends and neighbours, but the public at large elevated her to celebrity status. Perhaps it was because they felt that she had beaten the establishment, even though it had involved murder.

FANNY ADAMS

Another very well-known name associated with Victorian murder is that of Fanny Adams, although this time she was the victim. Most people have used the expressed 'Sweet Fanny Adams' on occasion, but how many actually know its origin.

Fanny's mother, Harriet Adams, had no reason to worry when her daughters wandered off to play with a friend on Saturday, August 24, 1867. Nothing much ever happened to disturb the rural tranquillity of Alton, Hampshire.

Eight-year-old Fanny Adams and Minnie Warner wandered off down Tan House Lane accompanied by Fanny's younger sister, Lizzie. Just as they were approaching Flood Meadow, they were approached by a man wearing a black frock coat, dark trousers and a light-coloured waistcoat. He offered Minnie three halfpence to go off and play with Lizzie and Fanny a full halfpenny if she would walk with him into the nearby village of Shalden.

There was something creepy about the way the man looked at the girls and Fanny told him she didn't want to go with him. Annoyed at the rejection the man promptly picked Fanny up and carried her to a nearby meadow well out of sight of the other children. By this time it was nearly 1.30 p.m.

Lizzie and Minnie made their way home for tea at about 5.00 p.m. after having played all afternoon. As they passed one of the neighbour's houses, a Mrs Gardiner leant over the fence and asked them where Fanny was. When the children told Mrs Gardiner about the man, the woman panicked, went to collect Fanny's mother, and the pair ran up the lane in the direction the children had come from. When they got halfway up the lane they met the man that the girls had described and shouted at him: 'What have you done with the child?'

Keeping his composure, the man replied in a calm manner, 'Nothing', and continued to say he had simply given the girls some money to buy sweets, which was something he often did. He then told the women that when he had last seen Fanny she was fine and that he had watched her run off to join the other girls. The man explained that his name was Frederick Baker and that he was a clerk to a local solicitor, William Clement. The women said they were sorry for doubting him but they were worried because Fanny had not returned home. The two women were totally taken in by his composed manner and air of respectability and simply bid him farewell.

When Fanny still hadn't returned home by 7.00 that evening, Mrs Adams called on her neighbours to help her search for her daughter. When they found poor Fanny's body lying in the middle of a hopfield, they were all sickened to their stomachs at the scene of carnage in front of them. It had been a sexually motivated assault that had turned into a frenzied butchery. In fact the attack had been so vicious that Baker had dismembered Fanny's corpse – the severed head lay on two poles and had been deeply slashed from mouth to ear, her right ear had been cut off and both her eyes were missing. Nearby lay a leg and a thigh and it took several days for the police to find all of the remains that hadn't been eaten by wild animals. Fanny's eyes were later recovered in the River Wey.

When George Adams heard of his daughter's death he collapsed in grief and then reacted by taking his shotgun and heading off towards the hopfield where Fanny had been found. The neighbours, on seeing the glazed look in his eyes, decided to stop him and managed to prise the gun out of his hands.

In the meantime, Frederick Baker was arrested at his place of work. As he was escorted back to the police station passing angry crowds that had gathered, he kept proclaiming his innocence. However, the twenty-nine-year-old clerk could not explain away the spots of blood on the wristbands of his shirt and on the front of his trousers. When the police searched him they found two small knives, one of them stained with blood, and Superintendent Cheyney was in no doubt that he had found the culprit. Cheyney locked Baker away in a cell while he went to check on his movement that afternoon.

Witnesses confirmed that Baker had left his office just after 1.00 p.m. returning just before 3.30 p.m. They said he went out again until around 5.30 p.m. which was when Mrs Gardiner and Mrs Adams had seen him walking away from the hopfield. It would appear that he murdered Fanny at around 1.30 p.m. and then returned to the scene of the crime later the same afternoon to carry out further depredations on poor Fanny's body.

When Cheyney searched Baker's office the following day, he discovered a diary which contained a damning entry stating that he had killed a young girl. On the hopfield, a local painter by the name of William Walker had found a large stone covered with blood and hair, which had been used as the murder weapon. After the coroner had the unenviable task of viewing the gruesome remains of Fanny Adams, Baker was remanded in Winchester Prison to await the formal committal hearing. The hearing was held at Alton Town Hall on Thursday, August 29, before local magistrates.

Baker maintained his innocence throughout but, because of the horrific nature of the crime, a large crowd had gathered outside the town hall and the prisoner had to be protected from the angry mobs wanting his blood.

The trial took place at Winchester Assizes on December 5, and the jury only took fifteen minutes to return a guilty verdict. A crowd in excess of 5,000 came to see him hanged outside Winchester Prison, a large proportion of them being women. A large cheer went up as the noose tightened around Baker's neck at 8.00 a.m. on Christmas Eve 1867.

It just so happened that the case of Fanny Adams coincided with the introduction of canned meat stew to the ranks of the British navy. As the contents of the cans were largely offal, fat and connective tissue, as opposed to good cuts of meat, it became a joke to suggest that they were parts of 'Sweet Fanny Adams'. In time, the phrase came to mean something of little value or nothing at all – Sweet F. A. So it was that black humour had immortalised the name of an unfortunate murder victim.

WINNIE RUTH JUDD AND RUTH SNYDER

The word 'ruth' means kindness, hence the word 'ruthless' meaning the opposite. This is the story of two Ruths who both turned out to be capable of murder, just like Ruth Ellis – Winnie Ruth Judd and Ruth Snyder. Both committed their heinous crimes in the USA in the early part of the twentieth century. Judd turned out to be insane and spent most of her life under lock and key in hospital. Snyder was found to be guilty of malice aforethought and duly went to the electric chair.

Winnie Ruth Judd, known as Ruthie, was the twenty-six-year-old wife of a fifty-six-year-old doctor. The couple had moved to Phoenix in 1930 in the hope that the warm, dry climate would alleviate some of the symptoms of Winnie Ruth's tuberculosis. However, the elderly doctor was unable to find work in Phoenix and left his bored wife behind while he went in search of employment in Los Angeles.

In an effort to try and kill the boredom of being on her own, Winnie Ruth made friends with two young women who shared a room close to where she lived. A short while after the doctor left Phoenix, one of the young women was taken ill and decided to return to her home town of Oregon to recuperate. Winnie Ruth said she would move in and take the girl's place.

This worked well until the girl returned from Oregon and tensions started to mount. Winnie Ruth decided it would be prudent to move out and rent another apartment, and this proved to be a wise move as the three girls remained close friends. They often went out socialising and it wasn't unusual for Winnie Ruth to spend the night with her two friends.

However, her two friends were not the only people with whom she shared a bed. Even before her husband had left Phoenix, Winnie Ruth had started a torrid affair with a notorious playboy by the name of Jack Halloran. Despite the fact that Halloran was married with three children, it didn't stop him visiting Winnie Ruth and her friends almost every night, often bringing friends and plenty of illicit alcohol with him.

One evening a violent argument broke out and the two young room-mates were shot to death. Winnie

Ruth panicked and left, heading back to her own apartment. She had only been back a few minutes when she heard Halloran's car pulling up outside. Halloran was very drunk while Winnie Ruth was hysterical and he found it hard to understand exactly what she was saying. When he eventually made sense through the uncontrollable sobs, he took Winnie Ruth back to the girls' apartment where he took care of the bodies. He told her to clean up the mess while he stuffed one of the girls' bodies into a trunk. One fitted easily, but he had difficulty in closing the second trunk and consequently had to dismember the body.

The following day, Winnie Ruth had regained her composure and returned to work as a receptionist, resuming her normal duties. When she had finished for the day, Winnie Ruth repacked the second trunk, putting some of the body parts into a suitcase to try and reduce the weight. Then she asked her landlord to arrange for the trunks to be taken to the local train station, explaining that they were full of medical books that her husband had asked her to send.

Winnie Ruth herself then went to the station and boarded a Union Pacific train to Los Angeles, after first checking the trunks onto the baggage car. She carried the suitcase containing the body parts and kept it by her side during the journey. What she hadn't allowed for was the heat on the train and during the 400-mile journey the trunks in the baggage car started to give off an offensive odour. Added to this the baggage handler noticed a liquid oozing from the trunks which looked like blood, so when they arrived at Los Angeles station, he decided to report it to the station agent. When Winnie Ruth went to fetch the trunks, the agent refused to release them and asked for the key so that he could see what was inside. Winnie Ruth told the agent that she would have to go and get the key from her husband, and promptly disappeared. When the agent forced the trunks open he was appalled at what he saw; all he had expected were some carcasses from an illegal hunting trip.

Winnie Ruth was found four days later sitting on a couch in a mortuary and a posse of heavily armed policemen escorted her back to Phoenix to await her trial. As she stepped back onto the streets of Phoenix, over 20,000 people lined the streets anxious to catch a glimpse of the now notorious murderess. The landlord of the apartments where the two girls had been murdered, made his own profit out of the crime by selling tickets to visit the scene of the crime.

The press had a field day and Winnie Ruth became dubbed as the 'Trunk Murderess'. She was tried for the murder of only one of the women – the one that hadn't been dismembered – and was found guilty and sentenced to death by hanging. She was moved to the state prison in Florence to await her execution, but the warden petitioned to have a sanity hearing and she was ultimately saved from her fate. Just seventy-two hours before her scheduled hanging, Winnie Ruth was pronounced insane and taken to the Arizona State Hospital where, according to records, she became a model prisoner.

Amazingly, she managed to escape from the hospital five times and in 1952, on her last spell of freedom, she returned when the administrator promised that she could appear before a grand jury. Her evidence regarding Halloran's involvement in the crime was so convincing that the jury recommended that her death sentence be commuted to life imprisonment.

Ten years later, she walked out of the State Hospital once again and made her way to Northern California. She became the companion to a wealthy doctor and his wife, and managed to elude capture for a further six and a half years.

Winnie Ruth Judd was released just before Christmas 1971, having spent forty years of her life in confinement. She returned to Phoenix in the 1990s where she lived under the assumed name of Marian Lane. She died peacefully in her sleep at the ripe old age of ninety-three.

Ruth Brown Snyder was a discontented housewife who went looking for excitement, but I don't think her search for thrills was meant to end up with her being executed in Sing Sing's electric chair. Ruth was married to Albert Schneider, an art editor on the magazine *Motor Boating*. Albert was a conservative character who loved fishing and the outdoor life and had had one great love in his life, Jesse Guishard. Unfortunately Jesse had died of pneumonia before he could walk her down the aisle, and Albert had made his home a shrine to his ex-fiancée. He adored his mother and was prepared to do anything for her, but he felt at the age of thirty-two that life was slipping him by.

Albert met Ruth when she was working as a telephone operator for a call centre. Albert had lost his temper with her when she failed to connect him to the number he requested, but regretted his outrage as soon as he had slammed the receiver down. To try and make amends he visited the call centre and asked to see the operator with whom he had lost his temper, and was taken aback when he was faced with the tall, blonde young woman with the sweetest smile. Smitten by Ruth, Albert started to meet her when she finished work and soon the couple were dating. However, Albert was frustrated as Ruth would not give in to his repeated sexual advances, but she told him she was a virgin and intended to stay that way until she became a bride. Eventually, possibly through frustration and loneliness, Albert asked Ruth to marry him. Ruth quickly accepted but said she had one request and that was that he change the spelling of his name to Snyder, as she felt it had more of an American ring to it. Albert agreed and the wedding went ahead.

Right from the start the marriage had its flaws. Not just because of the couple's age difference, but also because of Albert's refusal to remove any of Jesse's pictures and belongings from his house. Ruth found it hard living in the shadow of his past love and she was starting to find life a little dull to say the least.

When at last she fell pregnant, Ruth felt everything would change and that perhaps Albert would become the loving husband and father she had hoped for. However, she was in for a shock when she told her husband the good news. Albert was most displeased and told her quite bluntly that he had never wanted children and when baby Lorraine was born, she drove a deeper wedge between the couple.

In 1923 the Snyders settled in a substantial house in Queens Village, New York City. Ruth decided that she wanted to get out and socialise and invited her mother to come and stay so that she had someone to mind Lorraine. She started to attend parties and soon became a popular dinner guest with her witty talk and laughter. It was at one of these social occasions that she met a corset salesman by the name of Judd Gray. The couple were complete opposites – Ruth, now thirty-two, was tall, blonde and very good looking with an outgoing personality, whereas Judd was short, with a cleft chin, thick-lensed spectacles and, one could say, instantly forgettable. Despite these differences, there was a sexual attraction between them and it wasn't long before Ruth and Judd embarked on a torrid affair, despite the fact that Judd was supposedly happily married with children.

Albert, who was never at home during the day, left the way open for Ruth to fulfil her passions while her nine-year-old daughter, Lorraine, was attending school. She started to invite Judd round to her house and when that wasn't convenient they had their illicit liaisons in a hotel, leaving Lorraine to sit and wait for her in the downstairs lobby or ride up and down in the hotel lifts to pass the time. It would appear that Ruth and Judd could not get enough of each other and they would go to any means to spend time together, with Ruth playing the dominant role.

Soon the affair was not enough for Ruth and she started making outrageous accusations about her husband to Judd. She accused him of treating her badly and tried to convince her lover that Albert had to be disposed of. When Judd recoiled in disgust at her suggestions, Ruth would use her womanly ways to talk him round to her way of thinking. However, Ruth went too far with her persistence and she drove her lover to drink, until he spent much of his time inebriated on large amounts of Prohibition liquor. Judd continued to refuse to go along with her plans, that is until Saturday, March 19, 1927, when he had simply had enough and decided to give in.

They devised a plan, which they thought would be foolproof (but which turned out to be foolhardy), to murder Albert. Judd caught the train from Syracuse to New York and then took a bus to Long Island, and walked to where the Snyders lived in Queens Village. He had been drinking for most of the day, but his nerves still got the better of him and he hung around outside the house for a long time before daring to go in. He eventually plucked up the courage and entered through the back door, as previously arranged. Ruth, Albert and their daughter Lorraine were out attending a party, and Ruth had told Judd to go and hide in the spare room until they returned later that night. Inside the room Judd noticed that Ruth had laid out the 'tools of their trade' – a heavy sash window weight, a bottle of chloroform and a pair of rubber gloves.

Judd heard the front door open and looked at his

watch in the light coming from a crack in the door. It was two o'clock in the morning. He heard the family go upstairs and a little while later, after Albert had retired to bed and she had settled Lorraine in her own room, Ruth went to the spare room wearing only a very flimsy petticoat. Ruth kissed her lover eagerly and the pair made love while her husband and daughter slept peacefully in their beds. They lay for a while together, then Ruth jumped up and grabbed the window weight, beckoning for Judd to follow her. She led him down the hall to the master bedroom where Albert was asleep, his face hidden by the bedclothes. Ruth stood on one side of the bed, while Judd took the other, and as Ruth pulled back the covers Judd brought the weight crashing down on Albert's head. However, the blow was so weak that it simply glanced off the side of his head and Ruth was forced to grab the chloroform to render her husband unconscious as he tried to grab his attacker. As soon as he stopped struggling she grabbed the weight from her bungling lover and brought it down with full force on Albert's skull.

When they had carried out their deadly deed, the couple went downstairs and had a drink while discussing the final part of their plan. Firstly, they knocked over a few items and opened a few cupboards in an effort to fake a robbery and then Judd tied Ruth loosely by the wrists and ankles and placed a gag in her mouth. Then Judd left, but stupidly asked a policeman what time the next bus was back to Long Island.

Ruth crawled her way upstairs and started banging on her daughter's door. Lorraine opened her bedroom door to find her mother on her knees on the floor with a gag in her mouth, trying to speak. She removed the gag and Ruth told her to go as fast as she could to the neighbour's house so that they could alert the police.

Ruth and Judd thought they were home and dry and truly believed they had carried out the perfect crime. However, the police, who were used to visiting the scene of a burglary, were not convinced and said that something didn't look quite right. Ruth had told the detective that she had been hit over the head by a tall man with a dark moustache and had been rendered unconscious, and yet there was no bump or even a bruise to show that she had been attacked. Her wrists and ankles had been tied so loosely that there wasn't even a mark and, on top of that, there were no visible signs of forced entry which meant that the intruder must have had a key, or been let in by someone. Foolishly, the items which Ruth had said were missing, were found hidden under a mattress in one of the bedrooms and the sash weight, which was obviously the murder weapon, lay in the basement covered in blood. One thing the police did conceal from Ruth, however, was the fact that they had found a tie pin bearing the initials 'J. G.' on the floor of the room where Albert had been murdered. When the police looked in Ruth's address book they found an entry under 'G' for a man named Judd Gray and the investigators asked her, 'What about Judd Gray?'

Ruth was shocked at hearing his name and stupidly replied, 'Has he confessed?' The police, who up until that moment had never heard of the man, bluffed and said that he had. As soon as she heard that, Ruth started talking and confessed, blaming everything on Judd. She admitted to helping Judd make the arrangements and ransack the house, but she said that he had been the one to wield the sash weight. Her confession even led the police to the hotel room in Syracuse, where they found Judd Gray sitting on the bed still a little worse for drink.

When the police arrived to arrest him, Judd laughed at the accusation and said, 'Ridiculous.' However, he had been careless and thrown a train ticket into the rubbish bin in his hotel room and, when confronted with the evidence, he broke down and confessed. Just like Ruth he tried to blame everything on his accomplice, saying that he had been totally against killing her husband, but had gone through with it when Ruth had threatened to tell his wife.

It didn't take long for the newspapers to pick up on

the story and soon the front page of each tabloid carried pictures of Ruth and Judd, along with the full story of their confessions. As the trial commenced Judd's belief that Ruth had wanted her husband murdered so that they could be together was quashed, as it came to light that she had recently increased Albert's life insurance policy to $100,000 and had been paying the premiums on the quiet. Ruth and Judd both had separate lawyers to fight on their behalf and throughout the trial they continued to apportion the blame on one another.

Then it came to light that Ruth had tried to kill her husband on several other occasions. Twice by attempting to asphyxiate him by disconnecting the gas range, almost succeeding when she closed the garage door with the car engine still running and finally by poisoning his whisky – amazingly all without Albert being in the least bit suspicious. When the evidence was being given in court, Ruth sat with her face set in stone. Rudolph Valentino's widow, reporter Natacha Rambova, wrote of Ruth Snyder: 'There is lacking in her character that real thing, selflessness. She apparently doesn't possess it and never will. Her fault is that she has no heart.'

Ruth and Judd were both found guilty of Albert's murder and sentenced to death in the electric chair at Sing Sing prison. Appeals were filed but dismissed and Ruth Snyder was the eighth woman to be executed for murder in New York State. As the current surged through her body at 11.00 p.m. on January 12, 1928, a Daily News photographer uncrossed his legs and triggered a forbidden camera to take an unprecedented picture which appeared in the tabloids the following morning. It was a horrifying and graphic photograph which has become famous over the years, and which set a precedent for future executions whereby anyone entering the death chamber had to be thoroughly searched.

No one bothered to take a picture of the pathetic figure of Judd Gray who went to his death just six minutes later.

One footnote to add to this story is that the tie pin found on the bedroom floor bearing the initials 'J. G.' was in fact one given to Albert by his beloved Jesse Guishard – nothing to do with Judd Gray whatsoever.

DOROTHEA PUENTE

Some people will do just about anything for money! In the case of Dorothea Puente, life meandered for her in such a way that she was always impoverished and badly treated, so that she evolved into a criminal and a misandronist – a man-hater. This enabled her to prey on men as a source of income without any sense of remorse for her actions. She made something of a career of it, as she was sixty years of age when she eventually got caught in 1988, so prison became her comfortable retirement home.

Dorothea was born into an extremely disadvantaged background in California. Her father and mother both died of alcoholism when she was four and six years of age respectively. When they were alive they had abused and neglected her, so that she had had to scrounge food from neighbours to stay alive. The term 'cotton picking varmint' might have been invented for her father, for he was indeed a cotton picker and also a good-for-nothing. After a spell in an orphanage she was taken in by some relatives who also lived in California.

In 1946, at the age of seventeen, Dorothea married, but just when things were looking up, her husband died of a heart attack, leaving her destitute once more. Her solution was to forge some cheques in desperation, but she got caught and sentenced to her first stay in jail. Things weren't going well, and they were set to get worse upon her release, some six months later. Her only option was a life of prostitution, as she had nothing else to offer by way of skills and qualifications.

In 1952, she married for the second time, but for worse rather than better. Her new husband was a violent drunk who subjected her to violence for many years. As is so often the case with women of low self-esteem, she chose an aggressive man, mistaking his abuse for machismo and his shame for affection. In 1960, she fell foul of the law again, when she was arrested in a brothel and imprisoned again. No sooner had she been released than she was arrested and imprisoned once more for vagrancy, such was the vicious cycle of her life.

By the mid-1960s Dorothea had had enough and attempted to cultivate a proper career for herself. She found herself a job working as a nurse's aid in care homes for the elderly and disabled. She evidently made a success of it as she soon secured herself a position managing a boarding house for the socially dis-advantaged. It seems that she had turned her own unfortunate life experiences into assets, in understanding the plight of the people in her charge. However, her mind had already been influenced by the advantages to be had from criminality.

With her new-found public image of respectability, she realised that she was now in the perfect situation to continue with her wrongdoings unsuspected and unchecked. Her modus operandi was to steal the benefit payments of her boarding house customers. She did this by mothering them, so that they allowed her to look after their finances. She would then encourage them to get drunk and disorderly so that they got arrested and put in jail, and she could pocket the cash.

Inevitably things got more complicated. When the boarders returned from jail they would make accusations, so Dorothea had to play a shrewd game to keep from being arrested herself. This was when she realised that killing them was the best solution all round. It removed the problem and allowed her to entice new boarders under her motherly wing. Also, they were invariably old with no relations, so no one noticed when they disappeared.

In 1968, Dorothea took over a care home with sixteen bedrooms in Sacramento, California and got busy. Neighbours noticed that she had taken on a handyman, who would dig holes at all hours of the day and night, both inside and outside of the building. He was also seen pouring and levelling concrete pads that seemed to have no purpose. The handyman was a local drunk nicknamed 'Chief', to whom Dorothea had given shelter. Then one day, he was never seen again. However, Dorothea was such an innocent-looking and outwardly affable person that the curiosity of the neighbours didn't develop into suspicion of any unsavoury behaviour, so she was never questioned by police about the matter.

That didn't mean that she was immune from run-ins with the law, however. By the mid-1970s Dorothea had taken to chatting up elderly drunks in bars so that she could steal their benefit cheques and cash them in by forging their signatures. The police caught up with her in 1976, arresting her on over thirty counts of fraud. Nevertheless, she continued to do the same thing as soon as she was free to do so. She was pushing fifty and old habits die hard.

In the early 1980s Dorothea took an apartment in the same street as the care home. This is when things started to really hot up. A woman called Ruth Monroe began sharing the apartment but was soon found dead from an overdose of painkillers. When the police questioned Dorothea she spun a story that Ruth had taken her own life because she had discovered that her husband, who was evidently estranged to her, was suffering from a terminal illness. The police bought the story, due to her charming front, and the matter was duly treated as suicide.

Then, in 1982, Dorothea found herself in prison yet again. This time it was for theft. She had drugged a man named Malcolm McKenzie in her apartment and stolen his possessions. He duly went to the police to blow the whistle. While Dorothea was serving her time she developed a relationship by correspondence with a man named Everson Gillmouth. They set up home together immediately following her release, but love soon turned to hate and Dorothea ended his life.

With his body to dispose of, she hired the services of a carpenter named Ismael Florez to do some work in her apartment. She then asked him to construct a wooden crate, which she apparently wished to use for storage. This was in fact true, the object to be stored being Everson Gillmouth's corpse, which was why the crate looked rather like a coffin when it was finished. Having managed to hoist the cadaver into the crate and nail the lid down, she then asked Florez to deliver it to a storage depot. He obliged and set off with Dorothea and the crate. En route to the depot, however, Dorothea suddenly decided to jettison their cargo at a fly-tip by the side of the road. She told Florez that the contents were only worthless junk, so it wasn't worth paying for storage. They dumped the crate and drove away.

A month or so later, a fisherman noticed the coffin-shaped crate. Upon investigation he noticed the smell of death from within and put two and two together to make four. The police prized the lid off to find a badly decomposed man inside. Despite the material evidence of a murder or homicide, the police failed to identify the man or make any connection with Dorothea Puente. However, Everson Gillmouth's relatives had been trying to get in touch with him and Dorothea had repeatedly told them that he had fallen too ill to contact them in person.

Inevitably one thing led to another and the police arrived at Dorothea's door. Had she told Gillmouth's relatives that he had left her, then the police might have simply asked a few questions about his possible whereabouts and departed. But Dorothea had made the mistake of inventing his illness. In November 1988, two years after killing Gillmouth, the police discovered a body buried under Dorothea's lawn. An extended search found a further six bodies and Dorothea found herself charged with murder. She was actually convicted of three murders and began serving two life sentences at the age of sixty.

Dorothea Puente's defence was that the men had all tried to rape her. It may have been true, given her relationship history and the way she enticed them in, but her motive was the want of money above all else. It has been claimed by some that the police made little effort to find more bodies following her conviction, because they saw that their work was done and had no incentive to spend police time unearthing the bodies of people who had not been missed in the first place. Consequently, criminologists have estimated that she may have disposed of as many as twenty-five people in total.

RUTH ELLIS

Were it not for the fact that Ruth Ellis was the fifteenth and last woman to receive capital punishment in Britain, it is doubtful that anyone would know her name. After all, there can't be many who know the name of the penultimate woman to receive the death penalty – Styllou Christofi – or the one before that – Louisa Merrifield. Ellis was a very petite woman who did her best to imitate the film star looks of Marilyn Monroe. She made the error of falling in love with a man – David Blakely – who turned out to be something of a cad.

Ruth Neilson was born in Rhyl, in Wales, one of five children. She left school at the age of fifteen to work as a waitress and in 1941, right at the height of the Blitz, the family moved to London. When Ruth was seventeen, she became pregnant by a soldier and gave birth to a son, Andy, in 1944. The father was supportive, offering financial help until he had to return to Canada, leaving Ruth short of money and struggling. She decided to become a nightclub hostess, which paid significantly more than her previous jobs and she managed to support herself and her son until she met forty-one-year-old George Ellis in 1950. Unfortunately for Ruth, George was an alcoholic who became abusive when drunk. The relationship was doomed from the start, with Ruth being possessive and convinced that her husband was having an affair. When Ruth gave birth to Georgina in 1951, George refused to believe it was his and Ruth finally accepted the marriage was over and moved back home.

In 1953, Ruth became the manager of a drinking club called the Little Club, which was a favourite haunt with racing drivers. It was here that she met David Drummond Moffat Blakely, who was three years her junior. Blakely quickly moved into the flat above the club, despite the fact that Ruth was well aware that he had a reputation as being homosexual.

Ruth and Blakely had a passionate and stormy relationship which often erupted into jealous fights. They fought over money, which Blakely blew on his playboy lifestyle, and over each other's affairs. Ruth knew that Blakely had another mistress, while she had an older lover, Desmond Cussen, who hated Blakely with a passion. Fuelled by alcohol, their fights became more and more violent until Blakely caused Ruth to miscarry by punching her in the stomach during one of their frequent rows.

Blakely was a motor engineer by trade but also had a passion for driving racing cars. Along with some friends Blakely decided to build his own car, *The Emperor*, which caused further arguments as he spent more and more time away from Ruth. Convinced that Blakely was having an affair with a nanny that his friends had recently employed, in a pique of jealousy she called Cussen and asked if he could pick her up.

It was Easter Sunday, April 10, 1955, and Ruth managed to persuade Cussen to drive her to Hampstead, where she waited outside the Magdala pub where she knew Blakely was drinking with a friend. Blakely came out of the pub at around 9.30 p.m. and Ruth called his name. Blakely chose to ignore her which infuriated Ruth and, taking a .38-calibre revolver out of her handbag, she fired a shot at him. She then followed him round the car and fired a second shot which caused him to collapse on the pavement. Then she stood over him and emptied the remaining four bullets into him as he lay wounded on the ground.

When they heard the commotion, other drinkers came out of the pub to see what was happening. Ruth, still holding the smoking gun, was arrested by an off-duty policeman by the name of Alan Thompson and taken to Hampstead police station.

During her interrogation, Ruth remained calm and

gave a detailed confession. She appeared at a special hearing at Hampstead Magistrates Court on Easter Monday and was then remanded in custody of Holloway Prison to await her trial.

At the prison she was kept in the medical wing where she was examined to see if she showed any signs of mental illness. The examining doctors found no evidence and deemed that Ruth Ellis was fit to stand trial.

Her trial opened on Monday, June 20, 1955, at the Old Bailey in Court No. 1. Showing no signs of remorse, Ruth appeared in dock wearing a smart black two-piece suit and a white blouse. She pleaded not guilty and played on the fact that there had been some sort of conspiracy among Blakely's friends to keep him away from her. When the prosecuting counsel asked her, 'Mrs Ellis, when you fired that revolver at close range into the body of David Blakely, what did you intend to do?' she answered quite plainly, 'It was obvious that when I shot him I intended to kill him'.

The jury retired and, not surprisingly, found Ruth Ellis guilty of murder after deliberating for only twenty-three minutes. To convict a person of murder it is necessary to prove two things – one that the person actually killed the victim and two that they intended to kill the victim. Clearly there was no doubt from Ruth Ellis's previous answer that she was guilty of both.

Ruth stood silent and impassive as Mr Justice Havers read out the sentence – death by hanging – to which Ruth replied with a smile, 'Thank you'.

The case caused widespread controversy and was no doubt in part responsible for the abolition of the death penalty. Petitions to save her life were turned down and, having spent just three weeks and two days in the condemned suite at Holloway, Ruth Ellis was taken to meet her maker. She was executed by Albert Pierrepoint on July 13, 1955, aged just twenty-eight.

Although it has often been questioned whether Ruth Ellis deserved to die for her crime, there is no doubt that with the evidence presented to them, the jury had absolutely no option but to find Ruth guilty of murder.

Sadly, Ruth's death had many repercussions. Within weeks of her execution, Ruth's eighteen-year-old sister died suddenly, reportedly from a broken heart. George Ellis, Ruth's husband, became an alcoholic and hanged himself just three years later. Ruth's son, Andy, suffered irreparable psychological damage and committed suicide in a rundown bedsit in 1982.

KATHLEEN FOLBIGG

Sudden Infant Death Syndrome (SIDS) is one of those apparently modern phenomena attributed to the effects of polluting agents in the environment – airborne chemicals and gases, electromagnetic radiation, vaccinations, medications, dietary contaminants, and so on and so forth. It may actually be the case that babies have always died every now and then for no apparent reason, but people didn't react in the modern way because infant mortality was more commonplace and so death certificates gave the likely causes of death as non-specific conditions.

Anyone who has had a baby will know that babies are not particularly good at regulating their breathing while asleep. They frequently appear to stop breathing altogether and then suddenly come back to life with a deep breath. The reason for this is a phenomenon known as sleep apnoea – a temporary cessation of breathing. Thankfully, the body usually has an involuntary overdrive mechanism that ensures intake of oxygen before it is too late. It is this mechanism that appears to malfunction in some babies, so that they fail to revive themselves and die in their sleep. In Britain this is known colloquially as cot death and in the USA as crib death.

When SIDS first became a recognised phenomenon it was regarded as an extremely unlikely and therefore very unlucky thing to strike a family. It followed that two cases of SIDS in the same family were regarded as so unlikely that foul play should be suspected. Consequently a number of mothers were charged with filicide and imprisoned. Some of them were guilty as charged, with evidence available to show that they had committed murder, by smothering their infants for example. For others the situation wasn't so cut and dried – there was no evidence to suggest murderous intent at all.

Then, so-called specialists began to revise their opinions. They began to suggest that SIDS may be triggered by the genetic make-up of babies. This changed the complexion of things entirely. Suddenly, it became arguable that siblings of a SIDS baby might suffer from the same problem, even though a specific genetic flaw couldn't be identified. As a consequence, a number of imprisoned mothers were released as the mathematical argument of chance was no longer admissible in the complete absence of evidence – circumstantial or material.

Of course another consequence was the fact that filicidal mothers now had the perfect cover for their behaviour. That is what happened in the case of the Australian murderess Kathleen Folbigg. She managed to extinguish the life from her four infants over the space of nine years (1990–99) by disguising their deaths as serial SIDS. Everyone believed that her children inherited congenital traits that led to their deaths.

The first three infants – Caleb (twenty days old), Patrick (four months old) and Sarah (eleven months old) – all died apparently from breathing difficulties, and people thought that Kathleen was an extremely unfortunate mother. Then the fourth child – Laura – died at nineteen months, which the coroner considered too old for SIDS, so a police investigation was ordered.

In the early days of the investigation Craig Folbigg, the father of the four children, found his estranged wife's diaries. In them she had written numerous entries expressing the way that motherhood made her feel unattractive and ignored by her husband. Rather than loving her babies she had seen them as competition for her husband's affections. But the most damning entry read: 'One day Sarah left . . . with a bit of help'. Then of Laura she wrote: 'She's a fairly good-natured baby – thank goodness, it has saved her from the fate of her siblings'. Evidently her good nature didn't last in the mind of Folbigg.

The diaries were circumstantial evidence so the police had to find further evidence to reinforce a conviction. Another entry said, 'Obviously I am my father's daughter'. Upon investigation it turned out that her father had murdered her mother when Kathleen was eighteen months of age. It was these words that secured Folbigg's fate. She was eventually found guilty of all four murders and sentenced to ten years for each child. Craig commented that he had had his suspicions but had always loved her too much to take things any further until he found the diaries, which turned passing thoughts into cold reality.

Some doctors argue that women who kill their children in a disguised manner are suffering from Munchausen by Proxy (MhbP), just like Beverley Allitt, the killer paediatric nurse. This view is based on the notion that they enjoy the attention that surrounds them during and after the event. Folbigg's diaries certainly support this theory, as she wrote frequently about feeling marginalised by the presence of her babies.

In a way, it can be understood to be a form of perpetual immaturity, as the need for attention is a childlike quality in itself. So, in essence, such women don't view their offspring as their own children to be loved unconditionally, but rather as younger siblings with whom they need to compete. Ultimately, inflicting illness and death is the perfect solution for them, because it means that they remove the competition and get lavished with attention in the process. This is a very worrying conclusion that says a great deal about the fragility and selfishness of the human condition in these women.

Not all filicidal mothers kill their babies in a disguised manner attempting to feign SIDS. Dena Schlosser was an insane Texan who interpreted a television news story as a message from her god and duly removed the arms of her eleven-month-old daughter Margaret as some kind of sacrificial act. China Arnold was similarly maladjusted and caused the death of her newborn baby daughter Paris by cooking her in a microwave oven.

Some mothers turn on their children because the pressures and responsibilities of life build to a point where their minds cannot cope any longer. They undergo personality changes, and murdering their dependants becomes the choice they make. A very good example of this is Andrea Yates, another woman from the USA. She was a loving mother of five children when one day she flipped to the dark side. While her husband was at work she drowned all five of her children in the bathtub and calmly called the police to announce what she had done.

In the case of Yates she was diagnosed with that moot condition described as postpartum depression in the USA and postnatal depression in Britain, which is something that new mothers frequently suffer from. She was certainly suffering from psychosis, which is a detachment from reality in thought and emotion, and was presumably brought on by the demands that come with raising a young family – insufficient sleep, unrelenting routine, social isolation, infrequent respite, etc. That explanation is understandable, if not excusable, but it could just as easily happen to a man in the same situation, so it is by no means a gender-specific condition.

Other mothers kill their children in a more calculated way. Darlie Routier was a woman from Texas who enjoyed the high life. In fact she enjoyed it so much that she grew resentful of her two sons when the family fell on hard times. No longer able to live the life that she had grown accustomed to, she began to think of ways to cut back on spending domestically. That included feeding, clothing and schooling her two sons, so she murdered them with a knife and then went about pretending that an intruder had attacked them. Had she done it in the days of Lizzie Borden she might well have got away with it, but it was 1996 and forensics had moved on since Victorian times.

BEVERLEY ALLITT

While Dorothea Puente resorted to murder for money, Beverly Allitt did so for attention. She has been dubbed the Angel of Death, because she worked as a paediatric nurse and made her patients her victims. There is a condition called Munchausen's syndrome, whereby sufferers become obsessed with feigning illness, so that they enjoy being the centre of medical attention in hospitals. It is akin to hypochondria, except that hypochondriacs believe in their own maladies, although the crossover point might be described as something of a grey area.

Beverly Allitt had a very similar condition called Munchausen by Proxy (MhbP) syndrome, which meant that she made others ill so that she could bask in the sunlight of praise at having saved them from death. In short, she was the very worst kind of person you'd want looking after your child in hospital, for she was the exact opposite of the selfless altruist that a children's nurse should be. As if harming children wasn't bad enough, she ultimately took things too far and failed to save them, but even then she enjoyed the thanks of the grieving parents for trying her very best to save their children.

Allitt was one of four children born into an essentially ordinary home environment. But she was an attention-seeker from an early age. Sibling rivalry prompted her to feign illness and injury as a young girl and she quickly cultivated her craft of deception and self-delusion, even giving herself plaster casts for supposedly broken bones. So she reached adult life with Munchausen's syndrome/hypochondria well developed in her personality. The Munchausen component came to the fore when she faked the symptoms of appendicitis and actually had her appendix removed quite unnecessarily. She then prevented the appendectomy scar from healing by picking away at the sutures. She also self-harmed by lacerating her body with broken glass and bruising herself with hammers.

When Allitt left school her career choice was to train as a nurse. She was evidently drawn to a work environment with which she was already very familiar. While training she was considered to be somewhat of an oddity among her fellow students. She was absent from training college frequently and then relished the attention she got when she returned, having used illness as her excuse for being away. She was also suspected of being behind a number of unpleasant events involving the smearing of faeces in places where others took their refreshments. Presumably she found some kind of pleasure in witnessing the disgust and fuss it created. Clearly she would stop at nothing to be noticed and things were set to get a whole lot worse.

Despite her poor attendance record and having failed her nursing exams on numerous occasions, Allitt was given a six-month contract at the hospital she had trained in, due to staff shortages. It was the Grantham and Kesteven Hospital in Lincolnshire, England. She had actually applied for a nursing position elsewhere but had been turned down, so Allitt was determined to use her six months to impress the administration. Unfortunately for them, Allitt's idea of making a good impression was one that would lead to serial murder and attempted murder.

At the age of twenty-three, Beverley Allitt began work in Children's Ward Four. She was very attentive, perhaps overly attentive, but seemed to lack any emotional connection with her young charges. In hindsight her colleagues would remark that she displayed no feelings towards the babies and toddlers she nursed. She never held them when they cried and she showed no feelings even when they died, but she always did her job in a workmanlike manner, so everyone overlooked her lack of compassion.

Her psychological condition advanced to MhbP in February 1991. Her first victim was a seven-week-old baby boy named Liam Taylor. He was admitted to hospital with pneumonia. He was never discharged but left hospital dead from heart failure thanks to Allitt's intervention. Her attack on Liam Taylor was the first of thirteen, four of which were fatal. They lasted for a period of fifty-eight days until Allitt was finally arrested.

At first the medical staff at the hospital couldn't believe what a run of bad luck they were having, as there were no obvious signs of foul play. Even when they did begin to develop suspicions they simply couldn't get to the bottom of it because they couldn't identify a method of attack that pointed the finger at anyone. Following the fourth death, that of a baby girl named Claire Peck, staff alerted police simply because the number of cardiac arrests over such a short space of time was too high to be explained statistically.

To their enormous credit, the police began a systematic investigation using a chart. By a simple process of elimination they identified the presence of Allitt as the only component common to all thirteen attacks. The evidence was circumstantial but damning, so Allitt was arrested without further delay. Forensic work subsequently identified the use of insulin as the agent Allitt used to induce cardiac arrest in the children. She also interfered with their supplies of oxygen.

Initially people found it difficult to believe that a trained nurse could· be responsible for such heinous crimes. An angel of mercy had turned out to be an angel of death, thereby destroying the bond of trust that exists between the medical profession and the public. It wasn't until Allitt's life history had been disclosed that people realised just how serious her personality disorder really was. She had craved attention so badly that she had played with the lives of infants so that she might be thought of as a Florence Nightingale figure. And indeed, it worked, if only for a few short weeks.

What was worse was that she totally denied any wrongdoing and has never fully admitted her crimes, almost as if they never happened. It's as if she thought that her behaviour was normal and that she believed all people did similar things. Perhaps her mind works in such a different way to most that she cannot help but judge the world entirely by her own standards. To that extent it could be argued that she suffers fundamentally from a form of autism that happens to express itself as Munchausen syndrome and then develop into MhbP when all other avenues are exhausted.

In May 1993, Beverley Allitt was convicted of four murders and nine attempted murders. She began thirteen life sentences at the age of twenty-four in

Rampton Secure Hospital, Nottinghamshire, England. It isn't far from another hospital – the one she had hoped to work in, having impressed the staff with her nursing skills in Lincolnshire. Little did she realise that she was dangerously ill herself. Even incarcerated Allitt continues in her quest to attract attention. Waiting for her trial she stopped eating and developed anorexia nervosa, which caused delays to the proceedings. Since her conviction she has frequently self-harmed by whatever means available to her – piercing her skin with paper clips and scolding herself with hot water. It seems that she is hardwired by her condition to have a perpetual need for attention, come hell or high water.

Her sentence is the most severe ever given to a British female defendant and she has the dubious accolade of being one of the most prolific female serial deviants. She is in the company of such infamous killers as Rose West and Myra Hindley, except that she worked alone while they had male accomplices in their crimes. The case was such a high profile one, as is usually the case with female killers of children, that it is unlikely that Allitt will ever be released.

Insanely, it is an oddity of British law that results in thirteen life sentences not actually meaning what it suggests. Officially, Allitt has only been imprisoned for 'at least forty years' which means that she has to be considered for parole when she is sixty-four. That provides each 'life sentence' with a duration of a paltry three years and four weeks. In point of fact, several of her victims were older than that when she performed her evil work on them.

JUDI BUENOANO

Some women get divorced or separated, others simply kill their partners and move on. It is quicker, more convenient and cheaper than if divorce is involved, although it does carry the inherent risk of resulting in arrest for murder. Nevertheless, Judi Buenoano got away with it repeatedly and for many years before justice finally caught up with her. She has consequently been named the Black Widow, and with good reason. She has been described as a scheming, cold-blooded killer who preyed on her victims and all because of greed. In 1998, Judi Buenoano became the first woman to face execution for her crimes in Florida, USA, in 150 years, meeting her end at the hands of Old Sparky – the infamous electric chair.

Like so many of the criminals mentioned in this book, Judi Buenoano had a troubled childhood. She was born Judias Welty, in Quanah, Texas, on April 4, 1943. Her father was a farm labourer and her mother came from an ethnic background, with relatives in the Mesquite Apache tribe. Judi never really got to know her mother as she died when Judi was only four years old, which resulted in the family being split up. Judi and her younger brother, Robert, were sent to live with their maternal grandparents, while the two older children were put up for adoption.

Judi was happy living with her grandparents but it wasn't long before things were to change. Her father remarried and took Judi and Robert to live with them in Roswell, New Mexico. Judi didn't get along with her new stepmother and was constantly teased by her two stepbrothers. She was allegedly beaten, starved and forced to work long hours and by the time she reached the age of fourteen she retaliated. She attacked her father, stepmother and her two stepbrothers, for which she received a two-month prison sentence. When she was released, rather than have to face the misery of homelife, Judi chose to go to reform school and attended Foothills High School in Albuquerque until she was sixteen.

Having totally turned her back on her family, Judi sought work and managed to get a position as a nursing assistant in Roswell using the name Anna Schultz. In 1961 she became pregant, but would never divulge the name of the father and gave birth to a son whom she christened Michael Schultz.

Judi married an airforce officer by the name of James Goodyear on January 21, 1962. James was a loving, caring husband who adopted her son Michael. Their first child, James Jr, was born in 1966 and their daughter, Kimberley, in 1967. The family settled in Orlando, Florida, and it was here that Judi saw an opportunity to start her own business. With the financial backing of her husband, she opened the Conway Acres Child Care Center and worked hard while James Snr did his tour of duty in Vietnam. Three months after his return home, James was forced to spend a period in the US naval hospital in Orlando suffering from some inexplicable illness. He lost his fight for life on September 15, 1971, and Judi wasted no time cashing in on his three life insurance policies – netting herself a nice little sum. Later the same year there was a mysterious fire at the Goodyear home and Judi received a further $90,000 to add to her coffers.

Judi didn't stay on her own for long, very quickly moving in with her new boyfriend Bobby Joe Morris who lived in Pensacola. Things appeared to be going well, but Judi's son Michael was being a disruptive influence in the household and at school, and she decided to place him in residential foster care for a while.

In 1977, Bobby Joe moved to Colorado and Judi and her family, including Michael, joined him there after another fire at the family home. No prizes for guessing who claimed the insurance money. Bobby Joe became sick just a few weeks after Judi's arrival in Colorado and once again the doctors were unable to give an accurate diagnosis and discharged him from hospital. He had only been home for two days when he went into a coma and had to be rushed back to hospital, where he died on January 21. Once again Judi had made sure that his life insurance policies were paid up to date. The pattern was now becoming all too familiar.

However, Judi was not to be so lucky this time as Bobby Joe's family were highly suspicious about his death and, added to that, he was not the only victim. When Judy and Bobby Joe had been visiting his parents in Alabama in 1974, a man had been found dead in a hotel room. The local police received an anonymous phone call tipping them off and they found the victim who had had his throat cut and been shot in the chest. Allegedly Bobby Joe's mother heard Judi telling someone, 'The son-of-a-bitch shouldn't have come up here in the first place. He knew if he came up here he was gonna die'. Athough Bobby Joe confessed to the crime shortly before he died, the police could not find enough evidence to bring charges and the case was dropped.

Meanwhile, Judi legally changed her name to Buenoano, which was the Spanish equivalent of Goodyear – the name of her first husband – and she moved back to Pensacola with her family.

Michael joined the army in June 1979 but started showing signs of paralysis to his upper and lower limbs. He was given heavy metal braces in the military hospital and was discharged, being deemed unfit for duty. He was sent home to the loving care of his mother! Unable to walk or use his hands, Michael was totally reliant on his mother, and thought nothing of it when she suggested a canoe trip down the East River on May 13, 1980. Sadly, the canoe capsized – Judi and James were able to swim to safety, but Michael, weighed down by his heavy braces, drowned before anyone could reach him.

The police accepted Judi's version of events, but army investigators were not so easily convinced; after all, Judi had received $20,000 from her son's military life insurance. When the sheriff's office discovered that there were two other life insurance policies on Michael's life, they decided to take an interest in the case and discovered that the signatures on the policies had been forged.

Judi's next victim was a Pensacola businessman by the name of John Gentry II. It wasn't long before she was up to her old tricks and convinced John that they should take out life insurance policies on each other to the tune of $500,000. Judi also talked John into taking vitamin pills to keep him in the peak of health – except they didn't – and he started to complain of nausea and dizziness. Judy convinced him that he needed to take even more vitamins and doubled the dose.

Judi told John she was expecting their baby on June 25, 1983, and he said he would like to go out and get some champagne to celebrate the event. However, the celebrations never took place because, as he turned the key in the ignition, his car exploded causing him serious injury. He was taken to hospital where he recovered enough to answer some questions.

John told them that Judi had medical qualifications and yet when the police checked into her background this information proved to be false. It also turned out that Judi had been telling their friends that John had a terminal illness, which was also a lie, and when the vitamin pills were taken for forensic tests they found they had been laced with arsenic. Although the police did not really have enough evidence to charge Judi at this stage, when they found wire and tape in her bedroom which matched that found on the exploded car, they were able to take her into custody.

After exhuming the bodies of Michael, Bobby Joe Morris and James Goodyear, the coroner was able to confirm that their bodies all contained traces of arsenic.

Judi was tried separately for each of the murders and the attempted murder of John Gentry and was eventually found guilty and sentenced to death. It is believed that she collected as much as $240,000 in insurance money from the deaths of her husband, son and boyfriends.

Judi spent the next thirteen years on death row at the Broward Correctional Center at Pembroke Pines in Florida, passing her time by writing letters, crocheting blankets and baby clothes and, ironically, teaching Bible study to the other inmates. She continually appealed against her death sentence, but her last appeal on March 29, 1998, was turned down and her death warrant was signed.

Judi was finally executed at 7.02 a.m. on Monday, March 30, 1998 and when asked if she had a final statement, she simply replied, 'No sir'. She has been described by the Pensacola detective who looked into her past, as 'the coldest killer I ever knew'.

AILEEN WUORNOS

Just as Lizzie Borden was immortalised by the US media, so too was Aileen Wuornos, who became the subject of an Oscar-winning performance by Charlize Theron in the film Monster. The unusual thing about Wuornos is that she effectively cultivated her own image as a monster during her trial and while she waited for her eventual execution by lethal injection. In truth, Wuornos had led a life that took her to rock bottom in US society, so that she had lost all sense of dignity and moral code. In a way, she was a victim too, and her crimes were all about getting her own back on a world that she felt had dealt her a 'bum deal', as they say in the United States.

Aileen Wuornos's killing spree lasted between November 1989 and November 1990. In a little under a year she had killed seven men. It seems that she turned to murder because her first victim, Richard Mallory, had raped her despite the fact that she was in his car to provide sex as a prostitute. She was tried for his murder in early 1992 and used the rape allegation as her defence, but the jury found her guilty and convicted her of murder.

To say that Aileen had a bad start to life would be a gross understatement. She was born on February 29, 1956, Aileen Carol Pittman. Her biological father, Leo Dale Pittman – whom she never knew – was a convicted psychopathic child molester, who hanged himself while in prison in 1969.

Her mother, Diane, had married Pittman when she was only fifteen, but the marriage was a failure as she lived in constant fear of her husband. Aileen had an older brother, Keith, and Diane abandoned her two children in 1960, leaving them in the care of their grandparents, Lauri and Britta Wuornos. They were legally adopted, but Aileen did not discover the truth about her upbringing until she was twelve years of age, always believing that Lauri and Britta were her biological parents. Life with her grandparents had been tough, as Lauri drank heavily and ruled the children with an iron rod, often beating them with a belt when they misbehaved. Aileen also claimed that she was sexually abused by her grandfather from an early age.

Aileen was sexually promiscuous from her early teens and became pregnant when she was just thirteen. It was a disgrace to the family and she was banished from the family home and also disowned by the community. She gave birth at a Detroit maternity home on March 23, 1971, but the baby was put up for adoption as soon as it was born. Aileen had nowhere to go and was forced to live out of an abandoned car in the woods.

In the same year, Britta Wuornos died of liver failure, although Diane, Aileen's biological mother, accused Lauri of killing her. After their grandmother's death, Aileen and Keith were made wards of court. Although still at school, Aileen started working as a prostitute using the assumed name of Sandra Kretsch. In May 1974 she was arrested for driving under the influence of alcohol and firing a gun from a moving vehicle, and had to spend a period in Jefferson County jail.

In July 1976, she was arrested again for violent behaviour, when she threw a cue ball at a barman's head. Four days after her arrest, her brother Keith died of cancer and Aileen inherited $10,000 from his life insurance. She paid off her fine imposed by the court and then squandered the remainder of the money within a period of two months.

On the road and poor once again, Aileen hitched her way to Florida, where she met a wealthy but elderly president of a yacht club, Lewis Fell. He proposed to her and news of their wedding was listed in the society columns of the local newspaper. However, Aileen was still quick to lose her temper and she was sent to jail following a fight in a local bar. Her husband, who was unable to accept his wife's behaviour, had the marriage annulled and would have nothing more to do with her.

For the next ten years Aileen went from one failed relationship to another, unable to control her inner turmoil. She earned money any way she could, by prostitution, forgery, theft and armed robbery. Always struggling with depression, and a physical and emotional wreck, Aileen attempted to commit suicide. She was like an unexploded bomb, loading her body with drink and drugs, searching for a way to alleviate her feelings of anger and loneliness.

When Aileen met Tyria Moore in a Daytona gay bar in 1986, she had hit rock bottom and was flattered by the girl's attention. She decided to try something new and for a while everything was going well, for the first time in her life feeling that someone truly cared for her. There was no doubt that Tyria loved her and was prepared to follow Aileen wherever she went. Aileen supported their relationship with her prostitution earnings but little by little the magic went out of the relationship and they started to fight. They lived out of cheap motel rooms, struggling to survive on Aileen's meagre earnings. Frightened that she would lose Tyria, Aileen knew she had to do something desperate and her career changed from one of prostitution and theft to murder.

Aileen's first victim was a shop-owner by the name of Richard Mallory. Mallory was known to go off on drinking binges, so when he didn't turn up to open his shop in December 1989, no one thought very much of it. It wasn't until his Cadillac was found abandoned a few days later, that anyone knew that anything was wrong. Mallory's body was discovered on December 13, by two men looking for scrap metal along a dirt road. The badly decomposed body was wrapped in a piece of carpet and an autopsy showed that he had been killed by three shots to the head by a .22-calibre gun. After following several leads, including a stripper who went by the name of Chastity, the police came up against a brick wall and the case went cold.

Another naked body was found on June 1 in a wooded area in Citrus County, Florida. The victim was forty-three-year-old David Spears of Sarasota. He was a lorry driver and his abandoned vehicle was found on Interstate 75 with the doors unlocked and the licence plates removed. Spears, like Mallory, had been shot several times with a .22 gun.

Five days later, another body turned up just a few miles further up the same Interstate. The body was so badly decomposed it was difficult for medical examiners to determine exactly when the man had died, but they were able to confirm that he had been shot by the same gun.

The man was later identified as Charles Carskaddon.

On July 4, a woman was sitting on her front porch when she saw a car speed off the road and crash into some brush. Two women frantically climbed out of the car shouting abuse at one another. The taller, blonde woman had an injury to her arm and when the woman approached her, Aileen told her it wasn't necessary to call the police as her father lived just up the road. They climbed back into the car which, although badly damaged, started and took them a little way down the road before finally giving up.

They started walking and were stopped by a member of the Orange Springs Volunteer Fire Department who had responded to a call about an accident. He asked the two girls whether they were the ones that had been involved in the accident, but Aileen told him they knew nothing about it and he left them alone.

When the police discovered the abandoned 1988 Pontiac Sunbird, a computer search showed that the car belonged to a Peter Siems, who had disappeared on June 7. The sheriff of Orange Springs sent a sketch of the two women whom he believed were involved, to the Florida Criminal Activity Bulletin, along with details of specific evidence they had found in the abandoned car.

At the beginning of August a family who were taking a picnic at a beauty spot in the Ocala National Forest, found a body in a clearing. The body, although badly decomposed, was identified by a gold wedding ring, and it turned out to be Troy Burress, a delivery man who had gone missing on the morning of July 30. Like the other victims he had been killed by shots from a .22-calibre gun.

Dick Humphreys, who specialised in investigating cases of abused children, never made it home on the evening of September 11. His body was found the following night in Marion County – he had been shot seven times.

Approximately one month later the naked body of Walter Gino Antonio was found on a remote road in Dixie County. His car was found five days later, with the number plates missing, across the state in Brevard County.

The police gradually started to build up a picture, suspecting that women might be involved. They pointed out that as no one picked up hitchhikers any more, it could be assumed that the assailant had to be non-threatening to the victims. The police used the sketches supplied by the sheriff at Orange Springs and the following morning the newspapers across Florida ran the story that the police were looking for two women.

The policeman's hunch paid off and very soon they had numerous calls, all of them describing the same two women. One short with dark hair and the other, heavier built with long blonde hair. Two names kept cropping up, Tyria Moore and Lee Blahovec, both of whom were lesbians, and Lee a known prostitute.

Investigations led the police to a pawnshop in Daytona where a woman calling herself Cammie Marsh Greene had pawned a camera and a radar detector, leaving a nice thumbprint on the receipt. The two pawned items had belonged to one of the murdered men, Richard Mallory.

The fingerprint was the key to solving the case and within an hour records showed that there was an outstanding weapons charge against someone called Lori Grody. A bloody handprint found in the car of Peter Siems, also matched Grody's print as well and the information was sent to the National Crime Information Center. It soon came to light that the names Lori Grody, Susan Blahovec and Cammie Marsh Greene were all aliases for a woman known as Aileen Wuornos.

Aileen was eventually arrested using a clever ruse and Tyria Moore was located on January 10, living with her sister in Pennsylvania. Aileen was only being held on a previous weapons charge and the police needed a confession from her to make their murder charges stick. Their plan was to use Tyria as bait and they put her in a motel room in Daytona and asked her to make contact with Aileen in jail. The conversations would be taped and Tyria was to tell Aileen that she was worried that the authorities would pin the murders on her. The police hoped that, out of loyalty to Tyria, Aileen would confess.

It took three days of phone calls for Tyria to convince Aileen that the police were closing in on her ex-lover and eventually the plan paid off.

'I will cover for you, because you're innocent,' Aileen said down the phone. 'I'm not going to let you go to jail. Listen, if I have to confess, I will.' Aileen Wuornos confessed to murder on the morning of January 16.

At the trial Tyria testified against Aileen who was convicted of killing Richard Mallory, even though she claimed it was through self-defence. Ironically, it was later discovered that Mallory had in fact served ten years in jail for violent rape, but Aileen never got a retrial. Aileen eventually confessed to killing three other men and was given the death sentence. Unrepentant to the last, she was executed by lethal injection on October 9, 2002.

PART FOUR

VICTIMS OF
ASSASSINATION

ABRAHAM LINCOLN

Abraham Lincoln's assassination was motivated by events relating to the American Civil War (1861–65). In fact, his death came only days after General Robert E. Lee had surrendered his Confederate force to General Ulysses S. Grant of the Union, although hostilities would continue for another few months. Lincoln's assassin was John Wilkes Booth, a well-known stage actor and Confederate, who saw his opportunity when Lincoln came to watch a performance at Ford's Theatre in Washington DC.

To get a deeper insight into why Booth wanted Lincoln out of the picture, we need to look at the type of man he was. In his diary, Booth wrote of Lincoln:

Our country owed all her troubles to him, and God simply made me the instrument of his punishment.

John Wilkes Booth was born on May 10, 1838, on a farm near Bel Air in Maryland, one of ten children. His father, Junius Booth, was British but had moved to the United States in 1821 with his wife, Mary Ann Holmes. Junius was a famous actor, who had an alcohol problem and suffered from spells of madness.

As a young man, Booth became a member of the Know-Nothing political party, which was formed by American nativists who wanted to preserve the country for native-born white citizens.

When Junius died in 1852, Booth spent several years working on the farm, but his dreams went far beyond farming – he wanted to be a famous actor just like his father.

Booth made his stage debut in August 1855, when he was seventeen years old, playing the part of the Earl of Richmond in Shakespeare's *Richard III*. By 1858 he was a member of the Richmond Theatre, but often missed cues and forgot his lines, and consequently never played any major roles.

In 1859, Booth was an eyewitness to the execution of John Brown, who was the abolitionist who had tried to start a slave uprising at Harpers Ferry. The following year his career as an actor took off and, taking many leading roles, his income escalated to an estimated $20,000 a year. Over the next few years he starred in *Romeo and Juliet*, *The Apostate*, *The Marble Heart*, *The Merchant of Venice*, *Julius Caesar*, *Othello*, *The Taming* of *the Shrew, Hamlet* and *Macbeth*, to mention just a few, travelling all over the United States.

In 1862, Booth was arrested for making anti-government remarks and had to appear before a provost marshall in St Louis.

On November 9, 1863, Lincoln sat in the audience as Booth took the role of Raphael in *The Marble Heart*. Lincoln was in a box to the right of the stage accompanied by several other people. On a couple of occasions, when Booth had a particularly disagreeable line to play, he would walk up to Lincoln's box and point his finger directly at him. One of his companions, Mary Clay, who was the daughter of Cassius Clay, the US minister to Russia, commented: 'Mr Lincoln, he looks as if he meant that for you.'

In the autumn of 1864, Booth was known to stay on occasion at the McHenry House in Meadville, Pennsylvania. It is thought that he stayed there while he waited for a railroad connection, but more significantly, scratched on a window pane in Room 22 in the McHenry House were the words:

Abe Lincoln Departed This Life August 13th, 1864, By The Effects of Poison

There has been much speculation as to who actually

scratched the words on the window because Booth never occupied Room 22, and it still remains a mystery today.

However, what is certain is that in the summer of 1864 Booth started to make his own plans to kidnap Abraham Lincoln. His plan was to seize the president, take him to Richmond where he would be held in exchange for Confederate soldiers who were being held in Union prison camps. Booth recruited a gang of men who were prepared to help him with his plan – Michael O'Laughlen, Samuel Arnold, Lewis Powell, John Surratt, David Herold and George Atzerodt.

The whole group met at Gautier's Restaurant on March 15, to discuss the abduction of the president. Booth told them that he knew that Lincoln would be attending a play at the Campbell Hospital just outside Washington, on March 17, 1865. He told the men that he thought it would be an ideal opportunity to seize Lincoln while he was still in his carriage. However, at the last minute Lincoln changed his plans and decided to speak instead to the 140th Indiana Regiment to present a captured flag to the Governor of India. After this, the band of conspirators broke up and went their separate ways.

Early in 1865, Booth had a serious love affair with Lucy Lambert Hale, who was the daughter of John

Parker Hale, a former senator for New Hampshire's abolition cause. President Lincoln had appointed John Hale to be minister of Spain and the Hale family were making plans to sail to Europe. Booth became secretly engaged to Lucy and on March 4 attended Lincoln's second inauguration as a guest of his fiancée. He is known to have confided in a close friend, 'What an excellent chance I had to kill the president, if I had wished, on inauguration day!'

Of course this attempt never happened, and several other kidnap plans fell on stony ground. On April 9, 1865, General Lee surrendered to General Grant at Appomattox and on April 11, Lincoln gave his final speech from the White House. Booth was in the audience and became enraged when Lincoln started discussing the possibility of votes for a section of the black population. He is known to have said, 'Now, by God! I'll put him through. This is the last speech he will ever make.'

Three days later Booth learned that Lincoln was planning to attend the evening performance of *Our American Cousin* at the Ford Theatre. Booth started to make plans to assassinate Lincoln. He knew virtually every line in the play and figured out that the greatest laughter in the theatre would be about 10.15 p.m. He decided he would use this laughter to cover the noise of the gunshot and then went to find fellow conspirator Lewis Paine to tell him of his plans. Booth told Paine that he wanted him to assassinate the secretary of state, William Seward.

Booth then left and went to meet George Atzerodt. His plan for Atzerodt was for him to kill Vice-President Andrew Johnson.

Later that afternoon Booth went to Deery's tavern for a drink and then decided to write a letter to the editor of a newspaper called the *National Intelligencer*. In the letter he told the editor that he had changed his plans from kidnapping Lincoln to assassinating him, and signed it in the names of his own, along with those of Paine, Atzerodt and Herold.

After leaving the tavern, Booth met up with a fellow actor named John Mathews, and asked him to deliver the letter to the newspaper the following day. As Booth was walking home he met up with Atzerodt and told him what he wanted him to do – kill Andrew Johnson as close to 10.15 p.m. as possible.

Booth then went to Ford's Theatre to go over his plans for the assassination. Using a gimlet, he drilled a small hole in the door at the back of the box where Lincoln would be sitting so that he could get a good view of his head, and then he returned to the National Hotel, where he was staying, to have dinner.

After dinner Booth changed into calf-length boots, new spurs and black clothes. Booth loaded his derringer and then stuck a long bowie knife inside the belt of his trousers. Picking up his diary and putting on a black hat, Booth left his room at 7.45 p.m.

Although there is no record as to where the final meeting of the conspirators took place, Booth met up again with Paine and Atzerodt and told them he wanted the assassinations to take place simultaneously at 10.15 p.m.

Booth arrived at Ford's Theatre at approximately 10.07 p.m. and went up the stairs to the dress circle. Because he was such a famous actor no one questioned why he should want to arrive so late in the performance. Next to the outer door of Lincoln's state box sat Charles Forbes, the president's footman, and Booth was seen handing him a card. Booth then opened the door and went into the dark area at the back of the box. So that the door remained ajar, he propped it open with the wooden leg of a music stand he had placed there earlier in the day. Booth then opened the inner door, directly behind where Lincoln was sitting, put his derringer behind the president's head and pulled the trigger. Because of the noise of laughter, only those closest to the box heard the noise of the shot.

Major Henry Rathbone, another occupant of the royal box, started to wrestle with Booth, so the assassin pulled out his knife and stabbed Rathbone in the arm. Booth then climbed over the banister of the royal box and dropped the eleven feet onto the stage. The spur on his right foot caught in one of the flags draped across a balustrade, causing him to lose balance. He landed awkwardly and the fibula bone in his left leg just above the ankle made a loud snapping noise. Despite the obvious pain, Booth flashed his knife, ran quickly across the stage and out the back of the theatre.

Booth jumped onto his horse waiting outside the theatre, and escaped by crossing the Navy Yard Bridge. Booth met up with Paine, Herold and Atzerodt at Mary Surratt's tavern, approximately eleven miles south of Ford's Theatre. He was unaware at that time that Paine had failed to kill Seward and that Atzerodt had made no attempt to fulfil his part of the bargain. Mrs Surratt arranged for a doctor to come and strap up Booth's leg, which, in theory, made her an accomplice.

Union Cavalry eventually caught up with Booth on April 26, 1865, in a barn some sixty miles south of Ford's Theatre. The barn was set on fire, Booth was shot, and his body was dragged out and left lying on the grass. Booth was paralyzed and barely alive and when officers searched his body, they found a diary with several incriminating entries.

Within days the other conspirators were arrested and

tried by a military tribunal. They were all found guilty and hanged on July 7, 1865, including Mrs Surratt. The doctor who had attended to his leg, Dr Mudd, was given a life sentence, while Edman Spangler, a stagehand at the Ford's Theatre was convicted of helping Booth escape and sentenced to six years. There was much controversy over the convictions on Mrs Surratt, Dr Mudd and Spangler and, although it was too late for Mrs Surratt, Mudd and Spangler were later pardoned by President Andrew Johnson in 1869.

FRANZ FERDINAND

While it can be argued that the political ambitions of Adolf Hitler started World War II, so it can be argued that the political frustrations of Gavrilo Princip triggered World War I. Princip was a Bosnian Serb who had had enough of Austria–Hungary's hold over his country. In 1914 he joined a nationalist paramilitary group known as the Black Hand, which had the express aim of reuniting territories with Serb populations under independent rule. Princip and his comrades decided that the assassination of Austria-Hungary's heir to the throne, Archduke Franz Ferdinand, would be a good way to bring attention to their cause and their opportunity came when he visited Sarajevo in June 1914 with his wife Sophie.

Franz Ferdinand, born in 1863, was the eldest son of Carl Ludwig, the brother of Emperor Franz Josef. Ferdinand became the crown prince in line for the throne when the only son of Crown Prince Rudolf, Franz Josef, committed suicide. The Habsburg court was extremely orthodox in its views and frowned on the fact that the new prince had not only fathered two children out of wedlock, but also disapproved of his marrying someone beneath his ranks, Sophie von Hohenberg. Even though she came from noble blood, Sophie wasn't considered to be an appropriate match for the future emperor. To be an eligible partner for a member of the Austro-Hungarian royal family, you had to be descended from the House of Hapsburg or from one of the ruling dynasties of Europe.

Ferdinand ignored their old-fashioned rules and married his sweetheart anyway, but because of the court's disapproval Sophie was not allowed to accompany him on any state visits or appear in the public eye alongside her husband. For this reason, Ferdinand liked to go outside of Vienna on state visits, where this rule did not apply. Consequently, Ferdinand was eager to accept the invitation of Bosnia's general, General Oskar Potoirek to inspect the army manoeuvres being held outside Sarajevo. It had been four years since a prominent Hapsburg dignitary had made a goodwill visit to Bosnia and, as Inspector General of the army it made sense for Ferdinand to go. Added to this, the visit would coincide with his fourteenth wedding anniversary and he felt it would be a fitting present if Sophie were allowed to ride in the royal car beside him.

Ferdinand was aware that the trip could be dangerous because a large number of people living in Bosnia–

Herzegovina were not happy about the Austro–Hungarian rule and favoured union with Serbia. In 1910 a Serb, Bogdan Zerajic, had attempted the assassination of General Varesanin, the Austrian governor of Bosnia–Herzegovina, when he was opening parliament in Sarajevo.

Zerajic was a member of a secret society called Ujedinjenje ili Smrt (Union or Death), better known as the Black Hand. They wanted Bosnia–Herzegovina to leave the Austro–Hungarian empire and their leader, Colonel Dragutin Dimitrijevic, considered Ferdinand to be a serious threat to a union between Bosnia– Herzegovina and Serbia. Dimitrijevic was the chief of the Intelligence Department of the Serbian General Staff, and he felt that Ferdinand's plans to grant concessions to the South Slavs, would make it even harder for Serbia to become in independent state.

When it was learned that Ferdinand was scheduled to visit Sarajevo in June 1914, Dimitrijevic started to make plans to assassinate the heir to the Austro– Hungarian throne. He arranged for three members of the Black Hand group based in Belgrade – Gavrilo Princip, Nedjelko Cabrinovic and Trifko Grabez – to start training and then sent them fully equipped to Sarajevo.

Because the Black Hand had members in the government and the army, many of their activities were known to the Serbian government. When Prime

Minister Nikola Pasic, learned of the assassination plot, he had a difficult problem on his hands. He knew that if he took no action and the assassination was successful, that the tangled connections between the government and the Black Hand would come to light, fearing that it could mean war with Austria. Pasic was in a dilemma, aware that if he did warn the Austrians of the plot he would appear as a traitor by his own countrymen.

Pasic decided to have Princip, Cabrinovic and Grabez arrested as they tried to leave the country. However, it was only a weak attempt at trying to appease the situation, and needless to say his instructions were ignored. When this failed, Pasic decided that he would try and warn the Austrians in a diplomatic way without involving the Black Hand in any way. He gave the task to the Serbian Minister to Vienna, Jovan Jovanovic. On June 5, Jovanovic approached the Minister of Finance, Dr Leon von Bilinski, to advise him that it would be a good idea if Ferdinand cancelled his visit to Sarajevo. Bilinski did not seem to grasp the serious nature of the warning, simply saying, 'Let us hope nothing does happen' in a light-hearted manner. Jovanovic, who strongly suspected that Bilinski did not understand the gravity of the situation, chose to make no further effort to convey the warning.

Meanwhile the three Black Hand trainees worked their

way back to Sarajevo about one month before the proposed visit. A fourth man, Danilo Ilic, also joined the group in Sarajevo and, on his own initiative, recruited three other members. Vaso Cubrilovic and Cvijetko Popovic, who were still at school and only seventeen years old and Muhamed Mehmedbasic, a Bosnian muslim. The group were armed with four army pistols and six bombs.

Security on the day of the visit was relaxed. Ferdinand did not like to feel hemmed in by security guards, nor did he like a cordon of soldiers between the crowd and himself. For the most part, Ferdinand was greeted warmly and the crowds were overseen by Sarajevo's 120 policemen.

Ferdinand and Sophie arrived in Sarajevo by train just before 10.00 a.m. on Sunday, June 28, 1914. They were met by General Oskar Potiorek, who took them back to the City Hall for an official reception hosted by the mayor. The motorcade consisted of six vehicles and the car travelling directly in front of Ferdinand's car, contained Fehim Curcic, the mayor of Sarajevo and Dr Gerde, the city's Commissioner of Police. Franz Ferdinand and Duchess Sophie were in the second car with Potiorek and Count von Harrach. The third car in the procession carried the head of Ferdinand's military chancellor, Sophie's lady-in-waiting and Potoirek's chief adjutant, Lieutenant Colonel Merizzi. The fourth and fifth cars carried other members of Ferdinand's staff and various Bosnian officials, while the sixth car was a spare should any of the others break down.

The route went along a wide avenue called Appel Quay, which ran parallel with the north bank of the River Miljacka. The top of the car had been rolled back so that the crowds could get a good look at the royal visitors. The morning was warm and sunny and the atmosphere matched the weather. Crowds lined the Appel Quay waving flags and throwing flowers as the cars drove slowly by. Among the crowd, however, were seven young assassins, eager to get a prime position.

As Ferdinand's car passed the first assassin, Mehmed-basic, he did nothing. The next man they passed, Cabrinovic, hurled a hand grenade at Ferdinand's car. The driver of his car, Franz Urban, reacted quickly and accelerated away from the flying object, while Ferdinand raised his arm to deflect the grenade away from his wife. The grenade glanced off his arm and bounced onto the road, exploding under the wheel of the next car. Two of the occupants, Eric von Merizzi and Count Boos-Waldeck were seriously wounded, as were many of the spectators. The first two cars kept moving until they felt they were far enough away from the site of the explosion and then stopped to assess who had been injured.

After throwing the grenade, Cabrinovic swallowed his cynacide pill and then proceeded to jump into the river. The only problem was that the pill was out of date and it only made him sick, added to that, the part of the river where he had jumped in, was only a couple of inches in depth. He was seized by the crowd and finally arrested by the police.

The motorcade continued their journey on to City Hall passing the other assassins on the way, but for some unknown reason they failed to act. When Ferdinand reached the City Hall he was seething and flew at the mayor with all guns blazing. 'Mr Mayor, one comes here for a visit and is received by bombs! It is outrageous!' The Mayor stood open mouthed, not quite sure how to react and tried to pacify the situation. Ferdinand regained his composure, apologised for his outburst and the celebrations at City Hall continued as planned.

The mayor suggested that they might like to change the remainder of their schedule, but Ferdinand told him he had no intention of cancelling his visit to the museum or lunch at the governor's residence. However, he did ask to be taken to the hospital where those people injured in the explosion were receiving treatment. A member of Ferdinand's staff suggested that this might be a dangerous move, but Potiorek, who was responsible for the safety of the party, replied, 'So you think Sarajevo is full of assassins?' He did suggest that Duchess Sophie should stay behind, but she adamantly refused and said that as long as her husband was prepared to show himself in public, she wanted to be by his side.

The same group of cars set out along Appel Quay, but the mayor's driver and Ferdinand's driver had not been informed of the change to the planned schedule. The young assassins, who had counted on succeeding on their first attempt, unaware that Ferdinand would stick to his itinerary, had taken up various positions along the Appel Quay.

The mayor's car, followed by Ferdinand's car, turned off the Appel Quay and into Franz Joseph Street in the direction of the museum, as originally planned. Potoirek leaned forward to his driver and said, 'What is this? This is the wrong way! We're supposed to take the Appel Quay!' The driver, looking confused, started to reverse causing Ferdinand's driver to brake hard.

Gavrilo Princip was just walking out of a shop having bought himself a sandwich and couldn't believe his luck when he realised the car that had stopped about five feet away was the one carrying the archduke. Princip dropped the sandwich, pulled the pistol out of his pocket, took a step towards the car and fired twice into the car. Ferdinand was hit in the neck and Sophie in the abdomen, but because the couple remained sitting upright, General Potoirek thought that the shots had missed. He ordered the driver to take them directly to the governor's residence. What he didn't know was that the first bullet had pierced Ferdinand's jugular vein but before he lapsed into unconsciousness, he cried helplessly, 'Sophie dear! Sophie dear! Don't die! Stay alive for our children!'

Franz Urban drove straight to Konak, the governor's residence, but although the couple were alive on arrival they died soon afterwards from their wounds.

Princip, who like Cabrinovic, swalled his cyanide pill and then turned the gun on himself. However, before he could shoot he was mobbed by an angry crowd. Police had to drag Princip away before he was lynched and like Cabrinovic, his pill made his sick but did not have the desired effect.

The assassination of Franz Ferdinand and Countess Sophie brought tensions between Austria and Serbia to a head. The double murders were seen by the Hapsburg rulers as a case of Serbian state-sponsored terrorism. It was the last straw and they prepared for retaliation. Although the Black Hand involvement would not come to light for many years, Austria wanted revenge and did not wait for conclusive proof.

As Vienna took a hard line against Serbia, the rest of Europe took sides and the rumbles of war could soon be heard. There is no doubt that the double assas-sination helped an already tenuous situation spiral into a disaster and, in just over thirty days after the shootings, World War I was underway.

LEON TROTSKY

Leon Trotsky was a Ukrainian who became a leader of the Bolshevik movement that overthrew the monarchy of Russia in 1917 – the February Revolution. In fact, he was in New York at the time and didn't return to Russia until May 1917. He was close to both Lenin and Stalin at that time, but his political differences would prove to be his downfall. When Lenin died in 1924 Trotsky found himself in a difficult situation and fell victim to an assassination expressly ordered by Joseph Stalin himself.

Lev Davidovich Bronstein (Leon Trotsky) was born on October 26, 1879, the son of a hard-working Jewish farmer, in the southern part of Ukraine. Trotsky's family placed great importance on a good education so at the age of nine, the young Leon was sent to the city of Odessa to stay with his uncle. Leon proved to be a highly intellectual and capable pupil and in 1896 moved to Nicolayev to complete his education. He studied mathematics but it was also during this period that Leon turned revolutionary.

In 1897 he was involved in forming the South Russia Workers Union and the following year the Russian Social Democratic Labour Party (RSDLP), but he was put in prison for his political activities. In 1900 he was deported to Siberia, but two years later managed to escape, adopting the name Trotsky. He made his way to London which is where he met Lenin for the first time.

Lenin worked on the communist newspaper *Iskra* (The Spark) and was instrumental in getting Trotsky a job on the same publication. Lenin and Trotsky were both intellectuals and had a great amount of respect for each other. They parted ways, however, in 1903, at the Second Congress of the RSDLP when Lenin led the Bolsheviks and Trotsky went in the other direction with the Menshevik leaders.

Trotsky returned to Russia in 1905, where he actively took part in the first Russian Revolution. He was appointed President of the St Petersburg Soviet in December 1905, but he was arrested along with other members, and deported to Western Siberia in January 1907. Seemingly a master of escape, Trotsky once again managed to make his way to London, which is where he met Stalin for the first time. He spent his time working on several controversial papers, including Pravda, until, in 1917, he learned that the Tsar of Russia had abdicated.

Trotsky returned to Russia and by August 1917 he had become a member of the Central Committee of the Bolshevik Party, led by Lenin. Trotsky became second in command to Lenin and the following year was appointed People's Commissar for Military Naval Affairs, assisting with the formation of the Red Army.

Unfortunately for Trotsky, Lenin fell ill in 1922 and died two years later, leaving Stalin in control of the Soviet Union. Trotsky and Stalin did not see eye to eye, and in 1927 Stalin had him expelled from the Executive Committee of Comintern. To get Trotsky out of the picture, Stalin had him banished to Alma Ata in Kazakhstan and from there deported him to Turkey in 1929.

There was no doubt that although Stalin and Trotsky both represented Communism, their beliefs went in two totally different directions. While Trotsky liked to view his beliefs in writing, Stalin liked to put his into action and implemented policies that were extremely costly in terms of lives and freedom to the Soviet people. Trotsky used his writings to criticise Stalin and to try and turn communism in a different direction – gathering many followers on the way who became known as Trotskyists.

However, being a Communist who had been ousted from his own country, Trotsky found it hard to find a country that would allow him to stay permanently. He spent short periods in several different countries, until Mexico said he could stay in 1937. However, even here he was not safe from the power of Stalin.

On the afternoon of August 20, 1940, in a peaceful suburb of Coyoacán in the capital of Mexico, Trotsky was in his garden feeding his pet rabbits. He was approached by a nervous young man, who had recently wormed his way into Trotsky's entourage. The young man asked if he would accompany him to the study to read an article he had just written. Trotsky had no reason not to trust him, but wondered why he clutched a raincoat tightly to his chest when it was such a lovely day.

Inside the study were piles of books, many written by Trotsky, denouncing Stalin and Russia's alliance with Hitler, attacking socialist nationalism and urging a revolution.

Trotsky, now sixty years old, settled down at his desk to read the manuscript. The twenty-six-year-old man stood on his left side making sure that he blocked the panic button which would immediately alert Trotsky's security guards to any trouble. The man reached inside his raincoat and pulled out a mountaineer's ice pick and struck Trotsky from behind. In a few seconds, the brain of one of the most brilliant fighters for socialism was destroyed.

Trotsky died twenty-six hours later from a three-inch

hole in his skull. The assassin, Jaime Ramon Mercader del Rio Hernandez, was severely beaten, arrested, tried and convicted of murder. He served twenty years but was released in 1960 and immediately fled to Czechoslovakia.

Hernandez was the son of a middle-class businessman and a beautiful, but unstable, Cuban who developed into an ardent supporter of Stalin. She fought in the Spanish Civil War and later became the mistress of the Soviet secret police general who was later involved in the conspiracy to kill Trotsky.

With Trotsky and Lenin dead, Stalin was now ready to institute his revolution without any interference.

Martin Luther King, Jr

The original Martin Luther (1483–1546) was a German theologian who founded the Protestant faith in reaction to the excesses of the Catholic Church. The Catholic monasteries had become places of corruption and excess, which Luther saw as betraying the Christian message, hence the term 'Catholic tastes' which means to be too undiscerning and open-minded. The idea behind Protestantism was a return to simplicity and piousness, so that the emphasis was on worship of the Christian god. Luther was, in many ways, one of the founding fathers of the straight-laced and superior German cultural view, which would eventually lead to Nazism. It is perhaps ironic then, that Martin Luther King, Jr, a black American, should be named after him.

Martin Luther King, Jr (1929–1968) was one of the principle leaders of the American civil rights movement, a political activist, a pacifist, a Baptist minister and most importantly one of America's greatest speakers. From an early age, Martin experienced racism, which made him determined to do something to make the world a better and fairer place.

Martin Luther graduated from high school at the age of fifteen, receiving a BA in 1948 at Morehouse College, Atlanta, an institution attended by both his father and grandfather. For three years Martin Luther studied theology at the Crozer Theological Seminary in Pennsylvania, where he was elected president of a predominantly white class. Martin Luther proved to have a powerful way of speaking and his vision and determination had his fellow students spellbound.

Using a fellowship which he won at Crozer, Martin Luther enrolled in graduate studies at Boston University, receiving a degree in 1955. During his years at Boston, Martin Luther met and married Coretta Scott, a highly intellectual and artistic woman, who shared many of her husband's views. They had two sons and two daughters.

In 1954, Martin Luther took the pastorale of the Dexter Avenue Baptist Church in Montgomery, Alabama. He never stopped dreaming of what could be and became a strong supporter of civil rights. He also became a member of the executive committee of the National Association for the Advancement of Coloured People, the leading organisation of its kind in the United States.

By 1955, Martin Luther felt ready to accept the leadership of the first great African-American nonviolent demonstration – the Montgomery Bus Boycott. The boycott lasted for 382 days and was a formative turning point of the African-American freedom movement. One particular gripe among Montgomery blacks at that time was the segregation law of the bus system. The boycott was triggered by the refusal of a black seamstress, Mrs Rosa Parks, to take her place at the back of a city bus when the driver demanded it. Parks took a stand and refused to get up – minutes later she was arrested and sent to jail. When members of the black community heard about the arrest of Parks, they decided that a boycott of the bus system was long overdue. On December 21, 1956, the Supreme Court of the United States declared that laws requiring segregation on buses were unconstitutional, and from then on blacks and whites rode on buses as equals. However, during the days of boycott, Martin Luther suffered for his part. He was not only arrested, his house was also bombed and he was subjected to personal abuse.

In 1957, Martin Luther was elected as president of the Southern Christian Leadership Conference, which was formed to provide representation for the burgeoning civil rights movement. Martin Luther's ideals were based not only on Christianity, but also on the beliefs of one of his heroes, Gandhi. Martin Luther represented this organisation for a period of eleven years, from 1957 to 1968, travelled over six million miles and spoke over 2,500 times. He not only became the symbolic leader of African-Americans but also an inspiring world figure.

In October 1964, Martin Luther had to be admited to a hospital in Atlanta, as a result of extreme fatigue. It was while in hospital that he learned he was to receive the Nobel Peace Prize, a major achievement in itself, especially as, at thirty-five, he was the youngest man ever to receive this award. When Martin Luther learned about the presentation, he said that he would turn over the prize money of $54,123 to the furtherance of the civil rights movement. Later the same year he was named *Time* magazine's 'Man of the Year' and politicians from around the world turned to Martin Luther for his views on a wide range of issues.

Luther King's final fight for the civil rights movement was in late March, 1968. In an effort to raise money for his campaign, he accepted an invitation to speak in support of some Memphis sanitation workers. They had been striking for better pay and conditions, but their badly handled demonstration had been a disaster. Martin Luther spoke to an audience of 500 people at the Memphis Temple on April 3. He openly spoke about the possibility of his own assassination, which was a recurrent theme in many of his speeches. The following evening his life was cut short, when he was shot on the balcony outside his room at the Lorraine Motel in downtown Memphis.

On the evening of April 4, 1968, Martin Luther was getting ready to have dinner with minister Billy Kyles. Martin Luther was staying in Room 306 on the second floor of the motel and was in a hurry as he was running late. At about 5.30 p.m. Kyles knocked on his door to try and hurry him along.

At 6.01 p.m. Martin Luther and his close friend Reverend Jesse Jackson were standing on the balcony outside Room 306, when Martin Luther was hit in the neck by a sniper's bullet. He fell to the ground and Jackson saw a gaping wound covering a large portion of his jaw and neck.

Ralph Albernathy, another close friend of Martin Luther's, ran out of his room when he heard the shot and found his friend lying in a pool of blood. He held Martin Luther's head saying, 'Martin it's all right. Don't worry. This is Ralph. This is Ralph.' He grabbed a towel to try and stop the flow of blood while they waited for the ambulance to arrive.

When he arrived at hospital, Martin Luther was fighting for his life as the bullet had travelled through his neck and severed his spinal cord. Despite emergency surgery, Martin Luther lost his fight for life at 7.05 p.m. at the age of thirty-nine.

News of his death was greeted not only with immense grief but also rage, and riots erupted all over the United States, primarily in black urban areas. The worst riots occurred in Chicago, Baltimore and Washington, DC, and the police had to recruit federal troops to help them quell the violence. When the violence erupted in Chicago, Mayor Richard J. Daley imposed a curfew on anyone under the age of twenty-one, closed the streets to any traffic, and banned the sale of guns and ammunition. Daley also instructed the Chicago police that they were to 'shoot to kill'. Despite these measures it took days to restore order, resulting in eleven deaths and over 500 people injured.

Nearly forty years later the death of Martin Luther King, Jr. is still a matter of endless controversy. The accepted version of the assassination is that James Earl Ray, a known criminal and open rascist, committed the murder. Ray was an escaped convict who was renting a room directly opposite the motel room where Martin Luther was staying. Using a rifle with an attached sniper scope, he shot his target from his bathroom window. Witnesses say they saw Ray running from his boarding house just minutes after the shot was fired. Ray's fingerprints were also found on a pair of binoculars and the rifle, which he had purchased just six days before the shooting. After a massive manhunt which lasted for two months, Ray was eventually apprehended at Heathrow Airport after he had robbed a London bank.

To escape the death penalty, Ray pleaded guilty, which meant a trial was waived and he was given a ninety-nine-year prison sentence. Three days later, Ray recanted his confession but, despite many appeals, Ray's lawyers were unable to produce enough evidence to reopen his case. Many people believe that Ray was not alone in pulling the trigger and that he was simply part of a much larger conspiracy. Until the day he died on April 23, 1998, Ray continued to maintain his innocence, continually trying to put the blame on many people including the Memphis police, the FBI, army intelligence, the Mafia and even the Green Berets.

# MAHATMA GANDHI

The name Gandhi is synonymous with India. Some would say that it is also synonymous with bad fortune, for no less than three Gandhis have been assassinated while ruling the country. The first was the Gandhi. That is to say, Mahatma Gandhi, who took India into its age of independence from the British Empire. The other two were mother and son, Indira and Rajiv Gandhi, who were not in fact related to Mahatma Ghandi in any way.

India is a fundamentally troubled nation, due to its socio-cultural history. Before achieving independence India comprised a far larger area of territory, but ethnic and religious tensions arose following manumission from the empire. In August of 1947, Old India was partitioned into three new countries – west to east they are Pakistan, India and Bangladesh. The purpose of this was to provide the two major religions with their own territories and thereby prevent civil war. India is Hindu, while Pakistan and Bangladesh are Islamic. Nevertheless, there are further religious, ethnic and linguistic divisions in the Indian population.

From 1947 to 1948 a war was fought between the newly formed Pakistan and India over an area of territory called Kashmir. Gandhi, who followed an anti-war ethos, insisted that India make a promised payment to Pakistan to settle the disagreement, but this proved to be his undoing.

Many national heroes have gone down in history as valiant warriors, but not in the case of Gandhi. He was a peace-loving, frail man who devoted his life to achieving both social and political progress. Yet, despite his non-violent attitude, just six months after winning independence for India, Gandhi was assassinated by a religious fanatic.

He was born Mohandas Karamchand Gandhi on October 2, 1869, in Porbandar, near Bombay. His family belonged to the Vaisya, or Hindu, merchant caste and his father, Karamchand Gandhi, had been prime minister of several small native states.

In May 1883, following family tradition, thirteen-year-old Gandhi went into an arranged marriage with Kasturba Makhanji. However, at the age of nineteen he broke with tradition and travelled abroad to further his studies. He studied law at University College in London, but was rebuffed by his fellow students because of his race and spent many hours studying on his own. Gandhi took to reading books on philosophy and it was through these works that he discovered the principle of non-violence.

After graduating, Gandhi returned to India, but he struggled to work as a barrister and decided to go to South Africa. Working in Natal, Gandhi was the first so-called 'non-white' lawyer to be admitted to the Supreme Court. He managed to build himself a reasonably sized practice and his interest soon turned to the hardships suffered by fellow Indians who had sought work in South Africa. He had seen first hand how these people had been treated as inferiors, not only in South Africa but in England as well, and he was determined to do something about it. He founded the Natal Indian Congress for Indian rights in 1894, but managed to remain loyal to the British Empire throughout.

It seemed Gandhi's sole purpose in life was to do good and help his fellow man. During the Boer War he raised an ambulance corps and served the South African government. In 1906, he gave support against the Zulu revolt and later that year he began his non-aggressive revolution. He was resolute in his cause, vowing that he would rather go to jail or even die before he would obey an anti-Asian law. He had the support of thousands of Indians and twice he was imprisoned for his beliefs.

Gandhi returned to his homeland in 1914, and his reputation had won him many loyal followers. He worked ceaselessly to reconcile all classes and religious sects, in particular Hindus and Muslims, and in 1919 he became a leader in the newly formed Indian National Congress party.

In 1920, Gandhi began his campaign against Britain. He urged Indians to boycott anything British and to start spinning cotton for their own benefits. Because of this, Gandhi was forced to spend two years in prison, from 1922 to 1924. Undeterred by his years of incarceration, Gandhi led thousands of Indians on a 200-mile march in 1930 in protest against the salt tax imposed on his country. Once again he was imprisoned to literally put him 'out of the way'.

Gandhi retired as head of the Indian National Congress party, but to all intents and purposes he was still their leader and everyone looked to him for guidance. He believed that India would not be free until it could be released from the restrictions of the British Empire and, quite early in World War II, he demanded immediate independence in return for aiding Britain in the war. Once again he was imprisoned for his impudence and was not released until 1944.

Gandhi eventually saw his dreams come true when, in 1947, India won its independence. However, independence brought its own troubles when India divided into three separate countries, as explained earlier, which culminated in Hindu–Muslim riots. Gandhi, still using peaceful tactics, resorted to fasting until rioters would pledge peace to him.

This move was to be his downfall. On January 30, 1948, while travelling to Delhi for prayers, he was killed by a Hindu who was angry at Gandhi's attempt to reconcile two different religious sects. The assassin was a Hindu radical by the name of Nathuram Godse, who was known to have links with the extremist Hindu Mahasabha organisation. This group held Gandhi responsible for weakening India by insisting on a payment to Pakistan.

Nathuram Godse and his co-conspirator, Narayan Apte, were both executed on November 15, 1949, for the assassination of Gandhi.

Almost fifty years after his death, in January 1997, the ashes of Mahatma Gandhi were scattered on the Ganges River during a ceremony to honour his memory. Thousands gathered to watch the ceremony, wanting to remember the man who had succeeded, however briefly, in unifying their nation.

After Gandhi was shot, Jawaharlal Nehru, the leader of the Indian National Congress party, spoke to the people of India about the man who had strived so hard for his people and country:

*Friends and comrades, the light has gone out of our lives
and there is darkness everywhere, and I do not quite know
what to tell you or how to say it. Our beloved leader, Bapu
as we called him, the father of the nation, is no more.
Perhaps I am wrong to say that; nevertheless, we will not
see him again, as we have seen him for these many years,
we will not run to him for advice or seek solace from him,
and that is a terrible blow, not only for me, but for millions
and millions in this country.*

ALDO MORO

Aldo Moro was a highly successful and committed politician. As prime minister of Italy five times between the years 1963 and 1976, he had made an important contribution to Italy's political landscape and to his party: the Christian Democrats. The Christian Democrat party, or Democrazia Cristiana (DC), had its roots in the Catholic Conservatism which was once widespread in the Italian countryside, but in this unstable, postwar climate the party's ideology had begun to fragment and change, and so had that of the nation as a whole. The DC's policies, thanks to the input of left-wing members such as Amintor Fanfani, had begun to swing towards the centre left, and a third of the Italian population now supported the Italian Communist Party, making them one of the most powerful communist organisations in Western Europe, and they were busy making inroads into Italian government.

On March 16, 1978, Aldo Moro left his apartment in Rome to attend morning prayers at a local church. Later that same day he was due to inaugurate a new coalition government that would include, for the first time in thirty years, the Italian Communist Party. This was considered by many to be a controversial action. Moro received threats to desist in his attempts to unite Italy's political factions or pay dearly. In the end, he paid with his life.

The radical communist organisation, the Red Brigade, or Brigate Rosse, fiercely opposed the scheme. Previously, the Italian Communist Party had staunchly opposed the Christian Democratic rule in Italy during a period of serious economic, social and political crisis, and now the communists were preparing to join their former enemies in a coalition government. Aldo Moro had been a key player in bringing the two sides together in the name of 'national solidarity'.

Members of the Red Brigade considered the assimilation of the Communist Party into the capitalist establishment of the Italian government to be a huge mistake. It was impossible, they argued, for the Communist Party to make any real headway without out and out revolution. Anything less would mean compromising their left-wing principles. This was something the Red Brigade were not prepared to do and they did not understand why anyone of their political persuasion would want to enter into a deal with people of such disparate values to their own. To the Red Brigade, it was akin to selling your soul to Satan, or simply waving the white flag of defeat. They decided to take violent action.

On leaving his apartment Aldo Moro climbed into the back of his chauffeur-driven car, bound for church. He was accompanied in the back seat by his personal bodyguard. A second car carrying a driver and two more bodyguards followed the first. As the convoy was heading up a street called Via Fani, a Fiat 128 reversed suddenly from an adjoining street into the path of the first car. The car Moro was travelling in came to an abrupt halt and the second car, containing the two bodyguards, careered into the back of it. A male and a female then jumped out of the Fiat, shooting the driver and the bodyguard in Moro's car, but leaving Moro without injury. Then four men, quite bizarrely dressed in airline pilot's uniforms, who had been standing on the pavement outside a bar, pulled out semi-automatic machine guns and opened fire on the second car, killing everyone inside.

For all Moro's protection, none of his bodyguards were able to save him from the clutches of the Red Brigade on that fateful day. He was bundled into a getaway car, and then transferred into the trunk of a van parked nearby. From there he was transported to an apartment on Via Montalcini where a makeshift cell had been constructed especially for the purpose. He was to be interred indefinitely in a 'people's prison' until fourteen of Red Brigade's members, on trial in Turin, were released without charge. They were to have a long wait.

The Italian establishment reacted like any other government keen to stamp out terrorist activity. They refused to negotiate with the Red Brigade, but neither did they attempt to free him by force. Aldo Moro was on his own. As a man who did not believe that hard-line politics could ever be truly successful, and that negotiation was the only way to solve Italy's problems, Moro felt deeply frustrated and angered by his party's total refusal to negotiate. The Italian coalition government that Moro had worked so tirelessly to bring together, backed by the Americans and the West Germans, closed ranks and the nation's media followed suit. No public opposition of the government's hard line would be tolerated. Editors, reporters and columnists fell into line, and soon Moro was being painted as a madman in the press. In one of a series of desperate letters written to his family from his makeshift prison cell, he wrote: 'I face the solitary fate of the political prisoner condemned to death'. As one might expect, members of the DC party claimed that Moro was writing under the threat of torture, or under the influence of mind-altering drugs.

Some members of the Red Brigade claim that the

DC's behaviour so shocked and angered Moro, that he began to feel alienated by the party he had formerly led. He found sympathy with his captors, in particular its leader Mario Morretti, who is thought to have been the mastermind of the operation and the only Red Brigade member to speak to Moro during his fifty-four-day incarceration. This could have signalled the onset of stockholm syndrome, a psychological response whereby a captive begins to display signs of loyalty with the hostage taker. But according to Morretti, a genuine bond developed between the two men.

If Morretti's accounts are to be believed, the scenes that played out during this time would have been fascinating to witness. These two incredibly powerful and charismatic men from completely opposite political standpoints were in constant communication during this time. Moro, known as Italy's greatest political mediator, facing a possible death sentence at the hands of radical communists, and Morretti facing the possibility that, due to the DC's hardline stance, he would soon be forced to carry out that death sentence on a man he had come to respect. They engaged in an impassioned war of words. Moro used his ingenious wit, charm and natural intelligence, indeed everything he had, to bargain for his life. Morretti maintains that Moro was clear-thinking at all times, even in the most stressful situations. In a book by Morretti called *Red Brigades: An Italian Story,* he writes:

We didn't know a thing about how the power game is played. Moro taught me to understand it a little, clarifying what immediately became his battle against his party, the battle that in the end he'd lose. We were on opposite sides, but we worked together. I would pass along some information, a newspaper; all he would need was a few details, often a mere remark, to grasp what was going on. This was his universe, and he knew it to perfection.

Morretti continues to claim that it was the hard-line stance adopted by the DC party that ultimately forced the hand of the Red Brigade, that he had no choice but to carry out Moro's execution, but this is highly hypocritical. What of Morretti's own refusal to back down? When it finally became clear that DC would not negotiate to save Moro's life, there was disagreement within the ranks of the Red Brigade. Some members opposed the killing and wanted Moro released despite their failure to achieve their own goals. Morretti does not claim to be one of the members fighting for Moro's freedom and surely, as their leader, if he had argued for Moro's release, his opinion would have carried extra weight. When Moro realised what was to be his fate, he wrote a final letter to DC, demanding that no party members should be admitted at his funeral. He had finally resigned himself to the death of a prisoner of war.

When the time eventually came on May 9, 1978, Morretti was the man who led Moro from his cell to a nearby garage, where four members of the Red Brigade were waiting. He was bundled into a car, told to cover himself with a blanket, and told he was being transferred to another location. In this final act, the soldiers of the Red Brigade showed despicable cowardice, for they were not able to face killing Moro directly. By ordering him to cover himself, they were undoubtedly hiding from the reality of what they were about to do, just as the coalition government had distanced themselves from Moro's humanity in order to justify their non-action. The Red Brigade emptied ten rounds into Moro's chest. None of the members who stood trial for his murder ever admitted pulling the trigger.

By the time of Moro's assassination, Rome was under extremely close surveillance by the Italian police who were supposedly hunting high and low for any sign of the missing politician. Despite this, Morretti and his men were able to drive a van, carrying the dead body of Moro, through the streets of Rome to a site exactly equidistant between the DC party HQ and that of the Italian Communist Party, where they simply abandoned it. The enduring image of Aldo Moro's discoloured and cumbersome corpse lying slumped in the back of that van has appeared in newspapers and on television sets all over the world. It is a truly startling image which powerfully portrays the harsh reality of what had happened, or what had been allowed to happen. Many of Italy's political elite must have encountered that image with an overwhelming sense of shame. If one holds with any of the conspiracy theories that were rife following Moro's murder, the Red Brigade were not the only people with blood on their hands.

Many believe that, in an attempt to stop Italy's political system pursuing a communist manifesto, the CIA infiltrated the Red Brigade and recruited Morretti in order that he might create tension between the two factions, thus destroying the coalition. If this is the case, the plan backfired badly, as the DC and the communists were not divided over Moro's fate. The only real loser was Moro himself.

JOHN LENNON

On the evening of December 8, 1980, former Beatle, John Lennon, was murdered in front of his apartment building in New York City. One of the world's most famous rock stars, lay in a state of semi-consciousness, blood pouring from four bullet wounds. His wife, Yoko Ono, tenderly held his head in her arms and wailed in grief. Within the hour Lennon's Dakota apartment building was turned into a makeshift shrine, fans crying, bearing candles, all standing round in a state of disbelief. The scene was almost surreal and, like many assassinations, over twenty years later, people are still asking 'Why?'

John Winston Lennon was born on October 9, 1940, in Liverpool, England. He was raised by his mother Julia and his aunt Mimi, while his father, Freddie, worked on board a ship, spending many months away from home. In July 1946, Freddie returned saying that he wanted to take his son with him to New Zealand. John's mother was against the idea but gave her son the option of where he would like to live. He chose to stay in England

and didn't see his father again for twenty years. After his father left, John formed a much stronger bond with his mother and during this period he started to experiment with music. The first instrument he played was a banjo, moving on later to a guitar.

John's life was turned upside down when his mother was killed after she was struck by a car on July 15, 1958. It was a traumatic experience and one that haunted him for the remainder of his life. Music became John's comfort and he purchased his first guitar for the sum of seventeen pounds.

John played in many skiffle groups but his big break came in late 1960, when he set the foundation for the group that would change the course of music forever – The Beatles.

John and Yoko's limousine pulled up outside their apartment at 22.49 on December 8, 1980. The doorman stepped forward to open the car door for them and Yoko stepped out onto the street first. John followed close behind, carrying a tape recorder and some music casettes. As Yoko walked past a young man he turned and said 'Hello', causing John to give him a long, hard look to see if he knew him.

As John passed the man, he dropped into a combat stance and pulled a snubnosed .38 revolver out of his pocket. With his knees flexed and his arms outstretched, the man asked, 'Mr Lennon?' and, as John turned his head, the man fired two shots. The bullets caught John in the back and although he was already pouring with blood, the assassin took aim again. The gunman fired three more shots – one missed but the other two found their target and embedded in John's shoulder. There was the sound of shattering glass as the bullets passed through John's body and shattered the glass doors at the front of the Dakota apartment building. John, with blood spurting out of his wounds, staggered up to the lobby, his face grimacing in pain, before dropping to the floor in a state of semi-consciousness.

'John's been shot!', Yoko screamed and followed John into the lobby. The building's security man went straight to the desk and pressed the alarm button, which alerted the police at the nearby 20th Precinct station. Then he rushed over to John, removed his glasses which had been smashed in the attack, and covered his body with his own jacket.

By the time John was put into the back of a squad car, he had lost all control of his limbs and was unable to speak. The car sped through red lights and swung into the entrance of the Roosevelt Hospital. By the time John reached the emergency room his pulse was barely audible. The two bullets that hit him in the back had pierced a lung and passed out through his chest. A third bullet had shattered his left shoulder bone and a fourth had hit the same shoulder and ricocheted inside his chest, severing his aorta and windpipe. An emergency team tried every possible device and technique to save his life, but having lost eighty per cent of his blood John was just too weak to fight for his life.

Ironically, John had been having nightmares about violent deaths and gunshot wounds. He had become fascinated with numerology (the study of the occult meanings of numbers and their supposed influence on human life) and had even had visions of his own sudden death. He was so affected by these visions that one of the last songs he ever wrote mentions 'the angel of destruction' haunting his body.

Directly after the shooting, a chubby young man stood a few yards away reading the pages of a paperback novel, J. D. Salinger's *Catcher in the Rye*. The doorman of the Dakota apartment buildings called across to the man, 'Do you know what you've done?'

The young man casually replied, 'I just shot John Lennon'.

The gunman was Mark David Chapman, a man who suffered from severe delusional paranoid schizophrenia. Like most schizophrenics, Chapman was convinced that he had been chosen to fulful a special mission. He was convinced that he was being given clear signs that no one else could see, and that these signs were hidden in the text of books and magazines that he read. He also believed that certain songs contained lyrics that were words from false prophets and that he had to simply wait for the final signal.

John Lennon had become paranoid about appearing in pubic after almost five years of self-imposed seclusion, but he was starting to overcome his problems and was about to make a comeback. He had agreed to being interviewed so that he could promote his latest album, Double Fantasy, but what he didn't know was that he had unwittingly sent out signals to his assassin.

On October 20, 1980, Chapman read about John Lennon's return to the recording studios. He decided to resign from his security job and when he signed out for the last time he used the name 'John Lennon', then crossed it out. On October 27, Chapman went to a gun shop in Honolulu and brought a .38-calibre Charter Arms Special for $169.

On October 30, wearing a new suit and carrying the gun in a suitase, Chapman boarded a plan to New York City.

Chapman had been loaned $5,000 by his father-in-law and decided to live it up a little before carrying out his plan. He decided to check into the Waldorf Hotel and treated himself to a slap up meal. He was well aware that John lived in the Dakota apartment building across from Central Park, and Chapman spent much of the day walking round it and finding out from the doorman exactly which floor the Lennons lived on.

Chapman had forgotten to buy bullets in Honolulu and, not aware that New York's laws forbade the sale of them, he had to think of an alternative plan. He called a man called Dana Reeves, who was a sheriff's deputy in Georgia and told him that he wanted to visit some old friends. Reeves invited Chapman to stay in his apartment and he caught the first available flight to Atlanta. His story to Reeves was that he had bought the gun for personal protection while he was staying in New York, but he needed some bullets. Reeves was only too pleased to help and gave him five hollow-point cartridges. Despite the ban on military use, hollow-point bullets were one of the most common types of civilian and police ammunition, due largely to the reduced risk of bystanders being hit as they are the kind that expand as they pass through their target.

By November 10, Chapman was back in New York. That night he decided to go and see a movie called *Ordinary People*, in which Timothy Hutton played a suicidal youth trying to come to terms with his dysfunctional family. When he left the cinema, Chapman made a phone call to his wife in which he said, 'I'm coming home, I won a great victory. Your love has saved me.' Apparently, all of a sudden his demons were gone – but not for long. Back home he started behaving strangely and his wife, Gloria, was alarmed when he told her he was going back to New York. When she tried to stop him he told her that everything was fine and that he was going to find a job.

Chapman arrived in New York on Saturday, December 6 and immediately started to get into his character – the man chosen to assassinate John Lennon. He told a taxi driver that he was a recording engineer who had just come from a secret session with John Lennon and Paul McCartney. The taxi driver listened intently, not aware that it was all a pack of lies.

The following day Chapman spent many hours waiting outside the Dakota apartment building, then realising he was hungry, took a taxi back to the Sheraton Hotel, where he had booked in the previous day. Then he remembered he had forgotten to bring his copy of *The Catcher in the Rye* to New York and went off to a local bookshop to purchase the book.

On Monday, December 8, when Chapman woke he knew that this was to be the day. He dressed, picked up his copy of the *Double Fantasy* album, his copy of *The*

Catcher in the Rye and one other item, the pistol with a piece of cardboard over it to conceal the outline of it in his pocket.

Outside the Dakota building, Chapman leaned against the railings and started to read his book. He was so engrossed that he didn't notice John Lennon getting out of a taxi and walk into the building. In the afternoon, Chapman returned to the Dakota having had lunch with a woman called Jude Stein, who told him that she was a huge fan of John Lennon and that she had even managed to talk to him and his family on several occasions.

Back outside the Dakota, Jude and Chapman stood watching the front door when John's five-year-old son, Sean, came out with his nanny. Jude introduced Chapman to Sean and Chapman shook hands with the young boy.

Later the same afternoon John came out of the building and Chapman, dumbstruck, held out his copy of *Double Fantasy* and a pen. John smiled and wrote 'John Lennon, 1980' on the cover.

Just a few hours later Chapman killed the man with whom he was obsessed. When the doorman pointed Chapman out to the police, he didn't attempt to run away. He put his hands in the air and said, 'Don't hurt me'. The police put him in handcuffs and bundled him into the back of the squad car. 'I'm sorry I gave you guys all this trouble,' he said time and time again.

During his trial, the forty-five-year-old Chapman gave details of his mental state leading up to the shooting of John Lennon. He told the court that he had an overwhelming desire to kill Lennon after seeing photos of the pop icon standing in front his apartment buidling in a book called *One Day at a Time*. He also said that he had a list of other celebrities as a backup list in case he wasn't able to get to the legendary former Beatle. He spoke of an obsession, claiming that he had heard voices telling him to 'just do it'.

Chapman was sentenced to life in Attica prison, and the first few years behind bars were hard. Threats to his life were such a problem that the windows to his room at Bellevue Hospital had to be painted black in case snipers were waiting outside. He underwent dozens of tests and for many years experienced fits of rage which carried on into the 1990s.

The parole hearing in 2004, his third, brought a flood of protests. Yoko Ono said Chapman still posed a threat to her and her family, and a petition calling for him to live out his life in prison had 2,000 signatures.

In October 2006, the parole board held a sixteen-minute hearing and concluded that they remained 'concerned about the bizarre nature of his premeditated and violent crime . . . While the panel notes your satisfactory institutional adjustment, due to the extremely violent nature of the offence your release would not be in the best interest of the community' or his own personal safety.

On December 8, 2006, the twenty-sixth anniversary of Lennon's death, Yoko Ono published a one-page advertisement in several newspapers, saying that, while December 8 should be a 'day of forgiveness', she had not yet forgiven Chapman and wasn't sure if she was ready to yet.

Mark David Chapman is still a model prisoner in Attica Correctional Institution, seemingly free of his previous demons. For his own safety he has to remain in solitary confinement and as a New Yorker wrote, 'If he is set free, something will happen to him'.

Chapman's next parole hearing is scheduled for October 2008, but having killed one of the most popular singer/songwriters of our time, prison is most definitely the safest place for this assassin.

JILL DANDO

Jill Dando was a much loved and admired household name at the time of her murder in April 1999. The thirty-seven-year-old was at the pinnacle of her broadcasting career. An attractive and popular TV presenter for the BBC, she had worked in television for fifteen years, fronting prime-time programmes such as *Holiday*. Most prominently, she presented BBC1's *Crimewatch* with Nick Ross: a monthly magazine show that explores the nation's unsolved crimes and appeals for witnesses and information, often leading to the conviction of dangerous criminals. In the period immediately following her death it was generally supposed that Jill had been targeted by one of these violent criminals, perhaps somebody connected with organised crime, who was hell-bent on killing her as revenge for their conviction. It is true that Jill took none of the precautions one might expect of someone working in such a field, especially a high-profile television personality who had received threatening letters and phone calls in the year leading up to her death. She very publicly opposed the criminal under-world, had no minders of any kind, and made no special secret of her home address.

At first the murder seemed to carry the hallmarks of an assassination by a hitman. Indeed, the murder site showed none of the mess you might expect to find at the scene of a crazed-stalker attack. It was a fairly clean kill – if such a thing really exists – in that there were no eyewitnesses to the crime, even though it happened in broad daylight, no gunshot was heard by people in the vicinity, and there was no 'funny business' involved – that is to say no obvious sexual motive, or lust for violence evident at the crime scene.

On the morning of Monday, April 26, 1999, Jill left the house of her fiancé, gynaecologist Alan Farthing, where she had stayed the night and climbed into her blue BMW convertible. She drove towards her own home in Gowan Avenue, Fulham, stopping briefly at a couple of electrical stores and a fish market to pick up supplies. At approximately 11.30 that morning, a neighbour of Jill's, Mr Hughes, was alerted to the sound of a woman's screams coming from outside, and he ran to investigate. He found Jill slumped and bleeding in her doorway, as if crouched looking for keys. She had been shot once in the head at close range. The bullet had entered behind her left ear and exited behind her right, damaging the bottom of the front door to the right of the body. Hughes maintains he saw a well-dressed man standing outside another neighbour's house as he went to investigate, but this man disappeared during the panic that ensued. Jill was rushed by ambulance to Charing Cross hospital, but was declared dead later that day. Jill's friend and colleague, Jenny Bond, announced the news of Jill's death live on air a few minutes later and the nation went into a state of shock.

The investigation, named 'Operation Oxborough', began without delay. The crime scene was quickly cordoned off for forensic examination, and a team of forensic experts descended on Gowan Avenue. Jill's front garden yielded one single Remington brand cartridge from a short version 9 mm semi-automatic Browning pistol – a rare gun, and one similar to those used by drug dealers and professional killers. It was fired by someone with a knowledge of firearms, since the cartridge had been tampered with to remove some of the powder, thus deadening the sound of the shot. This was not the action of an opportunist, nor that of an unskilled amateur.

It was thought possible at the time that Jill's killing was meant as retribution for a UK/US-led air attack on a Serbian TV station that had, according to members of the Serbian military, killed a number of Serbian journalists and staff. Dando had just made a campaign film to raise money for Kosovar refugees, so this theory made sense. She had apparently reported receiving a threatening letter from a Serb source, criticising her appearance in the film a mere fortnight before the shooting. The police investigated the lead, but the trail led nowhere. It is, however, interesting to note that, in the weeks immediately following Jill's murder, Channel 4 stepped up security for their broadcast journalists, and other TV personalities John Humphreys and Alan Yentob also received Serbian threats.

Police soon ruled out the likelihood of a contract killing. It may have been a clean kill, but its neatness was really down to chance rather than meticulous planning. The killer came to Dando's own home, one she rarely visited because she spent most of her time at her fiancé's house in another part of London. This means the killer had either followed her there or come across her by chance. He had not allowed for a place to hide in the minutes immediately following the murder, there was no getaway vehicle and he had let the muzzle of the gun make contact with the victim's head, leaving a distinct imprint of the gun on her skin near to the entrance wound. This was not considered by police to be the actions of a hitman, and on May 25, a senior Scotland Yard source declared that an obsessive fan or a figure from Jill's private life was most likely responsible for her murder. The investigation changed direction.

Jill called herself 'Blando' Dando – because she was basically an attractive but uninteresting, conventional, girl-next-door type. Her televisual persona was not an elaborate creation, but a reflection of the safe, 'average' and homely person she really was. Perhaps it was these very qualities that attracted the sinister attentions of an obsessive killer. Her appearance also made her a target for unhinged elements of society. She bore a striking resemblance to the late Princess Diana, something which was often commented on in the media. Was it possible that a Diana fanatic had transferred his obsession to Jill following the princesses's own premature death? Some thought this was a distinct possibility. Having taken over 1,000 statements without anything concrete coming to light the police retraced their enquiries until one person emerged as their prime suspect.

Barry George lived half a mile away from the scene of the murder and was undoubtedly an oddball. George grew up in an unhappy home on a deprived London housing estate. His childhood was a difficult one, he was always restless, always striving for a more glamorous life which was completely out of reach – an existence similar to those he saw on television. As an adult he renamed himself Barry Bulsara after the Queen frontman Freddy Mercury's birth name, and sometimes claimed to be the singer's cousin. He also occasionally posed as Gary Glitter, and called himself Paul Gadd – the singer's real name. He was an obsessive compulsive who had developed fixations on the military, the world of celebrity and guns. He was also known to have followed countless women, sometimes as far as their front doors, and was once caught by police outside Kensington Palace wearing a balaclava and carrying a length of rope and a knife, along with a self-written poem to Prince Charles. In short, Barry George was most certainly a couple of b-sides short of a full back-catalogue, and he had made it known to police on a number of occasions. This was enough to put him squarely in the frame for murder.

George had been reported as behaving strangely in the crowd behind the police cordon immediately following the discovery of Dando's body. Witnesses had said that, in hindsight, George had mentioned details about the murder that hadn't yet been divulged by police to the public in their campaign to unravel the case. When the police investigated George in more depth they discovered a person whose profile made him a very likely candidate for the crime. The only employment he had ever had was as a messenger for the BBC for four months in 1977 and he had nurtured a particular

ABOVE: *A portrait of Vlad Tepes (Vlad the Impaler), from a painting in Castle Ambras in the Tyrol. He was infamous for having captured Turk soldiers and impaled them naked on ten foot poles.*

ABOVE: *Chinese leader Mao Zedong instigated several major socio-political programmes in an effort to achieve the perfect state. However, his programmes were a failure and he was blamed for the deaths of millions of his own countrymen.*

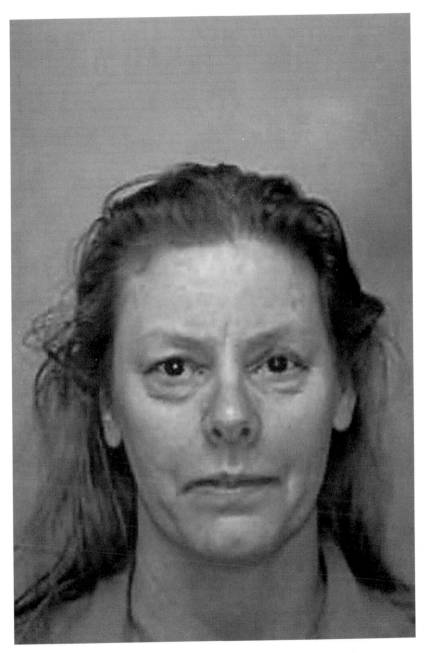

ABOVE: *Aileen Wuornos, dubbed the 'Damsel of Death', preyed on men while working as a prostitute. In a period of thirteen months in 1989 and 1990 Wuornos is believed to have killed seven men and was sentenced to death for six of these murders.*

ABOVE: *Olof Palme was assassinated around 11.20 p.m. on February 28, 1986, but the police investigation after the event was a major catastrophy. It has been said that: 'If the truth about the murder of Olof Palme is revealed it will shake the foundations of the nation'.*

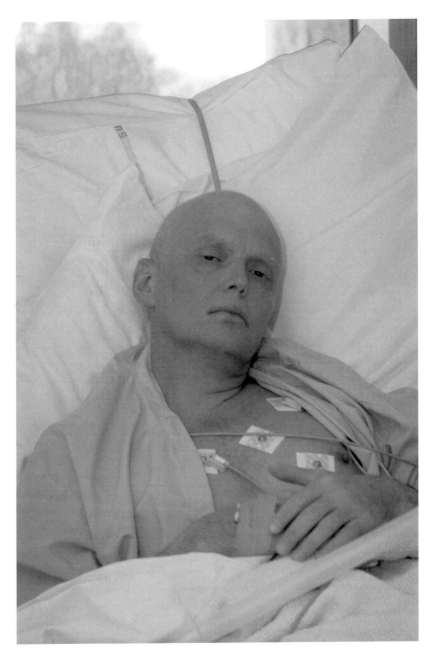

ABOVE: *Alexander Litvinenko is seen here in Intensive Care at University College Hospital in London in November 2006. The former KGB spy accused Russian President Vladimir Putin of being involved in a plot to poison him, which resulted in Litvinenko's death on November 23.*

ABOVE: *Jeffrey Dahmer was an American serial killer whose crimes were so repulsive his name is now synonymous with the word 'monster'. He killed at least seventeen times, not only dismembering his victims' bodies but often resorting to cannibalism to satisfy his insatiable urges.*

LEFT: *December 1969, the chained cult leader Charles Manson is led from court after hearing charges of possessing stolen property. He led a hippie group who were connected with the Sharon Tate murders and, on hearing his sentence, Manson said to the people of the United States, 'I am not the King of the Jews nor am I a hippie cult leader. I am what you have made me and the mad dog devil killer fiend leper is a reflection of your society . . .'*

ABOVE: *Bound bodies of Tutsi genocide victims lie on the ground in the Rebezo-Birenga sector (100 km from Kigali) of Rwanda in May 1994. Hutu militias seeking to rid Rwanda of Tutsis brutally murdered hundreds of thousands of innocent people.*

interest in the corporation and its employees for many years. George's enduring obsession with celebrities of all kinds, meant he had compiled dossiers on the individuals who aroused his interest – details of their appearance, addresses, employment, etc. were all listed. Princess Diana's name was among these, but Jill Dando's was not. Although George was a hoarder and collected newspapers for a number of years, only eight articles bearing any relation to Jill Dando were found in his flat. Jill had appeared on the cover of the *Radio Times* shortly before the killing, and she had recently become engaged. There were no copies of the *Radio Times* or articles pertaining to her engagement found at Barry George's flat. Regardless of these facts and, despite having been placed on a low priority list of suspects during the initial investigation, Barry George was eventually arrested and charged with Jill Dando's murder.

George was known to have been involved with gun clubs and the Territorial Army, he also owned a couple of air rifles and a number of gun magazines – but all this dated back to the 1980s. There was no evidence found in Barry's flat that his obsession with firearms had developed, or even continued into the 1990s. He was dismissed from the TA after failing basic training, and rejected by the gun club because he was unable to provide a suitable character reference. These are not the actions of a ballistics expert. The only forensic evidence presented at George's trial was that of firearms discharge residue found in the pocket of one of George's jackets. These were proven to contain the same elements as those found at the murder scene. What this means is that both compounds contained the same ingredients, but firework residue could also produce the same result.

In addition to this, it has been argued that Barry George's obsessions were exclusive. He could only be interested in one thing at a time, and when something, or someone, aroused his interest he was demonstrative and vocal about it – as with his interest in Freddy Mercury. Of George's few friends, those interviewed could not name a single incident whereby George had mentioned, or made particular reference to, Jill Dando – the woman whose life he is supposed to have been so obsessed with, that he went out and shot her dead in broad daylight. There are many who believe Barry George's conviction for the murder represents a huge travesty of justice, and it is not difficult to see why. But if Barry George didn't do it – who did?

THE ASSASSINATION OF OLOF PALME

The murder of the Swedish prime minister in 1986 was one of the strangest murder cases of modern times. Often in such cases a prime suspect is selected from a short list of suspects, and put on trial and convicted. It may later emerge that the wrong person was put on trial, or that more than one person was involved and the accomplices got away; often there is a sense that justice was not entirely done, and questions remain, as they still do over both of the Kennedy assassinations. What is extraordinary about this case is that there was never at any point a clear and obvious suspect, and that nobody was ever tried and convicted. It is a totally unsolved crime.

Sven Olof Palme was born in 1927 and served as prime minister of Sweden from 1969 to 1976 and again from 1982 until his assassination in 1986. The murder of Olof Palme was the first of its kind in modern Swedish history and had an impact in Scandinavia similar to that of JFK in the United States. Politically he was a Social Democrat. During his time at university, Palme became involved in student politics, working with the Swedish National Union of Students. Palme attributed his becoming a socialist to three experiences: a debate on taxes which he attended in 1947, observation of the wide division between the social classes in America in the 1940s, and seeing for himself in 1953 the consequences of colonialism and imperialism in Asia.

He was elected as an MP in 1958 and he held several cabinet posts from 1963 onwards. In 1967 he became Minister of Education, and the following year he was the target of fierce criticism from left-wing students protesting against the government's plans for university reform. When the party leader Tage Erlander stepped down in 1969, Palme was elected as his successor by the Social Democratic party congress; he also succeeded Erlander as prime minister.

Olof Palme's ten years as Prime Minister and his untimely death made him one of the best known Swedish politicians of the twentieth century. His protégé and political ally, Bernt Carlsson, was the UN Commissioner for Namibia in July 1987, and he also suffered an untimely death. Carlsson died in the Pan Am air crash on December 21, 1988, on his way to the signing ceremony in New York, in which South Africa finally granted independence to Namibia.

Palme led a generation of Swedish Social Democrats who stood much further to the left than their predecessors. Because of this he became a controversial political figure on the international scene. He was brave enough to condemn the United States for its participation in the Vietnam War. He campaigned against the proliferation of nuclear weapons. He criticised the Franco regime in Spain. He condemned apartheid and supported economic sanctions against South Africa. He supported the Palestine Liberation Organisation. Olof Palme therefore made many enemies abroad as well as friends. It may be that making these powerful enemies sowed the seeds of his assassination.

Another factor in the murder was the relaxed Scandinavian attitude to security for politicians. In spite of his position, Olof Palme was often to be seen walking about in Stockholm without any kind of bodyguard or other protection, and the night of his murder was one such occasion. Near to midnight on February 28, 1986, he was walking home from the cinema with his wife Lisbet along the central Stockholm street called Sveavägen, when the couple were attacked without warning by a lone gunman. Olof Palme was shot in the back at close range and a second shot wounded Lisbet

Palme. Police said a taxi-driver used his mobile radio to raise the alarm. Two young women sitting in a car nearby tried to help the Prime Minister. He was rushed to hospital but was pronounced dead on arrival, just after midnight. Mrs Palme was treated for her injury and she recovered.

Deputy Prime Minister Ingvar Carlsson immediately assumed Palme's duties as prime minister and leader of the Social Democratic Party.

The assassin escaped unobserved and vanished. A reward equivalent to five million US dollars was offered for information leading to the conviction of the killer, a reward that was to go uncollected. The revolver used in the murder was never found. The assassination remains an unsolved crime, though many different theories have been put forward. One is that right-wing extremists were behind it. A right-winger called Victor Gunnarsson, with connections to various right-wing extremist groups including the European Workers Party, was arrested straight after the murder but soon released after a dispute between the police and prosecuting attorneys. John Stannerman was another of the police's suspects, but he turned out to have a watertight alibi: he was locked up in prison on the night Palme was shot.

Viktor Gunnarsson, a thirty-three-year-old Swede and fanatical anti-Communist, looked a much likelier suspect. He was a compulsive liar and role-player. He had spent some time in America and claimed to have contacts with the CIA. Gunnarsson was arrested twice and Inspector Wingren, who was responsible for that part of the investigation, was convinced that he was the killer. Gunnarsson was nevertheless released after an intervention by senior police officers, and he left Sweden. In 1994, a short time after revealing that he was the one described as the killer in Inspector Wingren's book He killed Olof Palme, he was murdered in North Carolina. The motive for his murder remained a mystery to the American police. Gunnarsson had uttered threats against Palme. He was definitely seen by witnesses near the murder scene both before and after killing, and a man of his description was seen running away after the fatal shots. Unlike Stannerman, he had no alibi.

Over a year after the assassination, another suspect, Christer Pettersson, was arrested. He was picked out by Mrs Palme at an identification parade, and consequently tried and convicted of the murder. Later, on appeal to the High Court, Pettersson succeeded in gaining an acquittal; the murder weapon had never been found; there were doubts about the reliability of Mrs Palme's evidence; and Pettersson had no obvious motive. In the 1990s new evidence against Pettersson emerged, mostly from petty criminals who had changed their stories but also, startlingly, from a confession by Pettersson. The chief prosecutor, Agneta Blidberg, considered re-opening the case, but acknowledged that a confession alone would not be sufficient, saying rather oddly: 'He must say something about the weapon because the appeals court set that condition in its ruling. That is the only technical evidence that could be cited as a reason to re-open the case.'

The legal case against Christer Pettersson therefore remains closed, but the police file on the investigation into the Palme murder cannot be closed until both murder weapon and murderer are found. Christer Pettersson died in September 2004 of a cerebral haemorrhage after injuring his head. A recent Swedish television documentary investigating the murder claimed that Pettersson's associates had said that he confessed to them his role in the murder, but that it was a case of mistaken identity. Pettersson had intended to kill another man, a drug dealer who often walked, similarly dressed, along the same street at night. He had not intended to kill the prime minister. The television programme also said there had been police surveillance of drug activity in the area, with several officers on duty in apartments and cars near the scene of the shooting, but the police monitoring had ceased forty-five minutes before the murder.

Over thirty witnesses saw people, some identifiable as policemen, talking into walkie-talkies along the Palmes' route home from the cinema or along the killer's escape route leading up to the time of the murder. One interpretation is that Mr and Mrs Palme were being kept under observation for benevolent reasons; another is that they were being stalked as part of a malevolent conspiracy, an elaborate plot to assassinate Palme; another is that there was a police surveillance operation going on in the area that had nothing to do with the Palmes or the attack on them.

As a result of the documentary, the Swedish police decided to open an investigation into Pettersson's role in the Palme case. Then there were newspaper articles alleging that the film-maker had invented some of the material and left out contradictory evidence.

There was, alternatively, a possible South African connection. A week before he was murdered, Palme addressed the Swedish People's Parliament Against Apartheid in Stockholm, which was attended by hundreds of anti-apartheid sympathisers as well as leaders and officials from the ANC. In 1996, Colonel Eugene de Kock, a former South African police officer, gave evidence to the Supreme Court in Pretoria alleging that Palme had been shot and killed because he 'strongly opposed the apartheid regime and Sweden made substantial contributions to the ANC'. De Kock knew the person responsible for the murder of Olof Palme; he said it was Craig Williamson, a South African super-spy working for BOSS and who was in Stockholm during the days immediately before and after the murder. Brigadier Johannes Coetzee, who had been Williamson's boss, identified Anthony White as the assassin. Then it became more complicated still; Peter Caselton, a member of Coetzee's assassination squad, named a Swede living in Northern Cyprus since 1985 as the assassin; his name was Bertil Wedin. In October 1996, Swedish police investigators went to South Africa but were unable to substantiate any of de Kock's claims for a South African Operation Longreach.

There had certainly been a conspiracy to assassinate. In 1999, Coetzee, Williamson, de Kock and Caselton were to be granted amnesties by the South African Truth and Reconciliation Commission for their involvement in the bombing of the ANC offices in London in 1982. As it happened no-one was killed, but Oliver Tambo, who was supposed to have attended a meeting there at the time of the bombing, was their probable target. But the reality of a South African conspiracy to assassinate Oliver Tambo – if that is what it was – is no proof whatever of a South African conspiracy to assassinate Olof Palme.

Another possibility was that Kurds were behind the murder. The Stockholm police commissioner, Hans Holmér, arrested a number of Kurds living in Sweden, following allegations that one of their organisations was responsible for the murder. The lead led nowhere except to Holmér's removal from the investigation. Fifteen years later, in 2001, Swedish police officers interviewed the Kurdish rebel leader Abdullah Öcalan in a Turkish prison about his allegations that a dissident Kurdish group murdered Palme. But this lead also proved fruitless.

The Swedish police investigation was overall poorly organised, with bureaucrats and administrators making the key decisions rather than experienced police officers; meanwhile Sweden's most experienced murder investigators were left out or were brought into the investigation too late. Lisbeth Palme was only questioned by certain selected investigators and although she positively identified Pettersson at an identification parade she was apparently never called upon to identify Gunnarsson, the other prime suspect. Many police officers were shocked at the ineptitude with which the Palme case was handled. The investigation inspired a certain amount of black humour; 'The bad news is that the police are after us: the good news is that it's the Swedish police'. The implication was that there was no need to fear an early arrest.

Theories about the unsolved murder of Olof Palme

abound. Several of the theories link Palme's death to arms trading. One suggestion is that Palme built on his friendship with Rajiv Gandhi to secure Bofors, a Swedish armaments company, a deal to supply the Indian Army with howitzers. However, Palme did not realize that Bofors had used a company based in England to influence Indian government officials in concluding the deal. Bondeson alleged that on the morning he was assassinated Palme had met the Iraqi ambassador to Sweden, Muhammad Saeed al-Sahhaf. They discussed Bofors, which Muhammed Saeed al-Sahhaf knew well because of its arms sales during the Iran-Iraq War. The ambassador apparently told Palme all about Bofors' activities behind the scenes. Palme was furious. Palme's murder could have been triggered by this conversation, if either Bofors arms dealers or their middlemen had a prearranged plan to silence the prime minister if he should ever discover the truth and endanger the deal with India. Like many conspiracy theories, it makes a fascinating and compelling story but is ultimately unconvincing.

Another possibility is that the Red Army Faction of Germany assassinated Palme. Indeed it seems the Red Army Faction went so far as to claim responsibility for the murder by way of an anonymous phone call to a London news agency. They supposedly assassinated him because he was the prime minister of Sweden during the 1975 occupation of the West German embassy in Stockholm which ended in failure for the Red Army Faction.

The Olof Palme mystery may never be solved. It remains a possibility that more than one of the leads we have looked it is true. Perhaps BOSS (to take one example) was behind the assassination, and perhaps one of the 'lone gunmen' was hired to do the job – and take all the blame. But so much disinformation has been spread about that it is very difficult to get at the truth of what happened that night on an ordinary street corner in Stockholm, when a Prime Minister was shot and, incredibly, no-one was ever brought to justice for it.

JOHN F. KENNEDY

The assassination of John F. Kennedy is probably the most controversial case in the modern history of the United States. The question has frequently been asked – did Lee Harvey Oswald kill Kennedy by himself, or was he part of a larger conspiracy? There is no doubt that there were all the right ingredients for a conspiracy. It is strange that Kennedy was assassinated in front of thousands of people and while being filmed, yet the superfluity of witness evidence, from eye to lens, served only confuse matters enormously. Even the analysis of film footage was open to interpretation so that the result was a plethora of conflicting opinions that managed to muddy investigations.

Of Irish descent, John F. Kennedy was born in Brookline, Massachusetts, on May 29, 1917. He graduated from Harvard in 1940 and went straight into the navy. He was renowned for his bravery when, in 1943, his boat was sunk by a Japanese destroyer. Despite being seriously wounded, Kennedy led the survivors through dangerous waters to safety.

After the war Kennedy became a Democratic Congressman, advancing in 1953 to the Senate. In September 1953, he married Jacqueline Bovier and two years later wrote Profiles in Courage, while convalescing following an operation on his back. For this book he won the Pulitzer Prize in history.

Kennedy became the 35th President of the United States in 1960, the youngest man ever elected to this role. Major events during his presidency include the Bay of Pigs Invasion, the Cuban Missile Crisis, the building of the Berlin Wall, the Space Race, the American Civil Rights Movement and early events of the Vietnam War. However, above all Kennedy had a vision for the United States: 'a world of law and free choice, banishing the world of war and coercion'. His administration saw the start of new hope for both equality for Americans and the peace of the new world, but this was to be shortlived as his reign was truncated by an assassin's bullet.

Kennedy chose to visit Dallas in November 1963 for three main reasons: to help raise funds for the Democratic Party campaign, to begin his quest for re-election and to mend political boundaries (the Democrats had previously lost Dallas in 1960). Following a meeting with Vice President Johnson and Governor Connally on June 5, 1963, it was announced that Kennedy would definitely visit Dallas despite early concerns about security. Adlai

Stevenson, the US Ambassador to the United Nations had recently been heckled and struck by a protest sign on a recent visit.

The police were nervous and they prepared exceptionally stringent security precautions so that the demonstrations marking the Stevenson visit would not be repeated. However, for some reason Winston Lawson of the Secret Service, told the Dallas police not to assign the usual number of experienced homicide detectives to follow the president's car. This was standard protection for any visiting dignitary and had they been in place they could possibly have prevented the shooting. However, that is all hearsay.

The planned route for the motorcade was from Love Field airport, through downtown Dallas to end at the Dallas Trade Mart where Kennedy was to speak. The car to be used was an open-top, 1961 Lincoln Continental – no car with a bulletproof top was yet in service.

Dallas newspapers printed details and a map of the intended route, so anyone could have got hold of this information. Just before 12.30 p.m. Kennedy's car entered Dealey Plaza and then turned left directly in front of the Texas School Book Depository. As the presidential car passed the Depository and travelled down Elm Street, witnesses recall hearing three shots. There was little reaction as most people in the crowd thought it was simply an exhaust backfiring.

As Kennedy smiled and waved at the crowds to his right side, a shot entered his upper back, penetrated his neck and came out via his throat. His hands went to his neck and he leaned forward, while Jacqueline Kennedy put her arms around him, unsure of what had happened. Texas Governor John Connally, who was sitting in the front of the car with his wife, was also hit by one of the bullets and he yelled, 'Oh, no, no, no'. The first shot hit the governor in the back and the second in the chest, at which time he said, 'My God, they are going to kill us all'. The last shot hit its target as the car passed in front of the John Neely Bryan north pergola concrete structure. As the sound of the shot was heard, a hole the size of a grapefruit appeared on the right side of Kennedy's head, covering the inside of the car and a nearby motorcycle officer with blood. Of course anyone that can add up would make this four shots, but the consensus of opinion is that the first bullet left Kennedy's body and went on to hit Connally in the back.

Clint Hill, who was a secret service agent riding on the left front running board of the car following the president's limousine, jumped off as soon as he heard the shots and ran ahead. He climbed onto the rear of the president's car, pushed Mrs Kennedy down in her seat and then clung to the car as it sped off towards

Parkland Memorial Hospital. Governor Connally, although seriously wounded, survived the ordeal, thanks to the quick reactions of his wife who pulled him down onto her lap, thus closing his wound. John Kennedy was not so lucky.

When the shots were fired the cars had been passing a grassy mound to the north side of Elm Street, but when the police ran to the area with its high picket fence, there was no evidence of a sniper. However, Lee Bowers, a railway signalman who sat in a two-storey tower, had an unobstructed view of the mound and the rear of the picket fence. He said he saw a total of four men in the area at the time of the shooting.

Meanwhile, another witness, Howard Brennan, told the police that as he watched the motorcade go by he heard a shot coming from above and, when he looked up, he saw a man with a rifle make another shot from a corner window on the sixth floor of the Texas School Book Despository. He managed to give a description of the sniper, which was broadcast to all the Dallas police. Other witnesses came forward and said they had heard shots coming from the direction of the Depository.

The Depository reported that one of their employees, Lee Harvey Oswald, had gone missing. Oswald was arrested just one hour and twenty minutes after the assassination, when he killed a Dallas policeman, J. D.

Tippit, who had seen Oswald walking down a side road. Later that night he was charged with the murder of Kennedy and Tippit, although he adamantly denied shooting anyone. Oswald never made it to court, just two days later while being escorted to an armoured car on way to the Dallas County Jail, he was shot dead by Jack Ruby.

Jack Ruby lived in the Oak Cliff section of Dallas and shot Oswald in the stomach in the basement of Dallas police station. Ruby walked down a car ramp to get to the basement, managing to get past a police officer who was guarding the exit. Ruby was brought to trial and convicted to death. In 1966, the decision was reversed and he was granted a second trial. However, before his case could be heard he died from lung cancer, with Ruby claiming on his deathbed that someone had injected him with the disease. He has been described as a very volatile, very emotional, unbalanced person who thought he was doing the right thing when he shot Oswald. This of course did not stop people saying that he was just a small fry in a much larger conspiracy. In fact it later transpired that Ruby was a well connected businessman with friends in both the police force and the underworld. That led people to begin wondering about Ruby's true motive.

A 6.5 x 52mm Italian Mannlicher-Carcano M91/38

bolt-action rifle was found on the sixth floor of the Texas Book Depository and it was later identified as the weapon used in the assassination. It was also confirmed that the rifle had been bought the previous March by Lee Harvey Oswald under the assumed name 'A. Hiddell'. A partial palm print of Oswald was also found on the barrel of the gun.

Although the event was not captured by television cameras, Kennedy's last seconds were recorded on a piece of 8mm film for a little over twenty seconds before, during and immediately following the shooting. This famous piece of film was taken by an amateur camera-man Abraham Zapruder, in what became known as the Zapruder film. This film has been scrutinised many times and in great detail to see if investigators could learn anything more about the assassination of Kennedy.

Ballistics investigations then revealed the possibility of there having been two gunmen at the scene of Kennedy's assassination and the conspiracy theorists had a field day. In fact many different theories came out regarding the assassination of Kennedy, so President Johnson organised the first official investigation into the shooting, called the Warren Commission. It tried to give details of exactly what happened to try and alleviate further confusion.

The commission also concluded that:

- one shot likely missed the motorcade (it could not determine which of the three),
- the first shot to hit anyone struck Kennedy in the upper back, exited near the front of his neck and likely continued on to cause all of Governor Connally's injuries, and
- the last shot to hit anyone struck Kennedy in the head, fatally wounding him.

The commission also concluded that it could not find any persuasive evidence of a domestic or foreign conspiracy involving any other person, group or country. They reported that Lee Harvey Oswald had acted alone in the murder and that Jack Ruby had also acted alone in his killing of Oswald. However, almost as soon as the commission issued its report, people started to question its conclusions. Many books and articles have criticised their findings and yet subsequent investigations have all come to the same conclusion with the exception of one – the Dictabelt evidence. The Dictabelt evidence relating to the assassination of Kennedy, came from a recording on a police officer's motorcycle that was escorting the president's car. This then-common dictation machine recorded sounds in grooves pressed into soft vinyl, and the evidence of which opened the floodgates with conspiracy theorists.

They believe that it confirms that Kennedy was shot by two gunmen firing from perpendicular directions because of the force he slumped forward in his seat.

In the four decades since the assassination of John F. Kennedy, many many theories have been published that detail organised conspiracies. These theories implicate, among others, Cuban President Fidel Castro, the Anti-Castro Cuban community, President Johnson, the Mafia, the FBI, the CIA and the Soviet Bloc, and some even mention a combination of these.

Some of these theories claim that not only was Oswald definitely not the lone assassin but that he was not involved at all. One thing that is obvious in all of this is, that it doesn't matter how many films, books or articles are written about the assassination of JFK (as he became known), doubts will continue to plague regarding what really happened on November 22, 1963. It seems unlikely that we will ever know the full details of the assassination, simply because those involved are dead themselves.

ROBERT F. KENNEDY

President John F. Kennedy had fallen to an assassin in November 1963. His forty-two-year-old brother, Senator Robert F. Kennedy, seemed set fair to follow him into the White House. In June 1968, Robert Kennedy was in California campaigning to be nominated as the Democratic candidate for the Presidency. Voting took place on June 4 and after a hard-fought campaign Bobby Kennedy spent the day before he died swimming, sitting in the sun, talking to friends, playing with his children and sleeping.

He was so relaxed that he considered not attending his own election night party. He suggested that he and his family and friends might watch the primary results on television. In truth, he did not expect to win the election. Because the television networks refused to haul their equipment out to Malibu, Kennedy reluctantly decided to go into Los Angeles that evening to wait for the election result. Accompanied by John Frankenheimer and other members of his campaign staff, he drove to the Ambassador Hotel for the election night party. Kennedy had a suite reserved there and, with the election result still in doubt and Kennedy running behind, he went to relax in his suite.

It was announced at 11.40 p.m. that Kennedy had won. This was a completely unexpected result, and Kennedy made a short improvised victory speech from the podium in the hotel's Embassy Ballroom.

He was all too conscious that he could be the target of an assassination attempt, especially after the very high-profile assassinations of his brother and, only two months earlier, Martin Luther King Jr. Both had been shot dead in cold blood. Now that Kennedy was emerging as a real presidential candidate he was more at risk than ever. Yet in spite of the high risk, security at the hotel was almost non-existent. The hotel management had taken on eighteen security guards purely for crowd control, and as far as is known there were no police officers on duty. In 1968 presidential contenders were not provided with Secret Service protection, and relations between Kennedy and the Los Angeles Police Department (LAPD) were strained. Los Angeles police officers had found themselves wrong-footed when Kennedy was working a crowd; they had conscientiously tried to protect him and then been abused by his campaign followers for their trouble. A few personal bodyguards had been hired for the occasion from a local firm called Ace Security.

Shortly after midnight on June 5, Kennedy ended his speech with the words, 'And now its on to Chicago - and let's win there!' He started to make his way from the ballroom at the Ambassador Hotel to give a press conference in the Colonial Room. He moved forward through the crowd towards the front door, but then his Press Secretary Frank Mankiewicz turned him round and diverted him through the kitchen pantry, apparently because it was slightly less crowded and would therefore be a quicker and easier route.

He was led by one of the hotel staff, Karl Uecker, and followed by an Ace Security guard, Thane Cesar. A brown-skinned man of obvious Middle Eastern descent was pushing a steel food trolley towards the advancing crowd. When he was close enough, he shouted and began to fire a .22 revolver, apparently at Kennedy. He fired eight rounds, but a ballistics investigation showed that none of them hit Kennedy. All eight went wildly into bystanders, walls and ceiling. There was chaos as bullet after bullet whizzed around the confined space. Sirhan Sirhan, the man with the food trolley and the gun, was quickly restrained and disarmed, but Kennedy and five other people were wounded. The wounded were taken to the nearest hospital, the Central Receiving Hospital, but Kennedy was taken to the Good Samaritan Hospital for brain surgery. He had a three-hour operation and was thought to have a chance of surviving, but he died about twenty-five hours after the shooting.

Sirhan Sirhan was arrested immediately, and later charged and convicted of first degree murder. He was sentenced to death, but the US Supreme Court declared the death sentence unconstitutional before it could be carried out. Since then, Sirhan has been incarcerated at Corcoran State Prison, California. Sirhan was born in 1944, of an Arab family living in Jerusalem. When the state of Israel was created in 1948, the family became refugees. When he was twelve years old, he moved with his family to California. Sirhan continued to be deeply interested in the politics of the Middle East, inevitably empathizing with the Palestinian cause. He was outraged when the media and political leaders in the United States celebrated the Israeli victory in the Six-Day War in 1967. He began to see Robert Kennedy as a hate figure when he realized that Kennedy saw Israel as the injured party in the conflict. Sirhan himself said explicitly that he killed Kennedy to punish him for supporting Israel. With his biography and political background, Sirhan Sirhan looked like a perfect suspect for the assassination. Yet there were always some who doubted whether Sirhan was really the lone crazed gunman presented in court.

This was an assassination that took place in the close proximity of a great many witnesses; perhaps as many as seventy-six people saw it 'live' from close quarters and twenty million saw it on television. The problem is that the assassination happened with such speed, in such a melee and in such an emotionally charged context that people could not be sure what they saw or heard. On the face of it, the killing of Robert Kennedy looks like a lone gunman assassination, and there is much to recommend this interpretation. On the other hand there are reasons for doubting it. The physical evidence and eyewitness reports seem to show that Sirhan was forensically incapable of inflicting all of the wounds.

Thomas Noguchi, the Coroner, produced a post mortem report which showed that Senator Kennedy was shot three times. One shot entered the head behind the right ear, a second shot near the right armpit and a third roughly one and a half inches below the second. All the bullets entered the body at a sharply upward angle, moving slightly right to left. These are hard to square with the eyewitnesses' accounts of Sirhan's shooting.

Sirhan's .22 revolver contained just eight bullets and he had no chance to reload. This limit to the number of bullets caused a problem for the official version of the assassination. One bullet was lost in the ceiling space; two were lodged in a wooden door jamb. Five or six ceiling tiles were removed for tests. Los Angeles Police Department criminologist DeWayne Wolfer was quoted as saying 'it's unbelievable how many holes there are in the kitchen ceiling.' This strongly suggests that the LAPD found traces of more bullets than could have come from Sirhan's eight shot revolver. This in turn suggests that there were two or more people firing in the pantry.

There were reports of suspicious people in the area at the time of the assassination. The first police officer on the scene, Sergeant Paul Schraga, was approached by a couple who told him that they had seen and heard a young man and woman running out of the Ambassador Hotel shouting, 'We shot him! We shot him!' When asked whom they had shot, the young woman replied, 'Senator Kennedy!' Schraga sent out an All Points Bulletin on the two suspects. This was the start of what became known as the 'Polka-dot Dress Girl' controversy.

Within minutes of the crime the LAPD quixotically declared that Sirhan was the sole assassin, which was premature. Many observers were staggered that the police were so adamant; the official line from the beginning was, 'This is a solved case.' Schraga was asked to cancel his bulletin regarding two more suspects and when he refused it was cancelled by his superiors. The couple's story was plausibly explained by the LAPD as a case of mishearing, stating that the young woman must have said, 'They shot him!' Nevertheless, a young woman sitting on a staircase outside the Ambassador Hotel, Sandra Serrano, told the same story. Two witnesses in the pantry also saw armed men, quite apart from Sirhan and the security guard Thane Eugene ('Gene') Cesar. Lisa Urso noticed a fair-haired man in a grey suit putting a gun into a holster. Another witness saw a tall, dark-haired man in a black suit fire two shots and run out of the pantry. These men could have been assassins; they could alternatively have been Kennedy's bodyguards.

As the case was the responsibility of the LAPD, there was no pressure to release their findings. Researchers into the assassination finally forced the release of the report and the police department's files in 1988, a full twenty years after the assassination. This was extraordinary; the Warren Commission Report had been published in 1964, the year after JFK's assassination. After the long-delayed release of the files, it became clear that a huge amount of evidence contradicting the official version had gone missing, including 2,400 photographs, the ceiling tiles and the door frame from the pantry, and transcripts of over 3,000 interviews, including those for the fifty-one key 'conspiracy' witnesses.

Scott Enyart, a resourceful teenager who managed to take a sequence of photographs of the assassination, successfully won a lawsuit to have his photos returned in 1988. The courier who was returning the pictures to him in a rented car was involved in a minor accident; in the aftermath of the accident the envelope containing the pictures was stolen. They have never been seen since. One of the photos was taken at the moment when Kennedy dropped to the floor, and may show the smoking gun behind him.

Suspicion grew that the LAPD report was a cover-up. Files released to researchers in 1985 by the Los Angeles District Attorney's Office included a box of tapes, videos and documents. This box is said to have contained some of the evidence which conflicted with the official version, most conspicuously the filmed re-enactments that were staged in 1968 and 1977, which proved that Sirhan could not have inflicted the wounds found on Senator Kennedy's body. He was standing in the wrong place, too far away from Kennedy and on the wrong side of him, too. It was carefully selected stills from the reconstructions that were used to support the official version. If a deliberate cover-up was the result of the LAPD's investigation, it was almost certainly because the truth of what happened was beyond reach. The LAPD 'lone gunman' version of Bobby Kennedy's assassination seemed such an open and shut case that the House Select Committee on Assassinations did not even trouble to investigate it. Given the questions that have arisen subsequently, it looks as if there is a case for a re-investigation of the assassination.

Here are the reasons for believing that there was at least one other assassin besides Sirhan:

1. The powder burns on Kennedy's clothing show that all three shots came from a gun fired less than four inches away from him. The witnesses say that Sirhan's gun was never closer than twenty inches away. The assassin was standing very close indeed to Kennedy. Sirhan was simply too far away to have fired the fatal shots.

2. Sirhan's gun held a maximum of eight bullets. Seven bullets were found embedded in human tissue, in Robert Kennedy and the other victims in the pantry. An eighth bullet passed through two ceilings into an air space. A ninth and a tenth were lodged in the pantry door frame. Inexcusably, from the forensic point of view, the two expended bullets were dug out of the door frame, and the frame itself was burnt. In any case, Sirhan cannot

have fired more than eight bullets; at least two must have been fired by someone else. Some analysts thought there had been as many as thirteen bullet holes, so there must have been at least one more gun.

3. The three bullets found in Robert F. Kennedy and the fourth, which grazed his suit jacket, were fired almost vertically upwards. All the witnesses testified that Sirhan was not holding his gun vertically but completely horizontally for the first two shots, after which his gun hand was repeatedly slammed down on a table by Karl Uecker, who had been leading Kennedy forward by the right hand. It was not possible that Sirhan fired the third shot into Kennedy, because by then he was being tackled by Karl Uecker.

4. The four bullets which touched Kennedy all hit on his back right side, travelling forward in relation to his body. Kennedy was walking towards Sirhan, facing Sirhan while the shots were fired. Even when he fell, he fell backwards, and was therefore still facing Sirhan. It was not possible for any of Sirhan's shots to have hit Kennedy in the back. In a nutshell, Kennedy was shot from behind, and Sirhan was in front of him.

Obviously Sirhan was there; that has never been in

question. Irrefutably he fired gunshots in the general direction of Kennedy, but someone else was firing too. Once a second assassin is established, the complexion of the event is changed. Not only was a conspiracy involved, but it looks as though the second gunman, standing a little behind Kennedy and to one side, was given powerful and effective protection. Sirhan was allowed, perhaps even set up, to take the blame for the murder, while the other man was allowed not only to escape punishment but identification. Indeed, a second assassin strongly implies that a powerful US Government department was behind the murder itself – after the assassination, the evidence was consistently manipulated to keep the decoy, Sirhan, as the one conspicuous figure in the foreground while the other gunman was air-brushed from the background. New York Congressman Allard Lowenstein went public with the forensic information about the eleven or thirteen bullets in 1970, in an attempt to get the case re-opened. He was later shot dead in his New York office by 'a disgruntled client'.

Sirhan had his contacts. On June 2, 1968, Sirhan went into Kennedy's Campaign headquarters, where Larry Strick asked him if he needed help. Sirhan pointed at one of the volunteer workers and said, 'I'm with him.' At the time it seemed an insignificant remark, but the volunteer worker in question, who was only there for a few days, turned out to be a high-level international secret agent.

So – who was the second gunman? Who was it who was in the right position to have fired the three bullets into Bobby Kennedy? Thane Eugene Cesar, the Ace security guard, is known to have been pressed up against Kennedy's back right side and holding Kennedy's right arm in his left hand as Sirhan jumped out and fired his first two shots at Kennedy from several feet away. Don Schulman, who was the only eyewitness to observe accurately that Kennedy had sustained three bullet wounds, not two, saw this guard pull his gun and appear to fire back at Sirhan. Gene Cesar's clip-on bow tie, which was knocked off in the scuffle and lay near Bobby Kennedy as he died, was in just the spot where the gun needed to be located to deliver the fatal bullet up and forwards into Kennedy's brain. Gene Cesar owned a .22 (the same calibre as Sirhan's gun), but said he sold it before the assassination. Later he said he sold it after the assassination.

What of the couple seen running out of the hotel? Sandra Serrano was on the back stairs at the time of the assassination. She saw Sirhan walk up the stairs with a woman in a polka-dot dress and another man, and later saw the woman and man coming down the stairs without Sirhan, the woman saying, 'We shot him!'

Captain Lynch later claimed that he was on the back stairs at the time and that no one was there; this cast Sandra Serrano in the role of non-credible witness. The LAPD subjected Sandra Serrano to a lengthy and gruelling lie detector test in what looks like an attempt to intimidate a witness into backing off. The interviewer tried to persuade Serrano that the polka-dot woman did not exist – even though she was mentioned in the LAPD's teletype announcement of Sirhan's arrest.

Even so, a remarkable number of other witnesses went on insisting that a good-looking woman in a white polka-dot dress 'appeared to be with Sirhan' just before the assassination. If this 'polka-dot woman' scenario is true, we have a peculiar conspiracy, with a professional hit man, a decoy gunman and a very conspicuous woman in a memorable dress. There is no logical explanation for a member of an assassination team behaving in the way that this woman is alleged to have behaved. Why would she have given herself and her co-conspirators away like this? On this point I am more inclined to believe the LAPD's interpretation, which is that the people were running away from the scene of a shooting, possibly instinctively running away from danger, but also intoxicated and elated at having witnessed a sensational and historic event. 'They shot him! They shot him!' 'Who?' 'Senator Kennedy!' The alternative, which is to portray the couple as successful assassins, is absurd. If they had been part of a conspiracy to assassinate Kennedy, they might well have tried to leave the crime scene as quickly as possible, but they would hardly have been shouting 'We shot him!' as they fled.

Nevertheless, on June 4, the day immediately before the midnight assassination, Sirhan signed in at a firing range and was joined by a man and a shapely well-built woman, according to the range master of the gun club. The range master heard the woman say to Sirhan, 'Goddamn you, you son of a bitch, get out of here or they'll recognize us.' An explanation is available; a topless bar waitress came forward to testify that she and her husband had innocently met Sirhan at the range. On the other hand, what the waitress said was contradicted by the reports of other gun club witnesses. Those who favour the polka-dot woman as one of the assassins portray the topless bar waitress as a decoy who was part of a complex assassination network. This still leaves unexplained the absurd conspicuousness of the polka-dot woman, and the open admission of involvement. Assassins do not shout 'We did it!' as they leave the scene of the crime.

Sirhan meanwhile was left to take the rap for the murder. He has steadfastly maintained that he acted alone, yet what Sirhan thinks happened does not necessarily reflect what actually happened if an additional assassin network was in place. It is highly significant that Sirhan cannot remember the assassination at all, as if a segment of his memory has been entirely erased. As a jockey, Sirhan received a head injury in 1966, which may have made him especially susceptible to hypnosis. One interesting theory is that the CIA found this out when Sirhan later explored 'mind control' groups, and the CIA used hypnosis to ensure that he carried out orders and remembered nothing about his co-conspirators afterwards. He has been subsequently hypnotized in attempts to reconstruct his lost memory, and in his automatic writings he has come up with 'Pay to the order of one hundred thousand dollars' and 'My determination to eliminate RFK is becoming more and more of an unshakable obsession'. Was $100,000 the price for being part of the assassination team? Was Sirhan hypnotized into having a political motive?

Even so, the question still hangs in the air – was the twenty-six-year-old guard Gene Cesar involved? He asked not to be called to the witness stand at Sirhan's trial, a request which was unaccountably granted. He was probably the best person to give evidence of Sirhan's actions because of where he was standing, right next to Bobby Kennedy, and of course the post mortem evidence pointed to him as the likeliest suspect. He claimed he was not called to the Ambassador Hotel for duty until a few hours before the shooting. At 11.15 p.m. he was assigned to check credentials at the doorway of Colonial Room (where the press conference was to be held) and was to clear the way for the Kennedy entourage en route. He claimed to have been put next to Kennedy by his employers: he was not there out of choice. But perhaps this was a case of a lucky break – like the Archduke's car taking a wrong turning right in front of Gavrilo Princip in Sarajevo in 1914.

Gene Cesar said that when the shooting started he drew his gun and threw himself to the floor. Five witnesses confirmed that he drew the gun. Two witnesses said they saw him shoot, but Cesar insists that he did not do so. He successfully passed a polygraph (lie detector) test organized by Dan Moldea in 1994. Nevertheless, Cesar was standing directly behind Kennedy when Sirhan began firing and, according to his own admission, was in a position to shoot Kennedy at point-blank range. He also had been on guard duty in the pantry an hour earlier when Sirhan slipped into the area. The trajectory of the shots from the back, which went through Kennedy's jacket as well as into his head, were perfectly aligned with where Cesar said he was. If he did not fire, then he must have been right next to whoever did shoot and witnessed them do it. He was never asked and never volunteered that information during the polygraph.

Cesar admitted owning a .22 calibre handgun, but said he was not carrying it that night. He said he had sold it in February, but the sales slip showed that he sold it three months after the murder. Incredibly, it was never tested by LAPD for ballistics, and it subsequently disappeared. In 1993 someone salvaged a nine-shot .22 calibre revolver, serial number Y-13332, from a pond in Arkansas. Some believe this is Gene Cesar's gun, the gun that may have been used to kill Kennedy.

Gene Cesar looks like the perfect suspect, yet many are persuaded that he is innocent. He had no criminal record. He volunteered to be questioned. He offered to submit his gun for investigation. He voluntarily told the police about the .22 he owned or had owned. He was co-operative about questioning and undertaking a polygraph test. He was open and honest about his political sentiments, which were anti-Kennedy. He had not been scheduled to work that night, but was called in at the last minute. In all of these ways he comes across as innocent. Gene Cesar once said, 'Just because I don't like the Democrats, that doesn't mean I go around shooting them.' On the other hand, in purely forensic terms he was – uniquely – in the right place at the right moment to have assassinated Robert Kennedy.

THE POISONING OF ALEXANDER LITVINENKO

Alexander Litvinenko was a former Federal Security Service officer who somehow got caught up in the dark underworld of Russian politics. The years before his death he became relentless in his criticism of the Russian authorities and because of his outspokenness, died on November 23, 2006. Litvinenko was always considered to be a contradictory figure – some called him a traitor who betrayed his homeland and former comrades, others thought of him as a hero as he dared to tell the truth about Putin's regime.

Litvinenko was born in 1962 in the Russian city of Voronezh and many of his family had been prominent figures in the Russian military. On leaving school in 1985, he joined the army, quickly rising to the rank of lieutenant colonel. According to Litvinenko, while in service, he was involved in working with the KGB as an informer. In 1988, Litvinenko left the army and entered the counter-intelligence department of the KGB. He worked in such divisions as Military Counter-Intelligence, Directorate of Economic Security and the Antiterrorist Centre.

In 1991, when the KGB's directorates had divided, Litvinenko worked for the FSB (Federal Security Service) and was involved in fighting terrorism and organised crime. In 1997, he moved to one of the most top secret divisions of the service, a unit called URPO where he specialised in counter-terrorism and infiltration of organised crime. The nature of his job meant he would certainly have made enemies.

He assisted in the release of hostages seized by Chechen insurgents in Dagestan in January 1996 and also established confidential relations with the widow of the first President of Chechnya, Dzhokhar Dudaev, in April 1996. However, it was his association with the businessman Boris Berezovsky that played a pivotal role in his downfall.

Berezovsky was a former mathematician, turned businessman, who had made his fortune by selling cars and buying into state companies in some dubious, underhand deals. He was a shrewd and manipulative man who managed to inveigle his way into the Kremlin, quickly becoming an influential figure in the Russian leadership. As Boris Yeltsin's health and popularity began to wane, Berezovsky realised he needed allies to protect his position and he approached Litvinenko, who had previously investigated an earlier attempt on Berezovsky's life.

In 1998, Litvinenko called a press conference, in which he claimed that he had been instructed to kill the millionaire Berezovsky by the then head of the Russian security council. Protected by members of his FSB unit, Litvinenko claimed his superiors had threatened him with violence when he defiantly refused their order. Although the truth behind this accusation has been disputed, Litvinenko claimed it was just one tiny part of the corruption inside the FSB that he wanted to expose. Berezovsky, on the other hand, was allegedly using Litvinenko to strengthen his own influence within the FSB. Information also leaked out that Litvinenko had in fact been paid one and a half million dollars by Berezovsky for the press conference.

Following this conference, Litvinenko and a number of his associates were employed in the Executive Secretariat of the CIS, under the leadership of Berezovsky. Litvinenko took the position of a councillor of the Department for Security Issues.

At the beginning of 1999, the Russian authorities – in

particular the FSB – started a criminal prosecution against Litvinenko. He was arrested twice, in March and November, and spent a total of nine months imprisoned in the FSB prison at Fefortovo in Moscow. He was finally acquitted of 'exceeding his authority' in his place of work, but was rearrested in November. Again these charges were dismissed, but before they could bring a third criminal case against him, Litvinenko secretly fled to London with his wife Marina. He was immediately granted political asylum but in his absence Litvinenko was convicted back in Russia and given a three-and-a-half-year sentence.

However, in Britain, Litvinenko did not let the matter rest and began an active propaganda campaign against the Russian leadership and the FSB. His accusations went as far as saying that Russia even had ties with al-Qaeda and that they were involved in a wide range of criminal activities, including drug trafficking in Afghanistan. Litvinenko was reunited with his old friend Berezovsky, who was now also living in self-imposed exile.

Litvinenko not only spoke out verbally, he also published his first book in 2001 entitled *Blowing up Russia: Terror from Within*. His second book came in 2002, *Lubyanka's Criminal Grouping*, which was published in the United States and exposed even more underhand dealings. In one particularly damning part of the book he accused the FSB of co-ordinating the 1999 Russian apartment bombings that killed over 300 people. Litvinenko soon had a long list of enemies and as such was relying on the British law enforcement agencies to keep him safe.

Litvinenko said the first attempt on his life took place in December 1977 when he refused to carry out orders to kill Berezovsky. On his arrival in Britain, Litvinenko made it quite clear to the police that his life was in danger and had to contact them on several occasions warning them that he had received threats of physical violence.

On November 1, 2006, Litvinenko was mysteriously taken ill and had to be hospitalised. Although at first doctors were uncertain what was causing the illness, it was later attributed to a highly toxic form of radioactive poison, polonium-210. Not only were significant amounts found in his body, traces of the substance have since been discovered at various locations in London visited by Litvinenko. Polonium-210 was first discovered by Marie Curie at the end of the 19th century and, although everyone has a small amount in their body, at high doses it damages tissues and organs.

When interviewed, Litvinenko stated that he had met with three former KGB agents on the day he fell ill – Vyacheslav Sokolenko, Dmitry Kovtun and Andrei

Lugovoi. Lugovoi is a former bodyguard of Russian ex-prime minister Yegor Gaidar, who incidentally also suffered from a mysterious illness in November 2006. Litvinenko's wife, Marina, accused Moscow of arranging her husband's murder, although she didn't believe the order came from Putin himself.

Also on November 1, Litvinenko met with the Italian acamedic Mario Scaramella. Scaramella told Litvinenko that he had received a threatening e-mail and told the Russian that his life might be in danger. Scaramella had no idea who sent him the message, but having spent the past four years helping the Italian government with an investigation into Russian activities in Italy, knew full well the intricacies of the KGB. The meeting was brief, just thirty-five minutes, in a London sushi bar, and of course Scaramella was totally unaware that his ally had already been poisoned.

Litvinenko became weaker and weaker and eventually died on November 23 after suffering from a major setback which caused his heart to fail.

On January 20, 2007, British police announced that they had identified the man they believed poisoned Litvinenko. The suspect was captured on camera as he entered Heathrow airport. By January 26, the police were able to confirm the man they wanted for the murder, as they had discovered a teapot which contained an off-the-chart reading for polonium-210, in London's Millennium Hotel, where Lugovoi had stayed. The police said they wanted to charge former Russian spy, Andrei Lugovoi, believing that he administered the poison on November 1, when the two men met. The British government have prepared an extradition request asking that Lugovoi be returned to the UK to stand trial for Litvinenko's murder.

Litvinenko blamed the Kremlin shortly before he died, saying, 'You may succeed in silencing one man but the howl of protest from around the world will reverberate, Mr Putin, in your ears for the rest of your life. May God forgive you for what you have done, not only to me but to beloved Russia and its people.'

This statement came after the mysterious poisoning of yet another prominent opponent of the Kremlin, Ukrainian politician Viktor Yushchenko. In 1978 a Bulgarian dissident was assassinated by a jab from an umbrella tip bearing the toxin ricin.

Shortly before his death, Litvinenko had also been investigating the murder of Russian journalist Anna Politkovskaya, who was another critic of the Putin government.

Of course, the Kremlin denies any involvement in any of these murders, but a toxicologist who was asked to look into the death of Litvinenko, said that polonium-

210 is 'only found in government-controlled institutions'. Once it is administered there is absolutely nothing that can be done to save the exposed person.

Litvinenko's supporters say that Putin benefits by eliminating such a fierce critic but Nikolai Kovalyov, who once headed the Federal Security Service, defended the KGB by saying, '... defectors who did incomparably more harm to Russia than Litvinenko continue to live in the West safe and sound.'

PART FIVE

ATROCITIES

THE RAPE OF NANKING

For more than six weeks, the citizens of Nanking, the then capital of China, were held to ransom by unforgiving Japanese troops occupying the city. The Rape of Nanking, as it was quickly named, following the rape and murder of more than 20,000 women, showed that the Japanese soldiers had absolutely no regard for their victims and that the accepted rules of warfare and the welfare of prisoners in occupied territories had no place in the country's main city. Those who were raped were often mutilated and killed. Sometimes victims were kept captive so that gang rape and further abuse could be carried out on a regular basis. Not only were women at risk, including the elderly, even children as young as seven or less were subjected to this heinous brutality and then killed when they had outlived their usefulness.

The atrocities began in Nanking in December 1937 when the Japanese Imperial Army marched into the city.

More than 300,000 of the capital's inhabitants were murdered and the brutal slaying of innocent men, women and children would become regarded as the worst atrocity of the twentieth century so far.

A particularly tough battle at Shanghai began in the summer of 1937 where Chinese forces put up a particularly effective resistance to their Japanese enemy. The Japanese authorities had already announced that they would conquer China in three months, but fighting at Shanghai delayed their occupation until the late autumn. The stubborn resistance of the Chinese infuriated their enemy who were determined for revenge. Nanking became the centre for their exacted revenge which was metred out by the Japanese who defeated the Chinese in November the same year.

More than 50,000 Japanese soldiers marched on Nanking, which had taken on the role of the country's capital after Beijing had found itself under siege. As a result, the population in Nanking had grown quickly from 250,000 to nearer one million inhabitants with many of those arriving after fleeing the dangerous northern Chinese countryside. Refugees swelled the city's population and, by the autumn of 1937, Nanking found itself targeted by Japanese bombs which were concentrated on the downtown areas of the capital which were densely populated.

The trouble had started in September 1931 when a Chinese bomb – which was incidentally planted by Japanese secret agents – destroyed a Japanese express train. The Mukden Incident, as it was called, sparked an escalation in attacks from the Japanese who declared all-out war on China in July 1937. Japan defended its actions against China, stating that it needed additional territories for its overpopulation and that colonisation of other lands was a necessity. Japan stated that its own resources were inadequate and that it needed those that China could provide. Japan also defended its stance on the take-over of China by claiming that Japanese inhabitants in China would save the country from the 'inner turmoil' that it was suffering. Finally, the Japanese reasoned that claiming parts of China would strengthen the whole of East Asia.

When Japanese soldiers reached Nanking they were met with minimal resistance from tired and disorganised Chinese military units. On December 13, 1937, the Japanese assault, attacking the city from all angles, began and the soldiers started to go into hiding. Fearing the worst from their unforgiving captors, Chinese soldiers began to blend in like civilians. The 90,000 Chinese soldiers that surrendered to the Japanese were viewed and treated by their captors as subhuman, and the invading army looked on their prisoners of war with utter contempt. To surrender, as far as the Japanese were concerned, was the ultimate act of cowardice.

So determined was the contempt of Japanese soldiers for their weaker enemy, that they often documented their crimes in photographs. There was no civilised notion of mercy for these men and there is even filmed footage of Japanese soldiers practising with bayonets on live prisoners. It became usual practise to decapitate these prisoners whose heads were then lined up as 'souvenirs'. There are photographs of soldiers standing and smiling proudly with the mutilated bodies that lay all around them. The first few weeks of atrocities were the worst, with tens of thousands of men, women and children killed as they desperately tried to flee the occupied city. The assaults on civilians were barbaric, and those trying to escape by swimming the Yangtze River, were often victims of the grenades thrown by the Japanese troops into the masses who gathered at the water's edge. Meanwhile, Japanese soldiers were hunting down Chinese troops and anyone believed to be a member of the opposing army was shot or bayoneted. But hunting for hiding soldiers soon became an excuse for the killing of civilians at will, and while ordinary people were facing painful deaths, many buildings were burned and homes looted by the mercenary occupying army. Piles of victims were left in the city streets where

Japanese soldiers would randomly bayonet bodies in an attempt to ensure that all were dead.

The Japanese soldiers would also round up their victims and douse huge crowds in petrol before setting them alight. They were particularly fond of carrying out this type of crime on the prisoners of war who they brandished as cowards. It is well known that high-ranking Japanese officials were not only aware of the atrocities being committed on the Chinese people, they were regularly taking part. In one documented incident, a pregnant woman was gang-raped by soldiers. After the woman was murdered by her captors, her dead foetus was removed and bayoneted and brought before the soldiers' commanding officer. His response was to laugh at the misfortunes of the woman and her unborn child. This type of heinous activity was part of everyday life for the Chinese community in Nanking.

Once the Japanese felt that they had dealt with the prisoners of war and it was just a matter of rounding up stragglers, they turned their attentions to the women of Nanking. A woman-hunt ensued where the young and the old were treated as abysmally as each other. Although today the number of women estimated to have been abused by the Japanese stands at 20,000, some estimates put the number much higher at around 80,000. Gang rapes were common, with victims being shot following the savage brutality, so that they could never give evidence against the perpetrators who raped them. But families were equally humiliated and abused because the men were forced to rape their own daughters and sons were commanded to rape their mothers. Brothers were also made to rape their sisters while the entire family was made to watch the horrendous action. The Japanese soldiers took great pleasure in watching their victims suffer and it is well documented that the greater the suffering, the greater the pleasure taken by the occupying army.

Foreigners who found themselves caught up in the atrocity were mainly left alone. However, the safety zone for non-Chinese residents was regularly visited by the Japanese who would take away and kill anyone they believed to be hiding in the zone. Often these were young men deemed by the Japanese to be members of the Chinese army. Around twenty Europeans and American doctors, missionaries and other individuals set up the safety zone which encompassed a two and a half square mile area that they announced was a Japanese-free zone. These unsung heroes regularly risked their own lives as they intervened to stop the execution and rape of the Chinese men, women and children around them. It is due to the records kept by these eyewitnesses at the time that the world at large would hear far more of the massacre than the Japanese would have liked. But once the Rape of Nanking had become international knowledge, the powers in Tokyo started to restrain their troops and try and limit the extent of the savagery taking place. The safety zone became home to around 30,000 Chinese people.

By January 1938, much of the massacre was over as the Japanese army requested help from other countries to clear away the rotting bodies that lined the streets of the former Chinese capital.

The *New York Times* made a one-page report and while most Japanese news reflected the militaristic mood of the country and celebrated the imperial army's victories, other news reports began to surface which outlined the suffering that was going on. These came from eyewitness reports by Japanese military, who reported that the brutality shown to the communities in Nanking was aimed at the people whom the Japanese deemed as inferior. The US public were sceptical about the increased reports over the massacre, as the stories smuggled out of Nanking seemed too fantastical to be believed. The plight of the Chinese in Nanking was further overlooked by US and British authorities who were more concerned with Hitler's movements across Europe.

The utter carnage that ensued in Nanking and went unabated for more than six weeks, resulted in the streets of the city literally running red with blood. Even nearly seventy years later relations over Nanking are uneasy between the Chinese and the Japanese. The situation was not helped by an unrepentant Japan. However, some justice was served when twenty-eight high-ranking officials, including former foreign ministers, were tried in Tokyo by an international jury for their part in the leadership behind the Nanking Massacre or Najning Datusha as it was known by the Chinese. Of the twenty-eight accused, twenty-five were eventually found guilty on one or more charges while two died during the trials and one was admitted to a mental institution. Those found guilty were sentenced to death by hanging or life imprisonment in 1948. But, by 1956, all of them had been granted parole. Many years after the massacre, Japan tried to play down the events at Nanking and books were written to offer a very different view of the situation. Some even denied that Nanking had even taken place, and even in 1990 some high-ranking Japanese officials suggested that the massacre had been fabricated. However, there has been official acknowledgement of the atrocities carried out by Japanese soldiers during World War II. This was brought about by international pressure on the Japanese to own up to their barbaric behaviour. However, apologies and compensation have not been forthcoming.

Author Iris Chang was inspired to write the story of Nanking when she heard from her parents, who escaped China via Taiwan, before settling in the USA, how the Japanese '. . . sliced babies not just in half but in thirds and fourths', and she describes in the introduction to *The Rape Of Nanking: The Forgotten Holocaust of World War II*, how the events during the end of 1937 and the beginning of 1938 were a 'metaphor for unspeakable evil'.

GENOCIDE IN RWANDA

Between 6 April and mid-July 1994, the Tutsi people of Rwanda were the victims of one of the most heinous acts of genocide to be carried out in the modern world. As early as 1990, there was evidence to support the fact that the political, military and administrative leadership of Rwanda were plotting the demise of this ethnic community. The population didn't stand a chance against the factors that were being put into place and, by 1993, more than eighty-five tons of munitions had been distributed to another ethnic people, the Hutu. The Hutu – armed with machetes and other agricultural tools – were incited by a vicious hate campaign in the media. The world at large was shocked by the devastating events that would follow. However, governments across the globe ignored, or remained apathetic to, the plight of these innocent people and a conservative estimate is that more than 800,000 Tutsi people, or seventy-seven per cent of the population died during the atrocity.

Six hundred years ago the Hutus and Tutsis used to live in harmony. The Tutsis were a tall race of warriors who moved south from Ethiopia and invaded the homeland of the Hutus. Although not so many in number, the Tutsis managed to overpower the Hutus who, as a result, agreed to raise crops for the Tutsis in return for their protection. For many years the two groups managed to live almost as one, speaking the same language, intermarrying and obeying an almost god-like Tutsi king. That was until independence came along and that changed everything. The monarchy was dissolved and the Belgiums, who had ruled the area, withdrew. This left a large void which both the Tutsis and Hutus wanted to fill and fighting broke out between the two tribes. The fighting eventually exploded into a civil war in which hundreds of thousands of people were killed.

Today, there are around two and a half million Tutsi living in Rwanda and Burundi across central Africa and this group currently holds political power. Their history is complicated and the word Tutsi has evolved over the centuries to have many different meanings. Some refer to the Tutsi as people who have more than ten cows and a long European-looking nose, as opposed to the Hutu who have less than ten cows and a shorter, blunt nose. Other theories describe Tutsi people as having been associated with the ruling classes and the king, mwami, of Rwanda, and some document them as more impoverished than their fellow Hutus. Whatever their origins, the Tutsi and the moderate Hutu sympathisers that supported them, were categorically unprepared for the atrocity that would befall them.

There were mounting tensions across Rwanda during the early 1990s, fuelled by factions from both the established Tutsi, who are thought to have emigrated to the country around the sixteenth century, and the Hutu who are descended from the pygmy Twa populations who originally inhabited the land. By the end of the twentieth century, the Hutu were increasing their stronghold over Rwanda and Civil War broke out. Since 1962, Rwanda had enjoyed self-government and elections had advanced the Parmehutu, the Hutu political party. This, combined with the dissatisfaction of the Tutsis, who found themselves increasingly confined to refugee camps, led to the formation of the Tutsi-dominated Rwandan Patriotic Front (RPF) led by expatriate Paul Kagame who demanded the right for Tutsis to be given equal status.

In October 1990, the RPF invaded Rwanda from neighbouring Uganda, which led the Rwandan government to believe that the Tutsi wanted to take back political power. World government reaction to the events taking place was ambiguous and as violence and tension increased President Juvénal Habyarimana gave orders for the Tutsi to be immediately repressed. He justified his acts by claiming that the Tutsi wanted to enslave the Hutu people. For three years, between 1990 and 1993, the Kangura, a political journal, became instrumental in the rising ethnic violence and hatred.

The civil war ended on August 4, 1993, when the RPF and the government of Rwanda signed the Arusha Accords, and Habyarimana lost many of his powers which went to the newly formed coalition government. But the Committee for the Defence of the Republic (CDR), led by Habyarimana, was strongly opposed to sharing power with the RPF and refused to sign the accords. New terms were agreed, but by then, the RPF were unhappy with the proposals and they too refused to comply with the new conditions.

Radio Télévision Libre des Mille Collines (RTLM), along with top government ministers and newspapers, further instigated a campaign of hatred and fear. Training programmes were quickly set up to ensure that radical groups of Hutu people were prepared for battle and two factions – known as Interahamwe and Impuzamagambi – were established by secret meetings of government leaders and youth group organisations. Weapons arrived en masse and in January 1994, the UN Force Commander, General Roméo Dallaire, notified Major-

General Maurice Baril, Chief of the Defence Staff, that large caches of arms were available for the extermination of the Tutsis. The general asked for peacekeeping forces to be deployed, but none were sent. Demonstrations broke out in an attempt to remove the occupying Belgian forces and provoke the RPF. The killings that followed were well organised and involved a militia estimated at around 30,000. There were representatives of the militia in every neighbourhood across Rwanda and numbers were approximately one militia to every Tutsi family. Some troops carried AK-47 assault rifles, which were particularly easy to acquire, while other weapons, including hand grenades, didn't even require the militia to complete any paperwork. Many members of both the Interahamwe and Impuzamagambi were armed only with machetes, while government cabinet meetings openly discussed the forthcoming atrocity. In her book, *Conspiracy to Murder: The Rwanda Genocide*, journalist Linda Melvern cites that Colonel Théoneste Bagosora, General Augustin Bizimungu and other leading officials, including Prime Minister Jean Kambanda, were all aware of, and responsible for, what happened next.

The catalyst for the mass genocide took place when a plane carrying Habyarimana and Cyprien Ntaryamira, the Hutu President, was shot down over Kigali on April 6, 1994, and both men were killed. Rumours were rife and Paul Kagame of the RPF was blamed for the shooting, although other stories stated that Hutu extremists within Habyarimana's own circle were responsible. It is still not known with any certainty who ordered the attack on the plane. But the death of two presidents was enough to set off mass destruction, and Tutsi and moderate Hutus knew that they would become sitting targets. Local radio stations gave a coded message for Hutus to 'Cut the tall trees'. It was the signal that every extremist Hutu militiaman had been waiting for – it literally meant 'begin killing'. Tutsis were rounded up and executed by the military and Hutu militia groups. Political moderates were also captured regardless of their ethnic background, and many nations evacuated their staff from Kigali and closed down their embassies as the violence across the country increased. People were urged by radio stations to stay in their homes, while other reports over the networks talked of vitriolic attacks against the Tutsis and their moderate supporters. The network of cleverly devised roadblocks appeared in their hundreds and escape was both dangerous and futile.

From the centre of Kigali violence quickly swept across the country. In Nyarubuye, radio broadcasts and visits from local officials incited the populous to kill their neighbours. Those who refused were killed and there was very little choice for Hutus who wanted to survive.

It was kill, or be killed, and many fled to nearby churches to escape death. However, clergy and other church officials were unable to stop the rampage and in Ntarama, where 5,000 people sought refuge in the church, only twenty-five people survived. In what became a bloodbath, many ordinary citizens were killed by their neighbours in their own towns and villages, aided by militia. Death was usually delivered by a blow from a machete and many victims of the genocide were chopped into pieces by their attackers. Some were luckier and were killed by a bullet.

In the Catholic church of Kivumu, more than 1,500 Tutsis who were hiding there, were killed when the militia bulldozed the building. Those trying to escape faced the machete or rifle, while at a school in Kigali, the escaping Tutsis thought they'd be safe until the Belgian soldiers protecting them were ordered to withdraw and the militia and armed forces stormed the building killing everyone inside including hundreds of children. In the church at Gikondo, a mass was held on April 9, 1994, where more than 500 frightened men, women and children were hiding. While the mass took place, shots outside and exploding grenades could be heard. The church doors were flung open by soldiers of the Presidential Guard who demanded to see everyone's identity. A priest confronted the soldiers and said that the church housed Christian worshippers, but the soldiers continued their mission. Hutu worshippers were requested to leave the building. Not long after, 100 or so militia entered the church and began hacking at the congregation with their machetes, taking off limbs and slashing the faces of terrified people who were desperately trying to protect their children by hiding under the pews. For two hours the killing continued and even small children and babies were butchered. Unarmed UN military observers were present in Gikondo that day and the bodies stretched for more than one kilometre. As the killings began, Major Jerzy Maczka from the UN desperately tried to call for help, but the network was jammed and his pleas went unheeded being forced him to watch as the massacre unfolded with a gun held to his throat. In the Gikondo region alone, it was estimated that 10,000 people died in just two days.

Philippe Gaillard from Switzerland was present in Gikondo following the massacre, helping to look for survivors. He was responsible for realising that what was taking place was actually genocide. Seeing all the evidence and proof, he was shocked by the determination of the militia to exterminate this particular group of people. The killers had made no efforts to hide who they were and their victims had been slain in broad daylight. There was no doubt in Gaillard's mind that this was genocide on a phenomenal scale. The killings continued for a further two and a half months and Tutsis everywhere were in danger. The military, police, extremist Hutus and others were dogmatic in their search and destruction of a helpless people. As the major news networks across the globe reported on the atrocities being carried out, governments were reluctant to help or apathetic about the plight of the Tutsis.

The new Rwandan government tried hard to minimise an international scandal and the Rwandan ambassador, who had a seat on the Security Council, argued that the reports of genocide were widely exaggerated. France, who was responsible for training many of the militia in camps across the country, was also adamant that international intervention wouldn't be necessary. However, when the UN finally admitted that genocide 'may' have taken place and the Red Cross had estimated that more than 500,000 Tutsis had died in April 1994, the UN agreed to send 5,500 troops to the country and also requested a number of armoured personnel carriers from the US. The high cost of both troops and armoured vehicles led to arguments which delayed their deployment.

In June, with still no sign of back-up, the Security Council authorised French forces to be deployed on humanitarian grounds. The French were accused of the massacre of further Tutsis in the confusion that followed deployment. The RPF renewed civil war against the Hutu government and forces were sent into Rwanda from Uganda and Tanzania. The civil war and the continuing genocide raged side by side for more than two months. However, Tutsi rebels defeated the Hutu forces in July 1994 – 100 days after the genocide began. Hutu refugees eventually fled Rwanda taking up residence in Burundi, Tanzania, Uganda and Zaire, now known as the Democratic Republic of the Congo.

In May 1998, Jean Kambanda, Prime Minister of Rwanda, made history when he became the first person to plead guilty to charges of genocide in court. The extreme politician declared that he thought the Tutsis were racially alien and he had wanted a purely Hutu country to govern over. He was arrested the previous year after three years on the run. He gave a full confession in return for protection. He also testified against his fellow conspirators.

In March 2000, Paul Kagame (leader of the RPF) became Rwanda's President. Today, Rwanda is still in the process of prosecuting thousands of people who carried out genocide against the Tutsis.

ARMENIAN GENOCIDE

On April 24, 1915, the Turkish Ottoman government ordered the arrest and execution of an estimated 250 high-ranking Armenian officials in Constantinople. Although history had been playing a part in the demise of the ethnic Armenian community for some time, the execution of these influential men set the stage for what was to become the world's first genocide and the deaths of more than one million people between 1915 and 1917. Set against the backdrop of World War I, the horrific genocide, or Armenian Massacre, was clearly a carefully organised plan to eliminate and destroy a peaceful ethnic community who willingly believed and trusted in the government that was about to commit the most heinous atrocity against them.

The Armenian people were subjected to deportation, abduction, torture, starvation and eventually massacre as the great bulk of the population was forcibly removed from Armenia and Anatolia towards Syria, where a large majority faced dying of thirst and starvation in the desert. Others were methodically massacred throughout the Ottoman Empire, while women and children were often abducted and subjected to extreme abuse and their combined wealth was expropriated. What happened to these people would become the template for the Jewish Holocaust during World War II.

The government responsible for the atrocity was the Committee of Union and Progress (CUP), more popularly known as the Young Turks. Mehmet Talaat (Minister of the Interior), Prime Minister Grand Vizier, Ismail Enver (Minister of War) and Minister Ahmed Jemel were the four instigators within the government, who ordered the ethnic cleansing. These men set up a Special Organisation, Teshkilati Mahsusa, which comprised of troops and convicts headed by Dr Behaeddin Shakir. Organisation took place on a grand scale and there was widespread belief in the creation of a new empire stretching from Anatolia through Central Asia, but whose population would be exclusively Turkic. It is estimated that around one and a half million Armenians died as a result of the atrocities. This figure doesn't just include those who perished during World War I. After the initial massacre, the Turkish Nationalists overthrew the Young Turks in 1920 and, despite their differing views to the previous government, they too shared a common goal of ethnic exclusivity. Between 1920 and 1923 the Armenian population once again faced genocide.

World War I wasn't the first time that the Armenian population had faced this kind of atrocity though. For centuries, Armenians and Turks had lived peacefully side by side in the Ottoman Empire. But Armenians were not equal to their neighbours and endured a huge number of hardships including second-class citizenship. The rise of nationalism, however, increased self-awareness among ethnic groups, and the Ottoman Empire was in demise. Armenians became more isolated and called for independence. European leaders began to seek equal status for the Armenians, but the Sultan's government treated the populous with increasing brutality and between 1894 and 1896 hundreds of thousands perished in the Hamidian Massacres ordered by the Sultan, Abdul Hamid II. A successful coup by the Young Turks in 1908 replaced the government with the support of the Armenians. However, the promises of reform never materialised and the pan-Turkic dreams of the likes of Talaat, Enver, Vizier and Jemel were soon to become a reality.

Under the cover of war, the government was able to carry out its plans for the elimination of the Armenians virtually undetected. Leaving Armenians in Constantinople alone to start with, presumably due to the large foreign presence in the city, all other Armenians were ordered from their homes to be relocated 'for their own good'. They were asked to turn in knives and hunting weapons for the war effort and towns and villages were given quotas to meet. If they lacked enough weapons, Armenians were forced to buy them from the Turks to meet their quotas and all able-bodied men were 'drafted' to war. But these men were either killed immediately or worked to death by those they had trusted. With just women and children left in the towns and villages, people were told to assemble with only what they could carry, whereupon they were then escorted on death marches to the Syrian Der Zor desert.

Others were deported on trains and crammed ninety to a freight car that was only intended for transporting a small number of animals. They were shut behind bars, starving and terrified. Many people defecated themselves while the trains continued south and east. Many finished their train journey in the city of Konia before they were left to walk. These people were robbed, raped and murdered by killing squads who were waiting for them. In his book *The Burning Tigris*, Peter Balakian describes one German eyewitness who reported the train deportations as '...ironic that the Turks used the railway in ways that the Nazis would later...'. Then came the detention camps that were set up along the railway.

Konia had its own concentration camp, while the camps overall were responsible for the deaths of thousands from starvation and disease. Troops would kill many men, while the women were raped. Many women arrived at the camps naked and the bodies of those along the railway line showed that shockingly brutal acts had been carried out on them before they were killed. All men and boys over the age of twelve were killed, while other women and children were sold into slavery – many of the children had also been raped. More than 9,000 Armenian children were deported by rail and their future was short-lived and bleak. Abuse was rife, including the use of cotton-chopping tools to rip off flesh or sever tendons. Of course, needless to say, many of the children were left orphaned.

There were many eyewitnesses to the atrocities, although the government had taken precautions to impose restrictions on reporting and photography. The US diplomatic representatives and American missionaries were among the first to send news to the world at large. Many of the German eyewitnesses condoned the policy of the CUP and the fact Germany was an ally of the Turks. Russia, too, was aware, and bore witness to many of the events when the Russian army occupied parts of Anatolia. Syrian Arabs were also confronted with the brutality suffered by the Armenians and witnessed the deportations to the desert.

One man did more than any other to highlight the plight of the Armenians. Henry Morgenthau was appointed as US ambassador to the Ottoman Empire by President Woodrow Wilson in 1913. In his telegram to the US Secretary of State in July 1915 he warned of a 'campaign of race extermination . . . in progress under a pretext of reprisal against rebellion'. The ambassador worked with determination and courage to bring international attention to the plight of the Armenians. When he first took up his post in Constantinople, Morgenthau was appalled by the leadership of the CUP, particularly the likes of Talaat, Enver and Jemel, whom he described as running an irresponsible party that was ruled by 'intrigue, intimidation and assassination'.

At the beginning of the genocide, he had received detailed reports and telegrams outlining the atrocities that were taking place against the Armenian people. As the reports grew more frequent, Morgenthau became incensed at the major international human rights tragedy that was unfolding before him – many of the despatches were written by Armenians themselves who described in horrific detail the brutality they had witnessed. The reports all corroborated each story presented to the ambassador, of an ethnic minority who, at the time of their brutal treatment, were a prosperous, peaceful community based on thriving businesses and a commercial enterprise.

The *New York Times* began reporting on the genocide with slamming headlines designed to bring the true horror to the attention of the American people. The response from the nation was immense, with relief posters urging people to help. Sheet music was sold to enhance the cause and even US Sunday school children were urged to help save Armenia. Theodore Roosevelt was quoted as saying that the massacres were 'the greatest crime of the war'. He was responsible for US intervention to save the Armenians, while President Wilson proposed a US mandate. In 1920, Wilson drew up boundaries for an independent Armenia, however, his treaty was quashed by a revolution in Turkey.

The UK, France and Russia all condemned the Armenian genocide and advised the CUP that their leaders would be held personally responsible for the crime. As well as relief work in the USA, efforts were also made in the UK. However, despite the international outcry at the plight of the Armenians, no strong actions were taken against the fading Ottoman Empire and there was no pressure put on the postwar government to compensate the survivors and their families for the brutal treatment they had endured.

At the close of World War I, the Turkish government

held war crimes trials, but Talaat, Enver, Vizier and Jemel had all fled the country. They were found guilty of war crimes in absentia, and Talaat, Enver and Jemel were later executed by the Armenians. Turkey agreed to President Wilson's proposals for the drawing up of boundaries for an independent state of Armenia. Wilsonian Armenia included six western Ottoman provinces as well as coastline on the Black Sea. A further region was granted on the Mediterranean under French mandate. However, Kemal forces pushed the refugees from these lands and a new treaty was signed which ensured that Armenians could not return leaving them penniless with no home or belongings.

Today, Armenians all over the world commemorate the Armenian genocide on April 24 each year. There are many Armenian genocide monuments and memorials scattered throughout the world to mark the events that the Turkish government, even today, deny happened. The government has spent millions of dollars in their quest to destroy evidence and to try and change international views. Countries such as France, Argentina, Greece and Russia (where survivors settled) have officially recognised the genocide. In fact, twenty-one nations recognise the Armenian Massacre despite protestations from the Republic of Turkey.

GENOCIDE IN BANGLADESH

In 1971, Bangladesh, formerly East Pakistan, faced an extremely well manipulated genocide. In an attempt to quash the forces seeking independence, the West Pakistani military unleashed a campaign for supremacy and mass annihilation of a mainly Hindu population. After 200 years of British rule, East and West Pakistan were fighting for independence on the Indian sub-continent but, despite the attempts of Mahatma Gandhi and other influential figures to prevent division along religious and ethnic lines, there was pressure to create two states. One would be Hindu-dominated in India, the other Muslim-dominated in Pakistan. It is estimated that in the cleverly executed actions that followed, up to three million people were slaughtered. Of these, it is estimated that eighty per cent were Hindu.

The self-appointed President of Pakistan and Commander-in-Chief of the army, General Agha Mohammed Yahya Khan, and his top generals prepared a systematic military, economic and political operation in Bangladesh to murder the intellectual, cultural and political elite. The next stage was to eliminate hundreds and thousands of Hindus and drive the remainder out of the former East Pakistan and over the border into India. The underlying theme was to destroy economic foundations so that survivors would be subordinate to West Pakistan for at least a generation to follow. There was a well organised military presence in Bangladesh which grew steadily before the campaign was launched. Over time, the situation between East and West Pakistan had become more and more volatile. Corruption was rife and there had been rising opposition to the dominance of West Pakistan in the Bengali population. When catastrophic floods engulfed Bangladesh in August 1970, the regime was criticised for its meagre relief efforts. It gave Awami League leader Sheikh Mujibur Rahman the opportunity needed to demand autonomy for the East and bring an end to military rule. In December that year, the League won a landslide victory across its Bengali territory in the national elections.

But less than two months later, in February 1971, General Khan and his advisers decided to quash the Awami League and all its supporters. They quickly recognised that in order to meet their objectives, widespread genocide would be necessary. At the conference in West Pakistan on February 22, 1971, General Khan is reported to have said: 'Kill three million of them ... and the rest will eat out of our hands.' On March 25, 1971, the campaign was launched and the University of Dacca was attacked. Hundreds of students were killed as death squads roamed the campus and the streets of Dacca. More than 7,000 people were randomly murdered in one night. It was to prove to be the tip of the iceberg.

Within one week, half the population of Dacca had fled and more than 30,000 people had lost their lives. Those most at risk, apart from random killings, were teachers, scholars, professors, doctors, professionals and the Dacca elite. By April, more than thirty million people were lost and confused wandering across the former East Pakistan. More than ten million refugees found their way into India which would eventually lead to Indian military intervention as resources became overstretched and demand for aid was overwhelming.

According to eyewitness reports, there was no doubt about the militia's intended targets. These included the Bengali military, police, para-military Ansars and Mujahids, East Pakistan officials and Hindus. Only men were targeted at first with women and children allowed to go free. Awami League officials and supporters were next on the list followed by male university students, although militant women were also targeted. Many of the families of those targeted also fell foul of the brutality dished out by West Pakistan.

Young men and boys, those more likely to be a threat, were also singled out and killed. It was thought that they might become freedom fighters and consequently thousands were arrested, tortured and killed. Although some escaped to India, many young men joined the Liberation Forces. The bodies of those killed were found close to army camps, in fields or even floating down rivers. Many women encouraged their men, especially those aged between fifteen and twenty-five to flee, as the population became more and more terrified of the West Pakistan militia. In some cases, those who were circumcised were spared as they were more likely to be Muslim. All those who were not, were instantly killed. It was well-recognised that although women were being tortured and killed in some cases, on the whole this was a particularly systematic slaughter of men. The process was decidedly gender-specific according to many eye-witness statements of the time.

After the initial attack in the area surrounding Dacca, there were military experiments in mass extermination. These were unlikely to be witnessed by foreigners or journalists and the military concentrated their efforts on Hariharpara. Once a thriving village on the banks of the Buriganga River, Hariharpara had three essential elements that were ideal for experiments in mass murder. First, there was a large warehouse belonging to the National Oil Company which could act as a prison in which those arrested could be housed. Second, it offered a place where executions could be held and, third, it provided a method for disposing of bodies. The large, riverside prison banked down to the river where executions were carried out either on the river edge or in the shallow waters near the shore. Bodies were disposed of downstream.

Killing took place here on a nightly basis, where those chosen to die were usually roped together and forced to wade into the river. Most prisoners waded out in groups of six or eight where, under the glare of a powerful lamp, they were easy targets for the shooters who were assigned to kill them. In early morning, a boatman was responsible for hauling the roped prisoners' bodies into the midstream where their ropes were cut so that each body floated separately. It is widely documented that this type of execution style and disposal of bodies was also used in the genocide in Armenia (1915–1923) and the Rape of Nanking (1937–1938).

When women did come under extreme attack, the preferred form of abuse was gang rape and murder. Although there was recognition that Bengali men were the main targets, Susan Brownmiller highlighted the plight of women Bangladesh in her book *Against Our Will: Men, Women and Rape* where she likened the treatment of these women to the Rape of Nanking. It is estimated that between 200,000 and 400,000 women were raped, eighty per cent of them being Muslims. However, Hindu, and women of other religions, were also targeted and subjected to immeasurable brutality.

One story of a recently married young woman was particularly harrowing. Two West Pakistani soldiers entered the room built especially for the bridal couple at one dwelling while others held the young woman's family back with a rifle. The two soldiers raped the young woman in front of her new husband. The woman was raped by six soldiers in total. She was found unconscious and bleeding by her father, while her husband was crouched on the floor, clutching his stomach and surrounded by his own vomit. As in other atrocities committed throughout history, children – girls as young as seven – and elderly women were also the victims of rape. Some were raped in their homes, while others were abducted and held captive for ritual abuse. It is reported in Brownmiller's book that some women may have been raped up to eighty times in one night. Many died from their treatment and many more were murdered.

The atrocities raged on for nine months during which time abduction, rape and forced prostitution was only one humiliation faced by these women. When the Liberation Forces defeated the West Pakistani militia, Prime Minister Rahman declared that all victims of rape were heroines of the country as a way to integrate women back into society. However, many were left without husbands as few freedom fighters stepped forward to claim brides and those that did expected huge rewards from the government.

Estimates of how many actually died are varied. Some put the figure at one million, while a large majority claim it is much higher at three million. The campaign of terror lasted for 267 days and took place across eighteen districts in the former East Pakistan. There are reports that the West Pakistan army killed roughly one person in every sixty-one in Pakistan overall, and one out of every twenty-five in East Pakistan. More than eighty per cent of those killed were male and it is estimated that 600,000 children of both sexes died as a result of atrocities.

In a bold move, the surviving leaders of the Awami League declared Bangladesh independent on April 10, 1971. Liberation forces, Mukhta Bahini, were mobilised in an attempt to curb the West Pakistan military which they managed with skill and efficiency. However, the genocide continued side by side with the efforts of the Liberation forces who were fighting against arms provided by the USA. The USA was slammed when it was revealed that they had sent military equipment to West Pakistan after the genocide had started. They were further criticised when it emerged that this took place after a government minister had officially stated that all shipments to General Khan's militia had been halted.

Bengalis, particularly Hindus, were killed by soldiers who were fuelled by anti-Bengali racism. Seen as lower class citizens, Bengalis faced willing executioners in the name of General Khan's regime.

In December 1971, Prime Minister Indira Gandhi sought to return the Bengali refugees back to Bangladesh. A full scale military assault was launched on West Pakistan to secure Bengali independence. The West Pakistani militia, tired and demoralised, didn't take long to collapse and the final atrocities took place on December 16, after which there was an unconditional surrender. Awami leader Sheikh Mujibur Rahman returned to Dacca in January 1972 to a hero's welcome. Sadly, there were many reprisal killings and many Bengali men, who had been forced to collaborate with the Pakistani army, were killed in revenge attacks. No one has been brought to trial for the atrocities that took place in 1971 and several attempts to bring General Khan and his followers to court have failed.

SOVIET PRISONERS OF WAR

While the Nazis' treatment of Jews in concentration camps during World War II has been much publicised, especially in the high-profile Steven Spielberg film *Schindler's List* (1993), the fate suffered by millions of Soviet prisoners of war in eight short months of 1941–42 has perhaps not been brought to the level of worldwide attention that it deserves.

Preparations for the invasion of Russia and the overthrow of Joseph Stalin, codenamed Operation Barbarossa, began in July 1940, but it would be almost a year before the military might of the Third Reich was eventually unleashed on the Soviet Union. The goals were simple, to say the least: the political hierarchy was to be executed; the civilian population was to be reduced by twenty or thirty million; while those who survived were to be classed as slaves for the benefit of Germany. The newly acquired land was to be utilised as extra living space (*Lebensraum*) for the German population as the country waged war on Judaism and Communism.

Obviously, this directive went against the recognised and generally accepted rules of international warfare, but German soldiers were openly encouraged (and even ordered) to: treat Soviet prisoners of war as political criminals who had 'lost every right to treatment according to the Geneva Convention'; 'defend themselves ruthlessly against every threat by the hostile civilian population'; and 'finish off political commissars with weapons immediately as a matter of principle'.

It wasn't, however, just military personnel who were targeted in this manner. The German forces on the ground were working under the initiative that every man between the age of fifteen and sixty-five was a potential threat and should therefore be treated as a prisoner of war. Often, civilians were accused of being saboteurs and faced the same fate as their countrymen in uniform.

Such was the hatred that the Nazis felt for the Soviets, that soldiers on the battlefront had been given carte blanche to do whatever they felt was necessary at the time. They had also been informed that it was extremely unlikely there would be any retribution from their superiors for their actions if they claimed that they had carried them out in the name of Third Reich policy.

In the end, it came down to the opinion of the officer on the scene as to who was executed and who survived, but this blanket order was countermanded in May 1942 after the Soviet troops fought harder on the battlefield once this became common knowledge in their ranks.

The Germans denounced any responsibility to care for Soviet prisoners of war because the Soviet Union had failed to formally sanction the 1929 Geneva Convention on Prisoners of War. They had also failed to publicly commit to the 1907 Hague Convention and therefore Germany felt no international obligation to provide humane living conditions.

Operation Barbarossa, the largest military operation ever, was launched without a formal declaration of war on June 22, 1941, and the Soviet forces – made up largely of conscripts – crumbled in the face of the 6th Army. The attack was based on three spearheads intended to push quickly and deeply into the Soviet Union, with victory expected in a matter of weeks following the minimal resistance they had previously encountered during their Blitzkrieg of Poland and France. By September, the German army had gained control over Latvia, Lithuania and Estonia, and the following month claimed the Russian cities of Minsk, Kiev and Odessa, thereby cutting off the Soviet forces from their supplies. In a little over six months since the initial attack, the advance was already closing in on Moscow but that is as far as they progressed.

The unfortunate souls who had been captured by their enemies were treated appallingly and thousands died during their transfer to places of internment. Many were forced to walk hundreds of miles – and those who were too weak to complete the trip were shot where they had fallen – while others were crammed into open railway trucks that were simply too small for the numbers they contained. It was alleged that between twenty-five and seventy-five per cent of those soldiers who were sent to camps by rail were dead by the end of their journey.

Once the prisoners arrived, they were left to survive without shelter or proper food. Although officially given a ration of 2,200 calories a day, many received a meagre 700 (just twenty-five per cent of the amount a person needs to survive) and were still expected to labour for their captors. As a result, the prisoners began to eat the grass and leaves that were growing in their enclosures, in a desperate attempt to gain the nutrition that their bodies craved. Even when the Germans did prepare food for the prisoners, it wasn't enough to sustain life; around 65,000 perished in the concentration camp at Gross-Rosen after having been fed a diet of grass soup, water and salt for six months.

This systematic starvation was a premeditated strategy whose roots dated back to World War I. It was believed that many German citizens suspected the Great War was lost because of food shortages that led to riots in the homeland rather than because their military strategy was ineffective on the battlefields. So, it was decided by the High Command that there would be no risk of repeating this fate twenty years later, and prisoners of war would be forced to exist on subsistence rations in order for there to be sufficient food for the population in Germany.

But it wasn't just the unfortunate souls who were left to die in the prison camps who were suffering. The Germans had originally planned on utilising the vast amounts of Ukrainian crops to bolster their supplies, with their soldiers being able to live off the land as they were only issued with enough rations for twenty days. This, however, proved to be an unrealistic aim and the transportation of food back to Germany left soldiers on reduced rations and millions of civilians foraging for food. As a result, looting became commonplace and the advancing German forces razed entire villages as they progressed.

With thousands of prisoners of war dying in captivity, the survivors turned to cannibalism in a vain attempt to cling to life. This suited the German propaganda machine perfectly, as they had long described the Slavs as Untermenschen (subhumans). They began eating their dead comrades, and diseases like typhoid and dysentery were rife, but it was the arrival of the harsh Russian winter that decimated the numbers in the camps. Forced to live in the open air with temperatures often reaching -30°C, it wasn't long before the cold weather – added to the malnutrition factor – sent the death toll soaring. Indeed, it is estimated that deaths averaged 5,000 per day during October 1941.

One Hungarian tank officer later remarked: 'Behind the wire were tens of thousands of prisoners. Many were on the point of expiring. Few could stand on their feet. Their faces were dried up and their eyes had sunk deep into their sockets. Hundreds were dying every day, and those who had any strength left dumped them in a vast pit.'

Not content with the effect that 'natural causes' were having on the prisoners of war, the Germans also organised mass executions. Up to half a million men were shot then buried in trenches – locals in Mauthausen (Austria) complained that the waters of their streams and rivers ran red with blood – or were simply buried alive by the SS. But that inhumanity pales in comparison with the gas chambers that later claimed the lives of millions of Jews.

Heinrich Himmler organised the establishment of 'extermination' camps at Auschwitz-Birkenau and Majdanek, with the sole purpose of disposing of the Soviet prisoners of war. A total of 600 were chosen for execution in September 1941, as the Germans experimented with hydrogen cyanide. They realised they had discovered a way of carrying out mass murder with minimal effort and sought to perfect their routine. In early 1942, however, few of the original 10,000 Soviets who had been transported to Auschwitz were still alive – indeed, the Germans had succeeded in killing two million of the 3.3 million prisoners of war they had captured – so Himmler ordered that 150,000 Jews should be detained in the camp.

Other Soviet prisoners of war found themselves at the mercy of vivisectionists (practitioners who thought nothing of dissecting or operating on a living human) and were also used as guinea pigs for other scientific experiments.

Estimates put the death toll as high as nearly three million, with the victims dying mainly from starvation and exposure as well as execution. But some experts claim that a total of 5.5 million Soviet soldiers were captured by the Germans and more than 3.5 million of those had died by 1944 as the prisoners of war became the second largest group – after the Jews – that the Nazis killed as a result of their racial beliefs.

The Germans themselves fared little better at the hands of the Russians, with an estimated one third of the three million-plus prisoners of war perishing in captivity through starvation, exposure, overwork and execution.

In an unbelievable twist of fate, the two million prisoners of war who survived to see the end of hostilities were repatriated to their native country. On their arrival, the majority were arrested and accused of collaborating with the enemy. Having survived the German concentration camps, they were sent to the now notorious Soviet death camps where many perished during their sentences.

HIROSHIMA AND NAGASAKI

The art of modern warfare took on a sinister face on August 6, 1945, with the USA's decision to unleash the power of the atom on the people of Japan. That was the day when an atom bomb nicknamed 'Little Boy' was dropped on Hiroshima, while three days later a second trademark mushroom cloud was seen over Nagasaki as the USA continued in their efforts to batter Japan into surrender.

The race to design the first successful atom bomb had been contested by the USA and Germany throughout World War II. Instigated by a number of European scientists – several of whom later denounced the bombings – who had sought refuge in the United States (including Albert Einstein), it was codenamed 'The Manhattan Project' and, at its peak, employed the talents of more than 130,000 people. It was also granted a budget of around two billion dollars which made it the most expensive research programme at the time. As it turned out, Germany was eventually found to be lagging far behind the USA in terms of achievement and their atomic programme was nowhere near as extensive as that of the Americans.

Having terrorised the world for almost six years since their invasion of Poland on September 1, 1939, Germany capitulated to Soviet forces on May 2, 1945, just two days after the death of Adolf Hitler in a Berlin bunker. Today it is perhaps hard to comprehend but, by the time the USA dropped the first atom bomb on Hiroshima, a staggering fifty million people had lost their lives in the worldwide conflict that had been predicted two decades earlier. When the Treaty of Versailles was signed in 1919, several prominent people had labelled it as a 'peace for twenty years' and that turned out to be uncannily true.

The Japanese, however, refused to surrender and continued their own hostilities in the Pacific. Their political leaders realised that they had already lost the war but refused to accept the fact and were prepared to defend themselves on home soil if necessary rather than admit defeat.

World War II had been different from the Great War in that it was the first time it was deemed 'acceptable' for there to be civilian casualties, as the two sides sought to disable their enemies' vital industries and demoralise the general populace. German aircraft bombed European cities such as Warsaw, Rotterdam and London while the Royal Air Force had come in for severe criticism when 60,000 died in an air raid on the German industrial town of Dresden in February 1945. Japan had already been targeted by US planes and more than 100,000 people are thought to have perished in an attack on Tokyo in March 1945. With residences built close together and constructed out of paper and wood, it's no wonder that so many perished.

The USA tested their first atomic bomb on July 16 in the desert at New Mexico and, with its success, they began planning to utilise their new technology. A last ditch attempt at peace was brokered by the Allied forces with the issuing of the Potsdam Declaration on July 26, which outlined the terms of surrender for Japan but this was summarily rejected.

There were four choices of targets – Kyoto, Hiroshima, Yokohama and the Kokura arsenal – but the committee charged with deciding upon a city ruled out a strictly military focus because of the chance of missing. Hiroshima was eventually chosen as the drop site for several reasons: it was a city large enough to make the Japanese government sit up and take notice; it was a port and army base so had legitimate military targets; there were no prisoner-of-war camps there; and the terrain was flat in the immediate area but was surrounded by hills which would allow the full force of the atom bomb to be utilised.

As a military target, it had been expected that Hiroshima would be attacked at some point during the campaign but it had so far emerged virtually unscathed. On the morning of August 6, the inhabitants (estimates put this total between 255,000 to 320,000 at the time of the strike) were going about their business, oblivious to the terror that was about to descend from the skies. Commuters were travelling to work while schoolchildren were enjoying the day, helping to make firebreaks between buildings. If they had looked towards the heavens, they would have seen three tiny specks of silver in the sky – the B-29s that had come to deliver their deadly payload.

The plane that created history was the *Enola Gay* and the crew's observations and reactions were recorded. Tail gunner Sergeant Robert Caron described seeing fires 'springing up everywhere, like flames shooting out of a huge bed of coals... The mushroom is spreading out. It's maybe a mile or two wide and half a mile high... The city must be below that. The flames and smoke are billowing out, whirling out into the foothills...'

Once the bomb exploded at 8.15 a.m. local time, the first the inhabitants knew was a flash that was brighter than 1,000 suns. Thousands were annihilated instantly as they were vaporised, many leaving behind just a shadow burnt onto a wall. Further away from the point of impact, people had a chance of surviving but they paid an enormous price as their hair and skin was burnt off, their eyes were blinded or their clothes were fused to their skin. The blast that followed the flash flattened buildings for a ten-mile radius and killed even more civilians. With fires raging all around them, many jumped into the river only to drown in their attempt to escape.

Japanese forces were sent to the area to find out why there was no contact with Hiroshima and they could not believe the scale of the destruction. But it was not until the White House issued a public announcement sixteen hours later that they fully understood the nature of the attack.

The American President, Harry S. Truman, was ecstatic that the plan had worked and warned the Japanese that, 'If they do not accept our terms, they can expect a rain of ruin from the air the likes of which has never been seen on this earth'. That turned out to be partially true with the dropping of the second bomb on Nagasaki.

On August 9, the Soviet Union declared war on Japan and invaded Manchuria but the United States had already scheduled the attack on Nagasaki – one of the largest ports in the south of the country – for two days later. This was, however, brought forward to avoid bad weather and the 'Fat Man' bomb was dropped shortly after 11.00 a.m.. It exploded 1,540 feet above the ground and generated winds of over 600 mph and a temperature of 7,000°F.

Estimates of the extent of the casualties are vague and unreliable due to several factors: the Japanese allegedly inflated the figures as a propaganda exercise; the records kept at the time were not as accurate as they would be today; and it is not known how many died as an after-effect of radiation poisoning in the years following the attack. Needless to say, the 140,000 estimated to have perished at Hiroshima, added to the 74,000 who were killed at Nagasaki – mainly civilians – are probably conservative figures, and tens of thousands were also seriously injured.

The Americans had more raids in the pipeline and were anticipating another device to be functional in the third week of August with another six bombs being readied for September and October. As it turned out, these were not required because the Japanese government surrendered on August 15 with the treaty being signed on board the USS *Missouri* on September 2. In his declaration, Emperor Hirohito stated: 'the enemy has begun to employ a new and most cruel bomb, the power of which to do damage is, indeed, incalculable, taking the toll of many innocent lives. Should We continue to fight, not only would it result in an ultimate collapse and obliteration of the Japanese nation, but also it would lead to the total extinction of human civilisation. Such being the case, how are We to save the millions of Our subjects, or to atone Ourselves before the spirits of Our Imperial Ancestors?"

The survivors of Hiroshima and Nagasaki are called Hibakusha ('explosion-affected people') and as the twenty-first century dawned there were still more than a quarter of a million alive whose future was changed forever in August 1945. There is today a cenotaph in the Hiroshima Peace Park which bears the inscription 'Rest in peace, for this mistake will not be repeated.'

Apart from achieving the primary goal of forcing the Japanese into surrender, the United States' display of power was also intended to deter Russian leader Josef Stalin's political agenda. It could also be said that the attacks on Japan were still carried out despite the fact that a Japanese surrender was anticipated in the next few days as America's revenge for the unprovoked attack on Pearl Harbor on December 7, 1941, which prompted the United States' entry in the war. Around 2,500 people died in the surprise attack on the Pearl Harbor naval base that, according to rumour, could have been prevented by the British if they had been willing to admit that they had broken the Japanese code and so could have warned the Americans...

To be fair, these two bombs are the only time that nuclear warfare has been utilised in a conflict so it could be cited that the bombs dropped on Hiroshima and Nagasaki have prevented the major powers of the world from destroying each other. Indeed, in the years following the attacks, Japan led the protests against the race towards nuclear proliferation. True, there are still countries today who continue to test their nuclear arsenal and threaten their enemies but the Cold War that followed the end of World War II has thankfully ended, as each party realised that they could be blasted into oblivion simply at the push of a button.

MALMÉDY MASSACRE

The shooting of a group of unarmed Americans on December 17, 1944, at the Belgian town of Malmédy, stands out among the atrocities of World War II as one of the worst committed against prisoners of war in the West European arena during the conflict. This part of the country was about to become infamous for the epic Battle of the Bulge (later portrayed in a film) that took place between December 16, 1944, and January 25, 1945, which turned out to be the costliest engagement in terms of soldiers killed that the USA suffered during the whole war. In total, around 19,000 servicemen lost their lives in the attempt to defend Antwerp.

Sunday, December 17, began with the 6th SS Panzer Army being directed to break through the Allied lines and ultimately capture Antwerp. Under the command of General Sepp Dietrich, the offensive succeeded in breaching the American defensive positions and Waffen-SS Colonel Joachim Peiper (along with nearly 5,000 men and 600 vehicles) was charged with securing the Meuse bridges at Huy among other tactical objectives. He was forced to use minor roads that were not at all suitable for armoured vehicles and came across an American convoy.

Following orders, the men of the 285th Field Artillery Observation Battalion were heading for St Vith in the Ardennes and met up with Lieutenant-Colonel David Pergrin (291st Engineer Combat Battalion) who warned the officers in charge of the convoy that the route they intended to take could lead them straight to the advancing German forces, but for some reason this advice was ignored and they continued as planned. Their journey took them within two miles of Malmédy, to the Baugnez Crossroads (known to the Americans as 'Five Points' because of the five roads that met at this junction), and it was shortly before they reached this intersection that they were fired upon by two German tanks.

In the ensuing fire fight, the lead and rearguard vehicles of the convoy were targeted in order to prevent the column from scattering and the soldiers were taken prisoner. Adolf Hitler had given strict orders that nothing should stand in the way of victory and that the operation should be carried out with brutality in order to demoralise their enemy. As it was, Peiper – formerly Himmler's adjutant and the holder of the Knight's Cross with Oak Leaves – had already established a reputation during the invasion of Russia. It was well known that his men (known as the 'Blowtorch Brigade' after they burned around 200 villages in the Soviet Union having locked the inhabitants inside before setting the fires) were perfectly capable of killing civilians as well as military personnel.

The men from the convoy found that the Germans had already captured some of their countrymen and the whole group of 113 soldiers was ordered to stand in a field by the side of the road. It is not known to this day what prompted the events that followed but there is no record of an officer giving the order to execute the unarmed men. Some survivors later testified that they had heard an order given to kill the prisoners. It has been reported that Peiper was in an extremely bad mood because his progress had not been as quick as antici- pated as he had met with strong resistance from the Allied forces, but he had already left the crossroads before the massacre took place.

One theory suggests the prisoners were left to their own devices in a field as the Germans concentrated on their advance. When the later portion of the column arrived, they assumed that the group of Americans was a combat unit that had not yet been discovered and opened fire on them despite the fact that they were unarmed. Another possibility is that a handful of the prisoners decided to make a break for freedom and were shot. Other German soldiers nearby heard the shooting and joined in, not realising that they should only be targeting the individuals who were trying to flee. While international rules of warfare allowed captors to shoot escapees, it did not give them the right to massacre the whole group. This theory does not explain the actions that followed.

The most popular train of thought, however, is that the prisoners were deliberately executed. It would have been too troublesome for the Germans to have marched the men back to somewhere where they could more suitably be detained so they decided to rid themselves of their burden. Some of the Americans apparently tried to seek refuge in a nearby café to escape the shooting but it is alleged that the Germans set fire to the building and then shot anyone who emerged. They then examined each man to ensure nobody was left alive, shooting any survivors in the head or clubbing them to death, as autopsies later showed.

The first the Americans knew of the events was when three survivors were picked up by a patrol that had been sent to investigate after hearing gunfire. Pergrin took the wounded soldiers back to Malmédy and informed his superiors that a massacre had taken place. On the same day that the massacre happened, numerous statements were taken from witnesses and their accounts of the event were similar, despite the fact that they had not had any time in which to corroborate their stories. They all claimed (bar one man) that no escape attempt had been made and that the Germans had simply opened fire without warning. As they lay among their compatriots feigning death, it is also alleged that German soldiers who were driving past the scene were firing shots and using the bodies for target practice as they lay in the field. Eventually more than forty survivors from the massacre made their way back to the American lines but because of the continuing battle it was not possible to retrieve the bodies of those who had been killed.

It took almost a month for the US forces to advance far enough to claim the land around the crossroads, but when they did finally reach the site of the massacre, they found that the bodies were in a remarkably good state of preservation due to the snow that had fallen and blanketed the area. On January 14, 1945, seventy-one bodies were recovered and sent for autopsy. These investigations were carried out over the next three days and the evidence partly contradicted the survivors' accounts of Germans looting the dead bodies. It turned out that the majority of the dead soldiers were still wearing their rings and watches, while their valuables were still in their pockets.

What the autopsies did confirm, however, was that forty-three men had died from gunshot wounds to the head and several more displayed evidence of severe cranial blows. The investigation was hampered slightly due to the fact that many bodies had been hit by shell and mortar fragments as they lay in no man's land for almost a month. The army doctors who carried out the autopsies, also discovered that at least five of the men had had their eyes removed from their sockets, with one allegedly still being alive as he was maimed, though it has since been debated that this damage could have been caused by crows.

It was time for the recriminations to begin in earnest once the hostilities came to an end, with the surrender of Germany on May 2, 1945, and the men responsible for the Malmédy Massacre were tried at a subsequent war crimes court in Dachau during May and June of 1946. No clear evidence was produced, however, to back up claims that the Germans had been ordered not to take any prisoners, but to kill any enemy personnel they encountered.

A total of seventy people were charged with the massacre, including Joachim Peiper and his junior officers, and the court issued forty-three sentences of death by hanging once it had reached its verdict – each case took on average just three minutes to be decided –

with twenty-two of the remaining defendants sentenced to life imprisonment. As it turned out, none of the death sentences were carried out and they were commuted to life sentences. In fact everyone had been released from their internment by 1956. The last person to taste freedom was Peiper himself, when he was released in December 1956.

The events of December 17, 1944, still cause great debate to this day. Not because anyone denies that the massacre took place, but because the exact circumstances of the atrocity have never really been confirmed. Whether the Germans did indeed kill their prisoners of war in a deliberate act of cold-blooded murder, or whether the soldiers were killed in the confusion of an attempted escape, will probably never be known for certain. As well as in *The Battle of the Bulge* (1966), the events of that day have been immortalised in the film *Saints and Soldiers* released in 2004.

Today, there is a memorial at the Baugnez Crossroads in Belgium in honour of the men who were mercilessly gunned down by German forces.

THE HOLOCAUST

While the Nazis of Germany targeted many different population types during World War II, including Soviet POWs, gay men, Jehovah's Witnesses and disabled people, it was their treatment of Jews that they received most criticism and condemnation for. The Third Reich was responsible for the deaths of an estimated nine to eleven million individuals but an incredible six million of those were of the Jewish religion. This extermination has come to be known as the Holocaust (coming from the Greek words *olon* meaning 'completely' and *kauston* meaning 'burnt').

It wasn't just during World War II, however, that the persecution of the Jews began; it all started early in 1933 after Adolf Hitler was appointed Chancellor of Germany on January 30. He had written about his anti-Semitism (hatred of Jews) in his 1925 book *Mein Kampf* but few in the international arena could have foreseen the devastation that was to be unleashed on that race.

In less than three months, the former Austrian national had been granted dictatorial powers and ordered the setting up of concentration camps at Dachau, Buchenwald, Sachsenhausen and Ravensbrück. (Intended to provide slave labour, these are not to be confused with the extermination camps later set up to eliminate millions of people.) On April 1, the Nazis staged a boycott of Jewish shops and businesses and ten days later issued a decree categorising the Aryan race that they so revered. Basically, anyone who had 'non-Aryan, especially Jewish, parents or grandparents . . . classified the descendant as non-Aryan'. By the end of the year, Jews had been banned from owning land or being employed as newspaper editors.

The persecution escalated even further – although there was a temporary lull in the sanctions during the 1936 Munich Olympics as Hitler sought international approval – with Jews over the age of fifteen being forced to carry identity cards and being banned from trading or practising medicine (July 1938) before a law was introduced in September 1938 requiring all Jews to have a big red letter 'J' stamped on their passports. By this time, Germany had annexed Austria with its population of 200,000 Jews and the end of 1938 saw all Jewish pupils expelled from non-Jewish German schools, while laws were passed authorising the Aryan takeover of all Jewish businesses.

Nazi forces invaded Czechoslovakia in March 1939 but it was the invasion of Poland on September 1 that thrust the world into a second global conflict. Hitler's abhorrence of everything Jewish gained steam, and ghettos were established where the Jews could be contained and by 1941 Heinrich Himmler had ordered the expansion of the concentration camp at Auschwitz so that it could accommodate 100,000 people. Each territory that Germany conquered obviously included a percentage of the population that was Jewish and they targeted each and every nation they gained control over.

Such were the appalling conditions in the ghettos that starvation and disease killed hundreds of thousands, with 43,000 dying in Warsaw in 1941 alone. The following year saw the onset of deportation of Jews to the concentration camps, and within two months a staggering 300,000 people had been transported from Warsaw to the Treblinka extermination camp. The Germans had labelled the operation 'resettlement in the East' but more and more rumours were getting back to the ghettos and there were several attempted uprisings.

But Jews weren't just at risk in the concentration camps. It has been reported that there were mass executions throughout the newly formed German empire. One such instance took place outside Kiev in the Soviet Union where nearly 34,000 were killed in two days at the end of September 1941.

The Nazis soon found that they were unable to cope with the number of Jews that were being sent to the camps as they implemented 'the final solution' and decided to start gassing them to death. Initially, the victims were herded into a gas chamber where carbon monoxide was piped into the room, but the Germans soon found a way to improve on that system and used Zyklon-B (also known as hydrogen cyanide). In an ironic twist of fate, Zyklon-B had been developed as a pesticide by Fritz Haber (a German Jew who was forced to emigrate in 1933).

By June 1942, a second gas chamber had been set up at Auschwitz because the Germans could not cope with the number of Jews being sent there. Unlike Treblinka, where the ten individual gas chambers each only housed 200 people, the new set-up at Auschwitz meant that they could execute 2,000 people at a time. In reality, the lucky ones – though it can hardly be called good fortune – were the people who died during the transportation to the camps. Herded like cattle in freight trains, many often perished before reaching their final destination.

Once they reached the extermination camps that had been hastily constructed to kill as many Jews as quickly as possible, the prisoners were stripped naked and their possessions were confiscated with the explanation that they were going to have a shower to clean themselves up. Often they were handed a bar of soap and a towel to perpetuate this lie but they were eventually taken to the gas chambers where they took up to twenty minutes to die.

Their remains were initially buried but worries about contamination of the water supply, however, led to those bodies being exhumed and incinerated in huge firepits. Before this the Germans had already removed any items of value including gold fillings. In two weeks of May 1941, the SS collected eighty-eight pounds of gold and white metal from the teeth of those they had executed. This was the job of prisoners who wanted to delay their own execution, but spot-checks were carried out by the SS and if any filling was missed in a corpse then the person responsible was thrown into the furnace alive.

It wasn't just the mass extermination that the Jewish people faced, though. They were also the subject of medical experiments, with the most notorious practitioner being Dr Josef Mengele. He regularly conducted experiments on his 'patients' that included observing the results of high pressure and freezing temperatures, testing various drugs, attempting to change the colour of children's eyes by injecting chemicals and sterilisation along with amputations and other horrific surgical procedures.

He is reported to have enjoyed working with Romani children (who in their naivety used to call him Onkel Mengele) and twins were a fascination to him. One particular incident saw him adjoin two siblings back to back as if they were Siamese twins but they were in unbelievable pain and their wounds were infected so the parents managed to get hold of morphine and ended their children's lives rather than see them suffer.

Perhaps the Germans realised that they were losing the war because they closed the camp at Sobibór in Poland after an escape by 300 detainees in October 1943. Only fifty survived the ensuing pursuit but the Nazis closed the camp and removed all traces of their activities by planting an orchard of trees on the site. But this didn't stop the genocide, as the extermination camps worked at full pace during 1943 and 1944 with Auschwitz in particular responsible for killing and incinerating 20,000 people per day.

By the middle of July 1944, Soviet troops had liberated the first concentration camp at Majdanek in Poland, the site of more than 360,000 murders. That was the year when perhaps the most infamous of all those who died in the concentration camps was arrested. Anne Frank was a fifteen-year-old girl who had been hiding with her family in secret rooms in her father's office for two years before they were betrayed and given up to the authorities. She kept a diary of her life under the German occupation that was posthumously published in 1947, but she and her family were sent to Auschwitz. Anne and her sister were eventually transported to Bergen-Belsen where she died of typhus less than two months before the end of the hostilities.

As it became more apparent that Germany was going to be defeated, Himmler ordered an end to the final solution but such was the hatred for the Jews that this was mainly ignored. The gas chambers, however, were dismantled with the bodies that had been buried in the mass graves dug up to be cremated. Farmers were encouraged to plant crops on the sites in an attempt to hide the fact that the camps had ever existed, but it was an abomination that the Nazis simply could not hide.

The last tortuous fate that faced those that had survived the camps after they had been closed, was being forced to march miles to train stations in the dead of winter. Already weekend by hunger and disease, many fell along the way and were shot, with those who succeeded in making the trek being transported in open carriages. Once they reached their destination, they again faced a long march and around 100,000 Jews were killed in this manner towards the end of World War II. In the end, the camps were liberated but the scenes that awaited the Allied forces will never be forgotten by those involved. The survivors were malnourished and many had been driven insane by the conditions in which they were forced to exist. But they, unlike so many others of their faith, had at least survived to see the end of Adolf Hitler and his quest for world domination.

Of course there was a price to pay for this disregard of human life and many of the Nazi officers responsible for the atrocities were hunted down after the war. Rudolf Höß, the Commandant at Auschwitz who has since been labelled the world's greatest ever murderer, later testified at the Nuremberg trials that he had killed more than 400,000 Hungarian Jews in three months of 1944. Höß himself was found guilty of crimes against humanity and was hanged on April 16, 1947.

Today, several of the former concentration camps such as Auschwitz and Dachau are open to the public as museums and serve as a reminder of the atrocities that were committed there.

DARFUR ATROCITIES

In May 2007, Sudan resisted calls to withdraw the African Union peacekeeping force in Darfur and instead enlisted the help of the United Nations to put an end to the violence and abuse suffered by its citizens. As a reaction to this, the USA extended the sanctions already imposed following four years of fighting in the region.

Darfur – an area the size of France – is a western province of Sudan that is in turn the largest country in Africa. It is a country dominated by Arabs and there have traditionally been confrontations between the African farmers and the Arab herders as they compete for the best land around the Nile. The Fur people in the Marrah Mountains established an Islamic sultanate as far back as the late fourteenth and early fifteenth centuries, but they have suffered at the hands of invaders many times over the intervening centuries. Oppressors have included a Turco-Egyptian army and even the British.

It was on February 26, 2003, however, that the most recent conflict truly erupted when rebels began attacking government targets, claiming that the authorities were neglecting the farmers' rights. Credit for the attack in Golo was claimed by the Darfur Liberation Front, but in reality the rebellion ccould be traced back to an oath sworn by members of the Fur and Zaghawa tribes in July 2001, when they agreed to collaborate to end the attacks on their villages that were funded by the Sudanese government.

The rebels attacked police stations, army outposts and military convoys but the government ordered swift retribution with a massive air and ground attack on a rebel base in the Marrah Mountains. This failed to end the threat of more rebel action, however, as was demonstrated when they gained control of the garrison town of Tine. As well as replenishing their dwindling supplies, they also claimed a large quantity of arms. They began employing guerrilla warfare, using 4x4s to quickly get them to and from their targets, and it seemed that the government had no efficient response to these tactics.

As the conflict grew, so did the number of rebel factions opposing the government. The two main groups were the Justice and Equality Movement and the Sudan Liberation Army, both of whom were fighting against the Sudanese government and the Janjaweed militia. The authorities had utilised the services of the Janjaweed (armed Baggara herders) before, when they helped prevent a Masalit revolt in the late 1990s, although they denied controlling the militia with President Oman al-Bashir labelling them 'thieves and gangsters'.

That was little comfort to the Darfurians who accused the Janjaweed of riding into villages before butchering the men, raping the women and looting anything they could find of value. There were many reports of women who claimed to have been abducted by the Janjaweed and who held for a week or more while they were humiliated as sex slaves before their eventual release.

One particularly successful raid saw the rebels wipe out a garrison at al-Fashir where they destroyed planes and helicopters, killing seventy-five personnel in the process. The thirty-four out of their thirty-eight encounters with government forces during the summer of 2003, included killing 500 and capturing 300 at Kutum and killing another 250 in another successful raid on Tine. This forced the Sudanese government to change their tactics and they handed the responsibility for strategical decisions to the Janjaweed.

The militia soon turned things around, and within a few months had succeeded in killing several thousand people while driving 100,000 across the border into neighbouring Chad. They actually chased the refugees into Chad in an engagement that led to a clash with that country's forces which left many dead. But it was the report by a UN observer that brought the wider world a true picture of the ethnic cleansing that was taking place in Darfur.

The twenty-three Fur villages in the Shattaya Administrative Unit had been completely depopulated, looted and burnt to the ground (the team observed several such sites driving through the area for two days). Meanwhile, dotted alongside these charred locations were unharmed, populated and functioning Arab settlements. In some locations, the distance between a destroyed Fur village and an Arab village was less than 500 metres.

The reign of terror and the fear of the militia forced many people away from their homes and into refugee camps, but they found they were not safe there either. With aid agencies unable to get to the region because of the fighting, there was a lack of water, food and medicine, while danger also lurked outside the perimeters of these camps. The Janjaweed patrolled the area and men who strayed too far were murdered, while women were, once again, the victims of rape. One report in July 2006 described how seven women, who ventured out in search of firewood, were gang-raped and beaten by the militia before being stripped of their clothing and jeered by their attackers as they fled.

The Janjaweed's tactics have been compared to the genocide in Rwanda and the ethnic cleansing seen in the Yugoslav wars of the early to mid 1990s. These tactics have seen civilians murdered and dismembered including young children and babies. But they also used rape as a weapon of terror because in this culture a woman who has been raped is considered unclean and will be shunned by her community. In extreme cases, the militia also made the humiliation greater by raping the women in a public arena.

A UN party was sent to investigate claims that genocide was being systematically carried out but, while they did acknowledge that there were war crimes being committed, they didn't find any intent to commit genocide. It was claimed, however, by western observers and refugees that there was a definite plan to rid Darfur of black Africans, and many have used the terms genocide and ethnic cleansing as they describe the atrocities they have witnessed.

A peace deal brokered in May 2006 had little impact on the fighting, as not all parties concerned were willing to sign up to the agreement; only Minni Minawi's Sudan Liberation Army agreed to the terms but this organisation was then accused of collaborating with the government and attacking their former rebel partners. Indeed, Amnesty International accused the SLA of violence against opponents of the deal and Minawi was later installed as Senior Assistant to the President of the Republic and Chairman of the Regional Interim Authority of Darfur.

The 7,000 AU troops sent in to try and enforce the ceasefire, were given hardly any powers and were too few in number to effectively patrol the area which is why there were calls from the international community to send in a UN peacekeeping force. Unfortunately, the calls for sanctions had no effect because Russia and China both exercised their right to veto at the UN Security Council. The USA have denied Sudanese firms the opportunity of trading in US dollars since 1997, because of the country's ties to terrorist leader Osama Bin Laden.

The conflict intensified following the supposed peace deal and was particularly horrific in July and August 2006. It prompted the UN Security Council to approve Resolution 1706 thus enabling a 17,300 peacekeeping force to be sent to Sudan. Unfortunately, the government did not welcome this news and reacted by stating that it objected to the resolution and would treat any UN troops as invaders.

The Sudanese government have themselves been accused of trying to keep the truth from the wider world by imprisoning or killing witnesses and even tampering with evidence. They have disturbed mass graves and so invalidated any forensic evidence that might have been found and that might have eventually led to war crimes convictions.

By the end of 2006 there were more rebel factions engaged in the conflict such as the National Redemption Front and the Popular Forces Troops and UN observers were having trouble keeping up with the widespread killing. Indeed, the latter organisation were comprised of Darfurian Arabs who claimed that the Janjaweed were merely mercenaries.

Louis Arbour, UN High Commissioner for Human Rights, accused the Sudanese government in November 2006 of 'a deliberate and unprovoked attack on civilians and their property in the town of Sirba . . . with extensive wanton destruction and looting of civilian property'.

While the majority of estimates of the number of civilians who have died since 2003 stand at around 200,000, the United Nations believes that a more realistic figure is nearer half a million, although this figure would also include those who have perished of starvation and disease as well as those who had been murdered. It is also estimated that there are around two and a half million people who had been displaced by the fighting while some 200,000 have sought refuge in Chad.

April 2007 saw several incursions into Chad by the Janjaweed which left many dead after villages were surrounded before the militia opened fire. This led to the Sudanese and Chad presidents signing a peace agreement on May 3, but Russia came in for criticism from Amnesty International when it was claimed that they were supplying Sudan with arms and munitions, but the Soviets repeatedly denied breaking UN sanctions.

Only once peace has been secured, over this on-going attorcity can the true facts regarding the genocide in Darfur be revealed to the world but even when the conflict is over there will always be an uneasy tension in a region that has seen many turbulent periods in its history.

PART SIX

ORGANISATIONS

THE MAFIA

The word 'mafia' is a term used today to represent almost any organised crime group. The Mafia, which has been glorified by films and television, has controlled everything from street corner drug deals to the highest levels of government. It is a criminal organisation, or family, that is synonymous with oppression, arrogance, greed, power and violence that is governed by inexorable rules. Members of this family live by a 'code of honour' and usually have a brief, but violent existence.

The history of the *mafioso* can be traced back to the mid-nineteenth century in Sicily. The word 'mafia' is taken from an old Sicilian adjective *mafiusu* which means aggressive boasting or bragging. According to many *mafioso*, the real name is Cosa Nostra, which literally translated means 'our way', which was used to describe their way of life. Their activities have always been surrounded by a shroud of secrecy and members reportedly live by a code of silence known as the *omerta*.

By the early 1900s, organised crime had so thoroughly

infiltrated Sicilian life, that it was virtually impossible not to come in contact with it in some form or another. Dictator, Benito Mussolini, tried hard to control the brutal methods of the Mafia by placing many of its top men in prison, but when US troops occupied Sicily during World War II, they mistook the men as political prisoners and set them free. To make matters worse many were appointed in positions of responsibility within the government and police and consequently it didn't take long for the Mafia to get a firm grasp on Italy's political scene.

The Mafia is not in fact a single group or gang, it is made up of many families that have, at times, fought long and bloody gang wars. As the violence spiralled out of control, these families realised that their constant fighting was costing them dearly in terms of money and lives, and they decided to call a ceasefire. They formed a group that became known as the Cupola, which oversaw all the families and took control of major enterprises and assassinations. They started to cooperate in the interest of greater profits and although they worked together, to a degree, for the most part they simply agreed to stay out of each other's way.

Each group is made up of several different gangs, known as 'families' and the number of families can range from as little as ten to as many as one hundred. When a new family wishes to form, they need to be approved by the heads of other families, although as in any criminal setup there are often splinter groups that consolidate and form new families. Each family has their own separate business dealings, but needless to say, because of their close proximity to one another, these dealings often overlap causing friction. Each family is lead by the boss, or 'don', who is responsible for making all the major decisions. Their authority is vital to the smooth-running of the family, as they are needed to resolve disputes and keep the minions in line.

Directly beneath the don is the underboss. Sammy Gravano was a famous underboss for the Gambino family, who was notorious for turning state's evidence against Mafia boss John Gotti. The underboss has varying roles to help take pressure off the don, and many are groomed to replace the boss if he becomes too old or has to spend a spell inside.

Beneath the underboss comes the 'capo'. Their role can be described as a lieutenant who is responsible for leading one section of the family. The key to being a successful capo is making money for the family and this skill depends on the area to which they are designated. They usually organise rackets and illegal gambling and then pass their profits back up to the boss. The real dirty work, however, is carried out by the soldiers. They are the lowest rank in the family and hold little power. They are directly responsible to the capos and will be used on various criminal enterprises. In addition to the soldiers, the Mafia will also use associates. They are not actually members of a family, but merely someone who is prepared to work with the mob when required and can be anyone from a burglar, a drug dealer to a lawyer, banker, policeman or politician.

There is one final position within the family and that is the consigliere. He is a mediator who is there to act as an advisor who is supposed to leave personal feelings aside. Although, in reality, most consiglieres have shown that they are not always impartial.

Of course the Mafia is not strictly limited to Sicilian soils as many Sicilians and Italians immigrated to the United States in the nineteenth century. A huge proportion arrived on US shores early in the twentieth century and, although the majority just worked hard at building a new life for themselves, some of them brought the ways of the Mafia with them.

The first major incident of note, took place in New Orleans in the 1890s. A local chief of police was murdered after putting pressure on a particular Sicilian family. When the mobsters were tried, they managed to bribe many of the witnesses and the court had no choice but to acquit them. This resulted in much anti-Italian fervour and a lynch mob took the matter into their own hands, hanging or shooting sixteen men involved in the case.

Mafia families spread quickly throughout the USA in the first half of the twentieth century, emanating from New York City, where five families fought over who was to take control. Prohibition provided large amounts of money for the Mafia, as they sold illegal alcohol to the speakeasies and hotels and, as their power grew, so did the wars between the families. The violence reached a climax in the early 1930s, when bosses and underbosses were assassinated on a regular basis. The Luchese family, for example, got through four bosses in 1930 alone.

Right in the middle of all this bloodshed was a mobster by the name of Charles 'Lucky' Luciano. Luciano held a position of extreme power within the Cosa Nostra and he was behind the decision to form a multi-family commission to control Mafia activities nationwide. This idea was cemented at a meeting in Chicago where the commission was represented by five New York families, including the infamous Al Capone. They tried to iron out many of the problems surrounding the various Mafia families and decided that any large-scale money making activites, murders and kidnappings had to first be approved by the new commission. Membership of the commision was determined at national meetings that were held every five years.

One of these meetings became the scene of a famous event in the history of the Mafia – the Apalachin Raid – which took place on November 14, 1957. At the time Vito Genovese had recently taken over as boss of the Luciano family and in theory controlled almost half of New York's underworld. All he needed was approval by the commission as head of his family and for Carlo Gambino to be approved as boss of the Anatassi family. A meeting had been scheduled to take place in Apalachin, a small village in upper New York, about two hundred miles northwest of Manhattan, in the home of Joseph Barbara. The commission were concerned about what was taking place in New York and they were about to demand some answers.

Joseph Barbara, who had links with organised crime, was president of the Canada Dry bottling company in the area at the time. The police were aware that Barbara had connections in the drug trade and bootlegging rackets and had been keeping an eye on him for quite a while. However, what the police didn't know was that Barbara had also been made a member of the Mafia and had been asked to host the commission meeting. Barbara was flattered and arranged hotel accommodation for all the visiting dons and even invited some of them to stay in his own home. They came from as far away as Cuba, Los Angeles, Dallas, Chicago, Tucson,

Kansas City and Italy – in fact all the big bosses were there.

One of the major points under discussion at the meeting was the escalating prices being charged to the Mafia by drug dealers operating outside of the USA. Two mobsters whose names were on the list for discussion were Meyer Lansky and his partner, a man called Santo Sorge.

There are two schools of thought on how the police actually came to raid the meeting at Apalachin. One is that the New York don, Carlo Gambino – who was conspicuous in his absence from the meeting – actually tipped the police off in his own effort to take over the underworld. The other line of thought is that Mayer Lansky, fearful that the Mafia bosses were after his blood, decided to contact his friends within the federal government and told them about the meeting.

For whatever reason, the New York State police, who were curious about the large number of motel bookings, decided to place a stakeout outside the house of Joseph Barbara. The police knew they had to be careful because not only did they have no warrant to search the house, they were also aware that it could be exceedingly dangerous. Instead, they set up a road block on Route 17 and the McFall road, where they had a good view of the front door.

In the drive at the front of the house were almost thirty cars and the police decided to take down the number plates so that they could see to whom they belonged. As the police moved closer, Mrs Barbara yelled from inside the house, 'There's the state troopers!' causing complete panic.

One of the first men to run out of the house was Vito Genovese. The remainder of the visitors fled from the house and its grounds by running through the nearby woods, dumping guns and huge amounts of money as they went.

By 2.30 p.m. twenty-five people had been rounded up out of a possible fifty-nine, who the police believed were attending the meeting. All of those held by the police stuck to the same story – that they had simply come to pay their respects to Barbara who had been sick for some considerable time. Not one of the men wavered from their original story and eventually their convictions were overturned by the US Court of Appeals. Although it is believed that the commission is still in existence in some form, there is evidence that it is nowhere near as powerful as it was in the days of Lucky Luciano.

The Mafia has always been linked with gambling, the numbers game and betting, often bribing police to turn the other way as they reaped large rewards from their illegal casinos. When Nevada made gambling legal in

1931, needless to say mobsters seized the opportunity with both hands. Two of the first gang members to make their mark in Las Vegas, were Bugsy Siegel and Meyer Lansky, who offered dodgy loans to prospective developers who were keen to get in on the act. Many of the mobsters were so-called business partners with the casino owners, whether the owners wanted them as partners or not, while others simply skimmed cash after threatening the owners with their lives.

Even today the Mafia is still a symptom of Sicily's endemic political corruption, a situation which seems to have got worse in recent years. It has deliberately murdered judges, priests and even children in its search for supremacy. In March 2004 a fourteen-year-old Italian girl, Annalisa Durante, died from bullets intended for a Mafia boss. The twenty-year-old Camorra (the Naples version of the Sicilian Mafia) boss, Salvatore Giuliano, used the young girl as a shield when two men rode up on scooters and started firing at him. Annalisa was hit by bullets to her head, allowing Giuliano and his attackers to escape unharmed. She remained in a coma for several days before being announced brain dead – just another tragic victim of Mafia warfare.

THE YAKUZA

In a country where traditionalism is highly valued, the Yakuza's marks of individuality show their sheer disregard for conforming to Japanese standards. They have been described as the Japanese version of the Mafia and despite their rather garish appearance they are an organisation that have to be taken seriously. In fact, today, the Yakuza are one of the largest organised crime families in the world. In Japan alone there are more than 110,000 active members, divided into 2,500 families.

Just like the Sicilian Mafia, the Yakuza are divided up into families, but this is where the similarity ends. The Yakuza in their current role was formed in the nineteenth century under the son of a Samurai, Toyama Mitsuru. Mitsuri formed the Genyosha (Dark Ocean) Society and later Mitsuri's top aide Ryohei Uchida founded the Amur River Society (or the Black Dragons). Just like organised crime in other societies, the Yakuza started to take over control of construction and dockside enterprises. From there they moved into more illicit trades such as prostitution, gambling, distribution of alcohol and drugs and the world of entertainment. As their power increased, the Yakuza formed alliances with other organised crime syndicates including the Chinese Triads, the Sicilian and American Mafia, Colombian drug cartels and other organisations around the world. For the most part the Yakuza are accepted as a fact of life in Japan, and the government and the police tend to turn the back on their activities, including cold blooded killing.

Their origin can be traced as far back as the year 1612 to a band of men known as the kabuki-mono (or the crazy ones). Their unusual appearance and bad behaviour soon got them noticed as they wandered around Japan in large crowds plundering villages and small cities. However, if you asked a Yakuza about his origins, he would deny any connection to the kabuki-mono. They prefer to see themselves as ancestors of the machi-yakko (city servant), because they were seen as heroes for their help against the kabuki-mono, who were known for their ruthless behaviour and terrorising tactics.

The Yakuza, as they are known today, did not form until the middle of the seventeenth century. Their members were made up of bakuto (gamblers) and tekiya (street vendors) and they demanded total loyalty to the organisation even if it meant going against their own families. As the majority of the members had come from similar backgrounds – poverty, crime or simply being a society misfit – the Yakuza became their family. Possibly for the first time in their life they felt secure and safe in the knowledge that they had the full support of the other gang members.

When Japan began to industrialise, the Yakuza used this to their advantage and started to recruit members within the construction business and from the docks. They also started to infiltrate the political front and cooperated with the authorities to try and avoid any confrontations. When the economic depression came at the end of the twentieth century, it created doubts about the liberalism in the western world, and the Yakuza once again took advantage. They trained their members in warfare, different languages, assassination and blackmail. During this time two prime ministers and two finance ministers were murdered, while several politicians and industrialists were attacked – muscle power courtesy of the Yakuza.

When Japan was occupied by US troops following World War II, the Americans saw the Yakuza as an enormous threat and closely watched their activities. The US army started to ration food, little realising that they were playing right into the Yakuza's hands. The black market flourished and contributed to the wealth and power of the gangs, and a new type of Yakuza began to develop – the gurentai (or street hustler). The gurentai were mostly involved with the black market and robbery but they were also influenced by the US gangster movies and started to dress like their heroes. They wore black suits, white shirts, sunglasses and started to crop their hair. They also became tougher and more violent and the gun took the place of the sword. Soon honest businessmen were being exposed to violence and as more and as more gangs formed, street violence reached an all time high as they fought for their territories.

The Yakuza clans have a hierarchy structure. The head chief is called the Oyabun (father) and beneath him are the Wakashu (children) and Kyodai (brothers). All members of the clan must obey the Oyabun and in return for their loyalty he will protect them against any danger. The Oyabun's word is law and everyone, without exception, must obey him. Beneath the Oyabun is also the Saiko-komon (adviser) who has a staff of advocates, accountants, secretaries and advisers. The boss of the Wakashu is the Waka gashira, who is number two in the clan after the Oyabun. He acts as a mediator and ensures that all the Oyabun's orders are carried out.

The Yakuza is entirely made up of men with the exception of the Oyabun's wife who is called *o-neh-san* (older sister). In fact the Yakuza do not trust women at all with the exception of the *o-neh-san*, who they treat with equal respect as the Oyabun. The reason they do not trust women is because they believe they are weak and that women are unable to fight. Fighting is important to the Yakuza as is courage, because they are expected to fight to the death rather than lose a battle. Another reason the Yakuza distrust women is that no one is allowed to talk about the group to outsiders, and they do not believe that a woman is strong enough to remain silent under pressure.

It is normal within Yakuza gangs to have tattoos which normally cover their entire body. Very often it is the clan's badge and most are elaborate patterns containing dragons, flowers, mountainous landscapes, seascapes and abstract patterns. In fact if seen naked, the Yakuza member almost looks as if he is wearing very decorative underwear. The application of these tattoos is a long and painful procedure often taking as long as 100 hours to complete an entire back. It is not only considered a test of a man's strength but also to illustrate the man's affiliation to his clan. For the most part a Yakuza will keep these tattoos concealed under long-sleeved and high-necked shirts. However, they break this rule when playing Oicho-Kabu cards with one another, where they often remove their shirts to reveal their ornate tattoos.

The Yakuza have their own unique way of making an

apology when they make a mistake or do something that the Oyabun doesn't approve of. They call it *yubizume*, which is the act of cutting off their little finger and then giving it to the person to whom they are apologising. For example, when a younger member of the clan fell in love with the daughter of the Oyabun – which is something that is strictly forbidden – the couple started to meet in secret. They wanted to get married but knew that the Oyabun wouldn't allow it. Scared that the Oyabun would arrange to have him killed, the couple decided to run away, but they were found after a couple of days and returned to the base. The daughter was simply scolded for her behaviour, but the young man was made to apologise in the Yakuza way. He was given a knife and a piece of white string and the young man knew exactly what was expected of him. Without wavering, he picked up the knife, held one end of the string between his teeth while holding the other with his right hand, and tied it around the little finger of his left hand. After taking a deep breath, he chopped off the tip of his little finger with the knife and then wrapped it in a towel and gave it to the Oyabun. The Oyabun said nothing and took the finger which meant that the young man's apology had been accepted.

If a Yakuza member is jailed for any reason, this immediately elevates his position within the gang when he is released. Another practice carried out by the Yakuza in prison is pearling or genital beading. This is a form of body modification and involves the insertion of small beads, made from various materials, beneath the skin of the shaft or foreskin of the penis.

Another quite frequent Yakuza ritual is the sharing of sake. This is traditionally to seal the bond of brotherhood between individual Yakuza members or between two different Yakuza groups.

Unlike their counterparts, the Mafia and Chinese Triads, the Yakuza are not a secret organisation. They quite openly have an office with a wooden board on the front door, proudly displaying their group name or emblem. They are proud to be seen in public, often wearing colourful suits so that they stand out from the crowd. Many of their members also develop an arrogant, wide gait as they walk proudly among the less assuming members of the Japanese public.

The Yakuza make their living through illegal businesses including alcohol, drugs, prostitution and loan-sharking, but the majority of their funds come from gambling, usually in the form of card or dice games. Each family of Yakuza have their own gambling room which is usually behind a bar or cafe, and is kept quiet so that the police are not alerted. Each gambler must be a member of the Yakuza and the stakes are extremely high – up to ten thousand dollars just for one play. It is quite common for as much as one million dollars to change hands in any one day. The gamblers are all expected to be professional and are have to remain silent as they enter the gambling den, the only sound is the chink of the money and dice.

Prostitution is big business for the Yakuza, preferring to hire girls that are under eighteen years of age. There are various methods of making money from prostitution, but the most popular is the 'date club'. These clubs can turn over millions of dollars each month, and the membership fee is high – one thousand dollars. The majority of the members are rich, middle-aged men such as lawyers, doctors and company directors who can afford to enjoy the pleasures the young girls have to offer. The men are shown pictures of the girls and then the club will arrange a date. The men pay a fee and all expenses – to have sex with their escort costs an extra one thousand dollars. When the date is over the customer is expected to call the club and tell them whether they liked their date and this way the girls move up the 'professional' ladder. Although the hiring of high school students is strictly forbidden, many are willing to work as prostitutes because they can earn so much money and for the Yakuza they are a rich source of young, nubile girls.

The majority of the money made by the Yakuza is spent on buying weapons. Although it is illegal to carry a weapon in Japan without a permit, the Yakuza do not respect the law and many innocent people become the victims of their violent street battles, when one group clashes with another. Each group will fight to the death to protect their territory regardless of who gets in their way and for this reason it is easy to see why the Yakuza are so feared and hated by the Japanese public. Even today this continues to be one of the biggest social problems in Japan.

THE TRIADS

One of the most impenetrable of criminal organisations in the world today are the Triads of Hong Kong and Taiwan. They are best known for their involvement in the big business of drugs at every level, from the buying of the poppies, manufacturing opium and heroin, smuggling and finally dealing. However, their activities do not end there as they are also famous for being involved in contract killings, money laundering, extortion, all forms of racketeering and murder.

The Triads are believed to have been started as a resistance movement to the Manchu emperors of the Qinq Dynasty. The Manchu originated from a country north of China (Manchuria) and were looked upon as foreign rulers who had taken Peking (China's northern capital) by force. Their dynasty was established around 1674 and, in the thirteenth year of their rule, Emperor Kiang Hsi decided to recruit a band of fighting monks (Siu Lam) to try and defeat a rebellion taking place in Fukien. In return for their loyalty, the monks were offered a certain amount of imperial power. However, the monks themselves were then seen as a threat to the court and the emperor sent an army to suppress them.

Although the original numbers have not been recorded it is believed around eighteen monks survived the attack, five of whom set up separate monasteries. The monasteries were in fact secret societies – Tian Di Hui (Heaven and Earth Society) – who were dedicated to overthrowing the Manchu dynasty and restoring the previous Ming dynasty to power. Eventually the Manchus were overthrown in 1911, but sadly there were no Mings left to restore the dynasty to its former glory.

Over the centuries, what are today known as the Triads, developed from a patriotic society into a criminal organisation. Unable to revert back to a normal life after the years of fighting and extreme violence, many of the rebels got together and formed a cult which became known as the Triads. Having now lost the support of the public following the collapse of the empire, members of this newly formed gang resorted to extorting money by any means possible.

When China was invaded by the Japanese during World War II, the Triads offered their help and they started running criminal enterprises for the Japanese in Hong Kong. The gangs were united under an association called the Hing Ah Kee Kwan (Asia

Flourishing Organisation) and were paid through a company called Lee Yuen. These gangsters were used to help keep the residents of Hong Kong under control and also to suppress any anti-Japanese activity.

After World War II, when the Communist Party of China took power, mainland China came under strict law enforcement and consequently organised crime started to diminish. Triad members decided to migrate south to the then-British colony of Hong Kong and it is estimated that by 1947, there were 300,000 Triad members in Hong Kong alone.

The nine main Triad gangs were – Wo, Rung, Tung, Chuen, Shing, Fuk Yee Hing, Yee On, 14K and Luen – each having its own headquarters and its own splinter groups. However, in 1956 there was a major riot in Kowloon which was exploited by the Triads. The colonial government passed strict regulations to suppress the gangsters and 10,000 suspected Triad mobsters were arrested. For a while the Triads went underground with very little action, but the cultural revolution in China brought them back to the surface.

The Triads of Hong Kong are a very powerful organisation, with their own international drug syndicates and armed forces. Although the Triads do work under a system of hierarchy, where a father-figure controls all the other members, the Hong Kong Triads are generally composed of several independent groups. The actual power of the Triads seems to be at the lower level of the hierarchy ladder, with an 'official' (Red Pole) leading a group of fifteen or more active 'soldiers'. As in other criminal organisations these groups fight for supremacy and territory nearly always resulting in bloodshed. The Triads also use a form of numeric code to differentiate between the ranks within a gang. The Triad structure is broken down into ranks as follows: the Boss (Mountain Master) is the highest authority, under him is the Vanguard, the Deputy and the Ceremony Master, under these three come the Advisor, The Fighters and the Liaison Officer and then at the bottom of the hierarchy come the Ordinary Members and the Temporary Members. All the members live by thirty-six traditional Triad oaths whereby they swear allegiance to the organisation.

Present day Triads have become more business-like organisations, with their criminal activities being more diverse and complex than most other Asian mobsters. Their impact has been felt not only nationally but internationally, too, causing major upheaval with their extortion, murder, kidnapping, illegal gambling, prostitution, robbery and loan-sharking. Keeping up with modern trends the Triads have now moved onto drug trafficking, credit card fraud, theft of cars and computer equipment, counterfeiting, money laundering and piracy. They are now reputed to be among the most dangerous and powerful of the organised crime syndicates in the world, controlling much of the world's drug trade and operating in nearly every major city.

There are believed to be as many as fifty-seven Triad societies in Hong Kong and tackling the problems brought about by these gangs is still one of Hong Kong's greatest challenges. With Hong Kong being passed back into the hands of mainland China, it appears that more and more Triads are now fleeing their home town and seeking their fortunes elsewhere.

The Tong are a Chinese–American secret society whose activities flout the law. The very first Tongs modelled themselves on the Triads and dedicated themselves to the overthrow of the Qin dynasty. However, unlike the Triads, the Tongs formed without any clear political motives and soon found themselves embroiled in lucrative criminal activities. With the first wave of Chinese immigrants to the USA in the 1800s, many Chinatowns sprung up throughout the east and west coast. Soon certain inhabitants of these Chinatowns concentrated on providing vices to the Chinese population, including gambling, prostitution and opium. Prostitution became their most profitable business due to the high male-to-female ratio among the early immigrants. They would either kidnap or buy females from China and then smuggle them to the USA to work in brothels. However, because of the rich pickings, the various Tong gangs started to fight over territories which ultimately led to a period in history known as the Tong Wars. Fights broke out in almost every major Chinatown across the USA from the mid-1800s and lasted into the 1970s. The foot soldiers became known as *boohowdoy*, which is Cantonese for hatchetboy. Which was very apt as they always used a hatchet or a cleaver as their weapon of choice.

Although the fighting eventually dissipated, the Tongs continued their criminal ways and even today continue to engage in extortion, murder, gambling, prostitution, smuggling illegal immigrants and, of course, drugs from the Golden Triangle, which is one of Asia's two main illicit opium-producing areas.

Still operating the hierarchy principles, the Tong have *an an kung* (grandfather) or *shuk foo* (uncle) to oversee the group's activities. The top gang position is held by the *dai dai lo* (big big brother). Directly below the *dai dai lo*, in descending order, are the *dai lo*(s) (big brothers), the *yee lo/saam lo* (clique leaders) and at the very bottom the *ma jai* (little horses).

There do not seem to be any set rules that apply to

these gangs but they do appear to respect the ah kung, beat up members of rival gangs, follow the orders of the dai lo and finally, and perhaps most importantly, do not betray members to their own gang. Of course these so-called rules are frequently violated and the violators are punished, sometimes severely, usually by physical assault or cold-blooded killing.

THE BAYBASIN CARTEL

The Baybasin cartel have never been shy about telling people of their illegal activities, proudly boasting of their drug smuggling and violence. Added to this they had various political and intelligence links which they used to their own advantage. The Baybasin cartel, were a Kurdish gang, who controlled up to ninety per cent of the heroin which came into the United Kingdom. The cartel itself is enormous and straddles several international borders.

Their leader, Huseyin Baybasin, settled in the UK in the mid-1990s with his brother, Abdullah. Huseyin made his fortune by controlling the flow of opium which comes from Afghanistan, crosses his own family's lands in south-east Turkey, before being finally processed as heroin in the west. He is believed to have amassed a fortune of ten billion pounds from his drug smuggling empire.

When interviewed, Baybasin described himself as an 'International Man of Violence'. He was a self-made gangster who had financed not only the Turkish ruling classes but the PKK (Kurdish Workers' Party) as well, killing anyone who insulted his honour.

Although the Baybasins are believed to have entered the UK illegally using forged Dutch passports, there appears to have been no attempt to regularise their immigration status. Added to this the gang were allowed to move freely between Turkey and London, allegedly after Huseyin agreed to tell Customs and Excise investigators what he knew about the involvement of senior Turkish politicians and officials in the international heroin trade. Eventually the UK became a so-called sanctuary for the cartel members.

Abdullah, despite being bound to a wheelchair following a shooting incident in a bar in Amsterdam in the 80s, took over the helm of the cartel after his brother, Huseyin, was arrested. He was apprehended on one of his so-called 'business' trips to the Netherlands. Despite insisting that his drug trafficking days were over, Huseyin was jailed in 2001 for twenty years for conspiracy to murder, drug trafficking and kidnap. His sentence was increased to life following an appeal. Authorities believe that Huseyin Baybasin, despite sitting in a Dutch prison, is as powerful as ever.

In his brother's absence, Abdullah recruited a gang of young thugs known as the bombacilar (bombers) who spread fear throughout the Turkish and Kurdish community in London. They were a dangerous gang who ran a protection racket, forcing their way into shops and small businesses armed with weapons and demanding money. On one occasion, a gang of up twenty men, armed with samurai swords, metal bars, pool cues and a gun, forced their way into a Turkish cafe in Stoke Newington. One man had his index finger chopped off by the gang and several shots were fired, making sure that their 'customers' were duly terrorised into handing over their money.

It was the murder of an innocent family man, Alisan Dogan, however, that started a chain reaction which brought about the end of the reign of Britain's heroin godfather. Matters came to a head when some of the cartel's victims expressed their frustration to some members of the powerful PKK. On November 9, 2002, the bombacilar clashed with their PKK rivals. A massive fight broke out in the Haringey area of north London and one man, Alisan Dogan, was fatally stabbed and twenty other men were injured.

The murder triggered a new alliance of interests between the Kurdish and Turkish communities and the police. The Kurds told detectives that since the

Baybasins had moved into Edgware, they had been paralysed by fear. People were constantly being kidnapped against their will, brought to a special room at their headquarters and threatened with their life. The Baybasin foot soldiers (the bombacilar) were starting to wreak havoc, extorting money out of the local business-men by firebombing and inhumane forms of torture.

After this incident, Scotland Yard decided to step up their efforts to gather as much information about the Baybasin cartel as they could. It soon became clear that the battles on the streets of north London were being masterminded and funded by one of the wealthiest and most powerful families in the world of organised crime.

In the past five years it is believed that as many as twenty-five murders have been attributed to the cartel. In May 2001, twenty-six-year-old Oguzhan Ozdemir from Enfield, north London, was shot dead. Two months earlier Hasan Mamali, twenty-three, and his friend Sama Mustafa, twenty-six, were gunned down in east London. Mamali was shot in the head as he sat in the back of a car. Mustafa tried to run away, but was brought down by a volley of shots. All of the victims were east European and it is believed they were killed because they got on the wrong side of Turkish heroin suppliers. The police were certain that all the violence was connected with the increasing growth in the drug trade. Added to this was the fact that the gang members were getting younger and consequently more reckless. Many of the bombacilar were aged between fourteen and eighteen and proved to be a dangerous force when armed with guns. It is believed they were paid around £200 to oversee a drug delivery, supervise the arrival of illegal immigrants or make sure that protection money was paid. Although there had been constant complaints about the protection rackets, police struggled to infiltrate the gangs responsible because they were a close-knit community, often involving family members, who were sworn to secrecy.

The police discovered that most of the criminal activity in the area was centred around certain Turkish cafes, which were notorious for not actually selling any food. Instead, they were a front for illegal gambling, with the back rooms being used for the planning and delivery of drug shipments.

Meanwhile the Baybasin gang were busy making political contacts. The first man they used for their own purposes was a councillor by the name of Alan Sloam. Sloam was a well-known figure in the north London Labour party, who was later barred from holding office after some dodgy dealings with a neighbouring council. Abdullah asked Sloam if he could do anything to help Huseyin's wife, who was finding it difficult to visit her husband in the Netherlands. Sloam contacted MP Tony McNulty, who had been appointed a Home Office Minister in May 2005 with responsibility for immigration, nationality and citizenship. By writing several letters he managed to persuade Claude Moraes, the Labour MEP and former director of the Joint Council for the Welfare of Immigrants, to raise questions on Huseyin's behalf in the European parliament.

Apart from their illegal activities the Baybasin cartel were also involved in several legitimate business enterprises. They owned many residential properties in and around Edgware and also owned a car sales business in London. They purchased a former rest home for retired policemen on the seafront at Hove in East Sussex, which they turned into a hotel. Added to this they had numerous hotels on the Mediterranean and Aegean coasts which were visited by thousands of holidaymakers each year.

By early 2003 the National Crime Squad – a police agency responsible for tackling criminal organisations committing serious and organised crime – were starting to close in on the cartel. Detectives managed to hide a tiny video camera and microphones inside an office at the back of a sports club in Green Lanes, North London. It was where they believed Abdullah was running the Baybasin cartel's business transactions. Over the period of the next eight months, the police managed to obtain information on drug deals, distribution of guns, assembly of bombs and also evidence of the gangs violence. On one occasion they were able to watch footage of one of the bombacilar being stripped and threatened with a machete over some breach of gang discipline.

In December 2003, they carried out a series of raids and arrested several of the cartel members. They uncovered guns, machetes, stolen mobile phones and large amounts of counterfeit money and the police also discovered what they believed to be a torture room in Huseyin's large detached house in Edgware, north London.

Abdullah Baybasin now faces a twenty-two-year jail sentence after being convicted in London in 2006. Another ten members of the gang were also jailed at Woolwich crown court for up to fifteen years for crimes including blackmail, arson and firearms offences. A further six cartel members were jailed for conspiring to supply heroin.

Although other leading members of the cartel remain at liberty, they are being closely monitored to make sure they do not reassemble the bombacilar and renew the period of terror and violence that the Kurdish and Turkish people of north London have recently been subjected to.

PART SEVEN

COLD-BLOODED MEN

RICHARD KUKLINSKI: THE ICEMAN

There were a few things you just didn't do around Mafia hitman, Richard Kuklinsky. One was falling behind with payments to whomever Kuklinsky was working for. Another was getting his family involved in his business dealings. The third was to actually show up on his property and make threats. George Malliband was foolish enough to do all three.

One day while Kuklinsky was cooking a family barbecue, he saw a figure striding across the lawn of his house in Dumont. It was Malliband and he was making a big and fatal mistake that would be compounded by a later threat that he now knew where Kuklinsky lived, implying that he would do something to upset the rhythm of Kuklinsky's precious family life.

It wouldn't have been so bad if Malliband had not been falling behind in his payments to a man called Roy

DeMeo who happened to be a capo in the Gambino crime family. DeMeo was a butcher by trade, as well as by nature; a psychopath with a terrifying bloodlust. His henchmen followed his example. In a grimy apartment rented from a man known as Dracula, they would 'deal' with people who had somehow wronged them. Their procedure included stabbing the victim in the heart repeatedly to stop the blood from flowing. They would then hang the body above the bath until all the blood had drained away. At this point, DeMeo's former occupation would come in handy. The corpse would be cut into small pieces and these would then be wrapped and distributed in litter-bins and skips around the city.

George Malliband had been introduced to DeMeo by Kuklinsky; so, Kuklinsky was responsible for him, as DeMeo was at pains to make clear. Therefore, as was the way of these things, Kuklinsky would have to deal with the situation. Driving him back to New Jersey from Brooklyn one night, Kuklinsky calmly pulled over to the side of the road and shot Malliband five times with a .38. He then drove to Jersey City and tried to stuff the body into a steel drum. Finding it did not fit, he severed the tendons in Malliband's legs so that they would bend a little further back and forced it into the drum. He then drove back to Brooklyn and repaid Malliband's debt, out of his own pocket. Honour satisfied.

Malliband, however, was far from Kuklinsky's first murder. As a child he had delighted in killing neighbourhood cats, but, in 1949, at the age of fourteen he had beaten another boy, a bully, to death. His first kill, he later admitted, had made him feel 'empowered', as if he was 'someone'. From that point on he brooked no defiance or disrespect. The cold killer that became the Iceman was born.

Kuklinsky, a six-foot five, 300-pound mountain of a man, born on April 11, 1935, in Jersey City, had an uncanny means of detaching himself from the hundred or so people he killed. In one of two TV documentaries made about him, he described how when he made his first hit, using a car bomb triggered by petrol, he walked away from the scene, feeling nothing. He reckoned it was a result of the abuse heaped upon him and his brother during their childhood by a drunken father. His brother Joey went to prison aged twenty-five for the rape and murder of a twelve-year-old girl whose body he threw off the roof of a building. He got life in Trenton State Prison.

Kuklinsky was a master of his art and, over the years, he experimented with different ways of dispatching his hits. He used firearms, including a miniature derringer, ice picks, hand grenades, crossbows, chainsaws and even, on one occasion, a bomb attached to a remote-control toy car.

Once, while he was experimenting with the crossbow as a means of killing, he opened his car window as if to ask directions, and when a man approached, he fired an arrow which went straight through the man's head, killing him on the spot.

The Iceman's method of choice, however, involved cyanide. 'Why be messy. You do it nice and neat with cyanide,' he told Dominick Polifrone, an undercover Alcohol, Tobacco and Firearms agent. He would administer a cyanide solution into the face of his victim using a nasal spray bottle. Cyanide attacks the cellular enzyme system that processes the body's utilisation of oxygen. The victim experiences a burning in the mouth and throat, grows dizzy and disorientated and is, basically, asphyxiated. Best of all, cyanide is hard to detect, as it is rapidly metabolised by the body. The only way you know it has been ingested is a bitter almond smell that can be detected in the victim's mouth.

Nevertheless, he would happily use whichever method was appropriate to the situation and to his paymasters, and would then bring into use his special talents for the disposal of the victims' bodies. On one occasion, as with George Malliband, he stuffed a body into a steel drum again and left it beside a hot dog stand. Every day for weeks, Kuklinsky would stop, buy a hot dog and lean on the oil drum. Then one day it just disappeared and he never found out what happened to it and its grisly contents.

His most famous disposal gave rise to his nickname, the Iceman.

Robert Prongay was known as Mr Softee on account of the fact that he had an ice cream van. But as well as peddling ice cream, Prongay also worked as a hitman for DeMeo and did a few bits of business now and then with Kuklinsky, mostly in the pornography line. It was from Prongay that Kuklinsky learned of the efficacy of cyanide. To demonstrate it to Kuklinsky, Prongay walked up to a complete stranger in the street, sprayed him and they then watched the man collapse and die within a matter of seconds. It was from Prongay that Kuklinsky got his supply of the deadly poison.

Prongay and Kuklinsky wanted to refine the art of killing and wondered if it would be possible to freeze a body to disguise the time of death. It would ensure that the killer need not worry about an alibi. They decided to use a small-time crook called Louis Masgay as their guinea pig. Masgay wanted to purchase a quantity of video tapes from Kuklinsky and on July 1, 1981, he left home with $95,000 in cash, never to return. His van was later found abandoned, the secret cash compartment ripped out and the cash gone.

Masgay's carcass was reported to have hung for a time

in an industrial freezer in a warehouse rented by the Iceman. However, it is also believed to have spent some time in the freezer in Prongay's ice cream van, lying there while Mr Softee dispensed cornets to the children of North Bergen.

When Masgay's corpse was discovered, two years later, wrapped in plastic bags, the medical examiner thought it strange that the clothing he was wearing was the same as on the day he had left home with the cash. And yet, the body looked fresh. However, all became clear when, in the course of the autopsy, Masgay's tissue was found to contain crystals of ice and his heart was discovered to be still partially frozen. Kuklinsky had been either too careful in wrapping Masgay's body in layer after layer of plastic or too impatient to let the body thaw completely. He became the cops' chief suspect and the name 'Iceman' began to stick.

As for Prongay, he now knew too much and Kuklinsky shot him to death in his ice cream van in 1984.

In the midst of the mayhem he was creating, lay Kuklinsky's family. He maintained a normal, fairly affluent family life in a New Jersey suburb and his neighbours had no clue as to how he earned his living. In an interview with the writer, Anthony Bruno, he said: 'I'm not the Iceman. I'm the nice man.'

He had married his wife, Barbara, in 1961, but behind

closed doors she lived in constant fear of his fierce and violent temper. She disclosed after he had been imprisoned, that at different times he had attempted to smother her with a pillow, had pointed a gun at her, had tried to run her over with a car and had broken her nose no fewer than three times.

He had drifted into crime while working at a film lab, selling porn videos on the side to the Gambinos. At first they were suspicious of his enthusiasm for killing and they limited his activities to smaller crimes. But Kuklinski told DeMeo that he would do anything for money and to prove he had what it took, DeMeo took him for a walk. They were close to a man who was out walking his dog. Without a moment's hesitation, and on command, Kuklinski walked past the man and then turned and shot him dead. From that point on, they decided to exploit his love of killing. He would kill men he could lure into deals involving large amounts of cash being handed over for non-existent goods or fellow criminals who knew too much. He carried out contract killings for the Mafia or took care of people who just annoyed him.

Gary Smith, an associate of Kuklinsky, fell into the category of a man who knew too much. He would steal cars and Kuklinsky and he would re-sell them. But the police were on to him and, just before Christmas 1982, a warrant was issued for his arrest. The last thing Kuklinsky needed was for Smith to start talking. So, he shielded him, moving him from one New Jersey motel to another, helped by another car thief, Danny Deppner. Smith was hard to control, however, and it was just a matter of time before he would be picked up. There was only one way to deal with the situation.

Smith was holed up in the York Motel off Route 3, close to the Lincoln Tunnel. Kuklinsky brought hamburgers to him and Deppner and Smith grabbed the bag of food, not realising that Kuklinsky had rustled up a recipe of his own for the ketchup, adding just a dash of cyanide. Smith hungrily wolfed down the burger and at first nothing happened as the two men watched. Then, the poison began to work and Smith began to choke. It was taking time, however, so Deppner put a chord from one of the lamps around his throat and tightened it until Smith was no longer breathing.

The plan had been for Deppner's wife to show up with a car to remove the body but when she failed to show, the two men decided to hide Smith's body beneath the mattress and box springs of the bed. It took four days for the stench in the room to be reported and the mattress to be removed to reveal the bloated body of Gary Smith. In that time, three couples had used the bed.

Deppner, of course, now knew too much. His body was discovered in January 1983, only a few miles from a ranch at which Kuklinsky's family were known to go riding. The cause of death was stated as 'undetermined'. However, pinkish spots – a sign of cyanide poisoning – were noted and photographs of them were taken.

Kuklinsky became the chief suspect and the net began to tighten on him. It was decided that Special Agent Dominick Polifrone would lure him into a deal so that he could be caught on tape admitting something or be caught in the act of planning a murder.

When Polifrone eventually hooked up with Kuklinsky in 1986, pretending to offer an arms and cocaine deal, Kuklinsky began to brag about his methods, especially the use of cyanide. He asked Polifrone if he could get his hands on some cyanide for him.

To expedite matters, Polifrone asked Kuklinsky to help him take care of a 'rich Jewish kid' who wanted to buy coke from them and would be carrying a lot of cash. They decided to put cyanide in an egg sandwich. However, the 'cyanide' Polifrone brought was actually just quinine. On the day, however, Kuklinsky took the sandwiches and left. He failed to return and the task force that had been formed to manage the case, believing their undercover agent to be in mortal danger, moved in and Kuklinsky was arrested.

At his trial, he was found guilty of five murders, but the lack of eyewitness testimony meant he escaped the death penalty. He was given two sentences of life imprisonment, for each of which he would serve a minimum of thirty years. He would be 111 years old before he would be eligible for parole. He didn't make it, though. He died in Trenton State Prison – the same one in which his brother was incarcerated – in March 2006. He was seventy years old.

BIANCHI AND BUONO: THE HILLSIDE STRANGLERS

Kenneth Alessio Bianchi was born on May 22, 1951, to a seventeen-year-old alcoholic prostitute who worked the streets of Rochester, New York. A baby was the last thing she needed and Kenneth was immediately put up for adoption. He found a home within a few months with Frances Bianchi and her husband, a worker at the American Brake Shoe factory.

Bianchi was a difficult child from the start and it was not long before Frances realised that the child she had taken in was a compulsive liar. Not only that, he also did not sleep, was prone to anger and temper tantrums and was a chronic bed-wetter. When his mother took him to hospital to find out what was wrong, the doctor noted: 'Mother needs help'.

Frances sought help again when Kenny was five years old. She described how he would lapse into what seemed to be trances, his eyes rolling back in their sockets. The doctors diagnosed these episodes as petit mal syndrome or absence seizures. Frances was assured there was no cause for concern; Kenny would probably grow out of them.

However, by the age of eleven, he was being treated at DePaul Psychiatric Centre for a whole range of issues including 'involuntary urination, tics, absenteeism and behaviour problems'. To deal with his bladder problems, his mother made him wear sanitary towels.

His education also presented problems and he moved schools a few times around this time because of his inability to get on with his teachers. He was lazy, inattentive and angry, but not stupid – he had an IQ of 116. Nevertheless, his grades never reflected this and he was a chronic underachiever in class.

Kenny's father died of a heart attack when the boy was thirteen, but he received the news without any outward sign of emotion. Psychiatrists suggested that he was overly dependent on his mother.

He got through high school without any real problems; he was a clean-cut kid who seemed to respect his elders and he dated. At eighteen, a proposal of marriage he made to a girlfriend was turned down. But, he was still an odd kid. Around this time, in a letter to a girlfriend, he claimed to be the Alphabet Killer who was making a name for himself in the area. She didn't take his claim seriously.

When he graduated in 1971, Kenny married Brenda Beck, but the marriage failed after just eight months, perhaps because his wedding vows had never stopped him seeing other women. Nonetheless, when Brenda packed her things, left and filed for an annulment, Kenny felt betrayed. Another contributory factor to the marriage breakdown were the high standards he imposed upon his women. According to an acquaintance, his Catholic education led him to confuse ordinary women with the Virgin Mary, and their human frailties exasperated him to the point of anger. He did not like his women to wear V-neck sweaters or tight jeans and demanded absolute devotion and faithfulness, even while he was out playing the field.

He took courses in police science and psychology, but dropped out and, following a rejected application for a job in the sheriff's department, he worked as a security guard, using his position to steal things for girlfriends. But Rochester was a dead end for him and in 1975, aged twenty-six, he moved to Los Angeles, living initially with his older cousin, Angelo Buono.

Angelo was not a nice man. A car upholsterer and a

pimp, he had been married several times and had a number of children whom he abused both physically and sexually. Nonetheless, his course vulgarity and downright ugliness did not deter him from being a ladies' man. Like Bianchi, he had been born in Rochester but had moved with his mother and older sister to Glendale, California, following his parents' divorce. He, too, was a Catholic, but neither religion nor education can be said to have meant anything to him. He was into sadistic and brutal sex and he initiated Bianchi into his perverted world.

Kenny soon got a job, his own apartment in Glendale and a 1972 Cadillac sedan that he could barely afford. Before long he had moved in with a woman he had met at work, Kelli Boyd. When Kelli told him in May 1977 that she was having a baby, Kenny wanted to marry her, but his jealousy, immaturity and compulsive lying made her reluctant to share her future with him.

As well as his dayjob, Bianchi obtained a fraudulent degree and credentials, rented an office and set himself up as a psychologist, giving Kelli even more reason not to marry him. Fortunately, he did not have too many clients.

In late 1977, when the Hillside Strangler was starting to cause widespread panic on the streets of Los Angeles, Bianchi made a pretense of being seriously ill; he started coughing and saying that he was having difficulty breathing. He told Kelli that he had lung cancer and would require chemotherapy and radiation treatment. He took time off work and on one of his days at home he was questioned by detectives about the strangler case. One of the murders may have taken place in the apartment building he and Kelli lived in. They did not consider him a suspect, though, and he even managed to get himself recruited for the LAPD's ride-along programme which allowed civilians to travel in police cars. All Bianchi talked about to his police companions was the Hillside Strangler.

Not long after the birth of their son, Sean, Kelli decided she had had enough. She left Bianchi and went home to her parents in Bellingham. Bianchi found himself abandoned by yet another woman. Before too long, however, she agreed to give him another chance and he drove to Bellingham to be with her.

The killing had started a few months earlier, in October 1977, when Angelo and Kenneth had decided they would pimp out young girls. A couple of women, Deborah Noble and Yolanda Washington, sold them a list of potential male clients that the two men discovered to be fake. They went looking for revenge and eighteen-year-old Yolanda's body was discovered not long afterwards on a hillside close to a cemetery, with the cloth that had been used to strangle her still tied around her neck. She had been a part-time waitress and prostitute which meant that the police did not consider relevant the fact that she had had sex with two men before she died.

A few weeks later, on November 1, sixteen-year-old Judy Miller was found. She, too, had been raped and strangled and her ankles, wrists and neck bore ligature marks. Five days later, Linda Kastin's naked body turned up near a Glendale country club. The twenty-one-year-old waitress had been raped, sodomised and strangled, and she bore similar ligature marks to Judy Miller.

It was only when a couple of younger girls were murdered that the police began to really take the killings seriously. Until this point, the victims had been women who led lives that contained an element of risk. Now the victims were nice girls from middle class backgrounds. Dolores Capeda, twelve, and Sonja Johnson were schoolgirls who were last seen getting off the school bus on November 13 and going over to a large two-tone sedan to talk to someone on the passenger side. Their raped and strangled bodies were found by a nine-year-old boy and bore the Hillside Strangler's characteristic ligature marks.

Seven days passed before Kristine Weckler's nude body, complete with ligature marks, was stumbled upon on a hill near Glendale. Bianchi later told how she died: 'She was brought into the kitchen and put on the floor and her head was covered with a bag and the pipe from the gas stove was disconnected, put into the bag and then turned on. There may have been marks on her neck because there was a cord put around her neck to make a more complete sealing.' It took ninety minutes for her to be asphyxiated.

Bianchi and Buono had been busy. Twenty-eight-year-old Jane King turned up on a sliproad near the Golden State Freeway on November 23 and Lauren Wagner was found six days later. Both carried the tell-tale ligature marks, but Lauren's palms showed a new twist – electrical burns; she had been tortured before being strangled.

Police surmised correctly that more than one killer was involved. The bodies had been killed elsewhere and dumped. It would have taken two people to carry them to some of the locations. They also noted the elements common to each murder – bodies left on hillsides and death by ligature strangulation.

Kenny and Angelo took a break. There were no more deaths for a fortnight, but on December 13 it started up again when seventeen-year-old Kimberly Diane Martin, also known as Donna, was found – the strangler's ninth victim. The tenth was spotted by a helicopter on

February 16, 1978. Cindy Hudspeth's body was in the boot of an orange Datsun which had been pushed over a cliff.

Bianchi, by this time in Bellingham with Kelli and their son, now went solo. Working as a security guard, and looking after a house for some people who were abroad, he paid Karen Mandic and Diane Wilder a hundred dollars to housesit for a couple of hours. As he showed them round the house, he strangled them both and left their bodies in their car in a heavily wooded area. In January 1979, however, a woman called the police to complain about an abandoned car and they found the bodies of the two young women and vital evidence that tied Bianchi to the crime. In his home, they found jewellery belonging to Yolanda Washington and Kimberly Martin. The game was up.

When Bianchi was arrested, he claimed the killings had been carried out by one of his multiple personalities and, under hypnosis, his evil personality, 'Steve Walker' introduced himself. This character confessed to the murders and implicated Angelo Buono. The doctors were convinced at this point that Bianchi was indeed suffering from multiple personality syndrome. One was suspicious, however, especially when the Steve personality used 'he' instead of 'I'. He decided to test him. He told Kenny that it was unusual for there to be just one other personality. Kenny responded almost immediately by inventing another personality called Billy, and so was found to be faking it. Confronted with this fact, he agreed to testify against Buono in return for being spared the death penalty.

Explaining their methods, he told how he and Buono would pretend to be police officers and would tell prostitutes that they were being taken to a police station to be booked. Or, they would simply ask for directions and grab their victim. All were raped and strangled; some were tortured.

Before he went on trial, Bianchi dreamed up a scheme with Veronica Lynn Compton, with whom he had been corresponding from his prison cell. Compton offered to kill a woman and place Bianchi's semen at the scene, showing that the Hillside Strangler was still operating, thus causing confusion. He smuggled his semen to her in a rubber glove hidden in a book. She fluffed the attempt at murder, however, when her victim fought back, and was arrested and convicted in Washington in October 1980.

At Buono's trial in 1981, Bianchi agreed that he had faked multiple personality disorder and claimed not to know whether he had been telling the truth when he said Buono had been involved in the murders. He said he was not even sure that he was guilty. Buono was re-tried in

1982 and was convicted of nine murders, but was not sentenced to death. He died of a heart attack, aged sixty-seven, in Calipatria State Prison on September 21, 2002.

Kenneth Bianchi was given to two life sentences in the state of Washington. He was immediately transferred to California where he was sentenced to additional life terms. There he remains at the age of fifty-six.

DOCTOR CRIPPEN

Hawley Harvey Crippen was born in Coldwater, Michigan in the United States in 1862 to Andresee Skinner and Myron Augustus Crippen, a fairly prosperous couple who ran a dry goods store. As a child, Crippen had always wanted to be a doctor and by the age of twenty-one he had achieved his ambition, graduating from the University of Michigan before gaining an MD degree from the Homeopathic Hospital in Cleveland. He also received a diploma from the Ophthalmic Hospital in New York as an eye and ear specialist. Around this time, Crippen travelled to England with the intention of improving his knowledge of medicine, but discovered that he was insufficiently qualified to practise in the United Kingdom. Returning to the United States he worked in a number of different cities, and by the early 1890s he was married to Charlotte Bell, an Irish nurse. They had a son, Otto, but when his wife died of apoplexy in January, 1892, the boy was sent to live with his grandmother. He would never see his father again.

Not long after, back in New York, Crippen took the plunge again, marrying a nineteen-year-old girl who went by the name of Cora Turner. She was actually of Russian-German parentage and her rather more exotic real name was Kunigunde Mackamotsi. Cora had left home at the age of sixteen and had launched herself into a theatrical career, using her not inconsiderable sexual charms to get on. She had taken the stage name Belle Elmore. Critically, though, her talent was fairly negligible and her career never really amounted to very much. For Crippen, this larger-than-life character made for an unlikely mate; his upbringing had been rigidly Protestant and her life was far removed from his. For Cora, however, Crippen's status as a doctor offered a chance of wealth and respectability.

But Crippen's promise was largely unfulfilled. Homeopathy fell from favour with the American public and his income suffered as a result. He had to take a job with a mail-order company, Munyon's Homeopathic Remedies, and Belle became concerned that they would no longer be able to afford the acting and singing lessons she needed to achieve her dreams of being a star. Crippen fell on his feet, though, and his hard work impressed his superiors. Moreover, mail-order businesses were taking off in America and so he progressed. In 1895 he was promoted to general manager for the Philadelphia area and in 1897 he was given the responsibility of opening a Munyon office in London.

At first, Cora remained in Philadelphia, still enjoying numerous affairs, while Crippen set about organising their lives in London. She continued to collect diamonds and pink frilly clothes and Crippen had no choice but to put up with it. Scandal was, after all, unthinkable.

When she finally arrived in London, the couple lived in South Crescent, just off Tottenham Court Road, before decamping to Store Street, close to the British Museum. But Munyon's business began to struggle and Crippen was finally fired in 1899. The Crippens had to sacrifice their standard of living, which did not please Belle/Cora, and they moved from fashionable Piccadilly to down-at-heel Bloomsbury.

While working for Munyon's, Crippen had his fingers in several other pies and it was while working for a business called Yale Tooth Specialists that he took on a young typist called Ethel le Neve. It was not the first time he had met her; the pair had worked together before and were attracted to one another. It may have been because Ethel was the antithesis of the brash Belle. She was demure and quiet, and by 1903 there is no doubt that they were heavily involved with one another, although Crippen's strict Protestant morality prohibited him from making their relationship a physical one.

The Crippens relocated to a house in Camden Town, 39 Hilldrop Crescent, and Belle continued to work as a music hall performer, achieving some success. She became Treasurer of the Music Hall Ladies Guild and was described as vivacious and well-dressed. Her hair was dyed auburn and her New York accent added an exotic touch. Crippen, on the other hand, was a small, mild-mannered individual, rather dapper with a high forehead and prominent eyes blinking behind gold-rimmed spectacles.

The two began to lead separate lives and supplemented their income by taking in lodgers at Hilldrop Crescent. One night, Crippen came home to find Belle in bed with one. It was probably around this time that his relationship with Ethel became a physical one.

By December 1909, Belle had just about had enough of her insipid little husband. She was aware that he was having an affair with le Neve; her friends had reported seeing the couple having dinner together. Then, when Ethel fell pregnant Belle again found out through her friends. However, before Crippen could demand a divorce, Ethel had a miscarriage.

The marriage was now beyond repair and life at Hilldrop Crescent was intolerable. Crippen and Belle argued constantly, with Belle threatening to ruin his good name by spreading gossip about his relationship with le

Neve. When she announced that she was leaving him he should have been delighted, but Belle also let him know that she was planning to clean out their bank account and take all of their savings with her. She confirmed this by providing notice of withdrawal to the bank.

On the evening of January 31, the Crippens had dinner guests, a retired music hall performer called Martinetti and his wife. Following dinner, the two couples played several hands of whist and the Martinettis did not leave until around 1.30 a.m. on February 1. It would be the last time anyone would see Belle Elmore alive.

The exact events of that night have never been entirely clear, but at Crippen's trial it was surmised that he had intended to poison Belle with an overdose of a sedative, hyoscine hydrobromide, that he had purchased some weeks previously. Instead of becoming sedated, however, it was thought that Belle became hyperactive and extremely noisy. Panicking, and desperate to keep her quiet, Crippen shot her. Neighbours heard the sound of the gun going off but merely thought it was a door slamming.

Crippen's plan to pretend that Belle had suffered an overdose was in tatters. He decided to hide her corpse in the cellar of the house, but first he dissected her body, removing her long bones and ribs. These he burned in the kitchen fire. It is also thought that he removed her internal organs and dissolved them in a bath of acid. He removed her head and remaining organs and dumped these in a weighted sack in a nearby canal. What was left of Belle Elmore was buried beneath the brick floor in the cellar.

Next day, he went to work as normal, by this time in a dental practice. He told le Neve that Belle had finally left him and, later that day, pawned some jewellery, receiving £80 for it. Ethel le Neve spent that night at 39 Hilldrop Crescent.

A couple of days later, on February 3, the Secretary of the Music Hall Ladies Guild was in receipt of a letter, signed 'Belle Elmore'. In it, Belle resigned from her position as Honorary Treasurer, claiming that the illness of a family member back in the United States meant she had to return there. The handwriting, however, was not that of Belle Elmore.

Around this time, Crippen paid another visit to the pawnbroker, leaving with £115 this time. On February 20, 1910, he turned up at the ball of the Music Hall Ladies Benevolent Fund, accompanied by Ethel le Neve who was noticed to be wearing a brooch that belonged to Belle. The suspicions of the ladies of the Guild, already aroused, now went into overdrive.

On March 12, le Neve moved into the house in Hilldrop Crescent and around this time, Crippen gave his landlord three months' notice of his intention to move out. Belle's friend, Mrs Martinetti, was informed by Crippen that he had received news that his wife had become seriously ill in America and was not expected to live. He told her that he was going to take a holiday in France if she died. Unsurprisingly, she thought this was odd behaviour.

Thus, on March 24, 1910, Mrs Martinetti received a telegram sent from London's Victoria Station announcing that 'Belle died yesterday at 6.00 p.m.'. Crippen and le Neve had sent it shortly before boarding the boat train to Dieppe.

On his return, Crippen had to somehow deal with the fact that Belle's friends wanted to send tokens of remembrance to her funeral. He got round this by telling them that her ashes were being returned to England and the tokens would arrive too late. Meanwhile, Ethel le Neve was swanning around in Belle's furs and jewellery, something that was considered to be in very poor taste.

All of this proved too much for the ladies of the Guild and Belle's friends. They took their suspicions to Chief Inspector Walter Dew at Scotland Yard, known as 'the blue serge' because of the blue suit he seemed to wear every day. However, he told them that there was not enough evidence to proceed with an inquiry. But this did not stop them from making their own enquiries and they turned up some useful information. Firstly, shipping records told them that there had been no sailing for America on the day Crippen had said Belle had left. Secondly, no one called Crippen had died in California at the time Crippen said she had.

Dew had no choice but to call on Crippen and question him. But the doctor had already prepared his story and admitted to Dew that, yes, he had lied about his wife's death, but only to avoid scandal; his wife had actually left him for an American boxer called Bruce Miller. Dew believed him, but Crippen was, unaccountably, thrown into a blind panic. He immediately went to Ethel and told her about the policeman's visit and the pair decided to leave the country until the scandal had died down. The next day they left for Antwerp, planning to take a boat from there to Quebec in Canada.

Dew called round to Crippen's dental practice on July 11, to discover that Crippen and le Neve had disappeared. He immediately ordered a search of the house in Hilldrop Crescent. It uncovered the grisly remains of Belle Elmore in the cellar. A warrant was issued for the arrest of Hawley Harvey Crippen and Ethel le Neve.

The case immediately became a huge news story in the British press and pictures of the fugitive couple also appeared in the European papers. Knowing the police were looking for them, Crippen and le Neve, in disguise, boarded the SS Montrose, bound for Canada, on July 20. He was not wearing his spectacles, he had shaved off his moustache, had grown a beard and was going by the name of Mr Robinson. She disguised herself, very badly, as his young son. In fact, the disguise was so bad that it drew the attention of fellow passengers and especially that of the ship's captain, Captain Kendall, who recognised the pair from newspaper photos.

The SS *Montrose* was one of the few liners of the time fitted with a wireless telegraph and on July 22, Captain Kendall sent a telegram to the White Star Line in Liverpool informing them that he believed the fugitives were on board his ship. His message read: 'Have strong suspicions that Crippen – London cellar murderer and accomplice are among Saloon passengers. Moustache taken off – growing beard. Accomplice dressed as boy. Voice manner and build undoubtedly a girl.' This was the first time that this new technology had been used to catch a criminal. Chief Inspector Dew was informed immediately and boarded the SS *Laurentic*, a faster ship than the *Montrose*, leaving Liverpool for Quebec the next day.

The newspapers went into a frenzy, page after page filled with the story of Belle, le Neve and Crippen. They avidly followed the chase across the Atlantic.

The *Laurentic* arrived in Quebec a day before the

*Mon*trose and as the *Montrose* approached Father Point, where pilots were to be taken on board, Dew boarded the vessel, disguised as a pilot. On approaching Crippen and removing his pilot's hat, he said: 'Good afternoon Dr. Crippen, remember me? I'm Inspector Dew with Scotland Yard.'

Shocked, Crippen could only reply: 'Thank God it's over', holding out his wrists for the handcuffs.

In October 1910, at the Old Bailey, Crippen and Ethel were tried separately. Crippen immediately scuppered his chances by refusing to allow Ethel to be called as a witness for the defence, seeking to protect her reputation. He might also have avoided the death penalty if he had pleaded guilty and had used Belle's serial adultery in his defence. The prosecuting counsel, R.C. Muir QC, relied on the lies Crippen told to Belle's friends and the police.

Thus, on October 22, it took the jury a mere twenty-two minutes to return a guilty verdict. Crippen was sentenced to death by hanging.

Things went better for Ethel le Neve. She was charged with being an accessory to murder but it took the jury only twelve minutes to find her not guilty.

Crippen was to be hung on November 23, 1910 and, until that day, Ethel visited him every day in his cell, without fail. On the day of his execution he asked that the letters she had written to him while he had been incarcerated and a photograph of her, be buried with him.

She left the country that day, by ship for New York. She settled in Toronto for five years before returning to the UK where she married and lived quietly in Croydon. She died in 1967, aged eighty-four.

The house at 39 Hilldrop Crescent remained un-occupied for thirty years and was destroyed in a bombing raid during World War II.

ANDREI CHIKATILO

Only bones remained. A few pieces of skin clung here and there and patches of matted black hair hung from the skull. It lay amidst the spindly trees of a lespolosa, a forested strip of land, not far from the village of Novocherkassk in the Rostov-on-Don area of the USSR. The corpse lay on its back, the head turned to one side. The victim was a female. She had been stabbed many times in an apparently frenzied attack, and had been gouged with a knife in the pelvic area. Disturbingly, she had also been stabbed in the eyes.

Major Mikhail Fetisov, the region's chief detective, determined that the victim was a missing thirteen-year-old girl, Lyubov Biryuk. Unfortunately, that was about as much as could be gleaned from the scene. It looked like that most difficult of cases – a random attack.

The police started to look for suspects amongst the usual groupings – people suffering from mental illness and known sex offenders. One man, learning that he was a suspect, promptly hung himself and the police breathed a sigh of relief, believing they had their man.

Two months later, however, another pile of bones was discovered. It was near the railway station at Shakhty. The victim, a woman, had received multiple stab wounds and, once again, the killer had attacked the eyes.

A month passed before a soldier, gathering firewood, stumbled across the body of yet another woman. She had been mutilated in the same way.

There was little doubt that a serial killer was on the loose. But this was the Soviet Union and such things did not happen there. Serial killers were a manifestation of Western decadence, after all. Consequently, the press were not briefed and no warning was given to people to take precautions. Instead, a special task force was assembled. It included a second lieutenant from the criminology lab, thirty-seven-year-old Viktor Burakov, an expert in the analysis of crime scenes and physical evidence. This case would consume him for the next few years.

Victim number four turned up that same month, although she had been killed about six months previously. The body, a woman again, bore the same wounds as the others.

What was the issue with the eyes, Burakov and the team wondered? What it did suggest is that the 'Maniac', as they had started to call him, did not just kill and run; he spent time with the victims after they were dead. He was sexually motivated and his hunger for the kill seemed to be increasing. Still only a very few in the police force and high-ranking officials were aware of what was really happening.

Ten-year-old Olga Stalmachenok had gone missing in the town of Novoshakhtinsk, on her way to piano lessons. Now when someone went missing, everyone feared the worst and sure enough it happened, although it took four months for her body to turn up. This attack had been particularly frenetic, the knife having been pushed into the girl's body countless times, to the extent that it moved her internal organs around inside the body. The heart, lungs and sexual organs had received particular attention and, as usual, the eyes were gouged. Olga's parents had been sent a card while she was missing, signed 'the Black Cat Sadist', and police began to check the handwriting against everyone in the town, a thankless and, ultimately, pointless task. They looked yet again at sex offenders and the mentally ill.

Nothing happened for four months, but a group of boys playing in a lespolosa close to Rostov, found the remains of a thirteen-year-old girl who had suffered from Down's Syndrome, in a gully. As if things had not been bad enough, to harm a child with such a condition seemed to take this killer's cruelty to a new level of degradation.

Suddenly, however, someone was arrested. Nineteen-year-old Yuri Kalenik had spent years in a home for children with special needs, but now worked in the construction industry. He was arrested on the basis of an accusation by an inhabitant of the home, but everyone was convinced they had the Maniac. Kalenik, at first, denied the charges. Then, in order to stop the beating he was taking, he confessed to all the murders, even adding some others that had been carried out locally.

Burakov interrogated Kalenik. He seemed a likely candidate. After all, he had a history of mental problems and also used public transport, just like the Maniac. He also led the team to the sites of several of the murders, but as far as Burakov could make out he was almost being guided to them by a team of policemen willing him to be their murderer. Burakov was convinced Kalenik was responding to coercion.

In the meantime, the body of another young woman was discovered. The mutilation of the body and the eyes were similar, but this time her nipples had been bitten off. She had been there for several months. So, Kalenik could have murdered this girl, but, unfortunately for the police, not the one found on October 20. She had been killed three days earlier, while the boy had been in custody.

This woman had been disembowelled, but, strangely, the organs were nowhere to be found. He had taken them away with him. Unusually the eyes had not been attacked. Was it the same killer?

A few weeks later another body was found. She had been killed months before and the killing bore the hallmarks of the Maniac. Number ten was a fourteen-year-old boy, found near railway lines. He had been stabbed no fewer than seventy times and he had been castrated and raped. During it all, the killer had gone to a place nearby and had a bowel movement. Kalenik was in the clear.

Another boy, another former pupil of a home for children with special needs, had apparently taken the same train as the dead boy. Mikhail Tyapin was a big and powerful young man who could barely speak. Nonetheless, the police got him to talk and obtained yet another confession. Tyapin, like Kalenik, had a violent fantasy life and, like him, claimed responsibility for other murders in the area. What he failed to mention, though, was the damage to the eyes.

Semen found in the murdered boy's anus provided them with a break. They could find the killer's blood type from it. Now they were able to eliminate all the suspects they had had so far; their blood did not match. The lab, however, announced that it had mixed up the sample and that it did, indeed, match Mikhail Tyapin. Now they were convinced they had their killer. Or at least, they would have been, if the killer had not carried on killing.

Throughout 1984, woods in the region disgorged bodies, lots of them. And they all bore similar wounds. One of them was an eighteen-year-old and on her clothing were semen and blood, left, presumably, by the killer who it seems had masturbated over her dead body. A forensics expert from Moscow confirmed that two semen specimens found on different bodies were type AB and that immediately eliminated every suspect to date. He was still out there.

In March he struck again, killing ten-year-old Dmitri Ptashnikov. He cut off the tip of his tongue and his penis. Close to the body was a large footprint, the same size thirteen that had been found at an earlier scene. For the first time, however, he was seen. A tall, hollow-cheeked man with a stiff-kneed gait and wearing glasses had followed the boy.

Victims followed in quick succession, one killed by a hammer blow, another stabbed thirty-nine times with a kitchen knife; a mother and daughter killed at the same time; the eyes were stabbed and now sometimes the upper lip and nose were cut off and deposited in the corpse's mouth or stomach. The death toll rose to at least twenty-four.

The police were lost and confused. They split into factions and Burakov argued with his superiors. Two hundred officers were by this time working on the case.

They worked undercover at bus and train stations, they walked the streets and parks on the lookout for the tall, hollow-cheeked man.

At Rostov bus station an older man was spotted taking an interest in a young girl. The undercover officer became suspicious and brought him in for questioning. It was a man called Andrei Chikatilo, the manager of a Shakhty machinery supply company. When questioned about his behaviour, he told police that he had once been a teacher and missed the company of the young. They let him go.

He was followed, however, and when he continued to act suspiciously, accosting women and even receiving oral sex from a prostitute in the street, he was picked up. In his briefcase was a jar of Vaseline, a long knife, a length of rope and a grimy towel. Hardly the accoutrements of a businessman.

But his blood type was A and not AB. They held him for a few days, but he persisted in his denials. There was nothing untoward in his background and he was a member of the Party. He was released again.

Burakov, in the meantime, asked a psychiatrist, Dr Bukhanovsky, to create a profile of the killer. He was a sexual deviant, the psychiatrist said, twenty-five to fifty years old and around five feet ten in height. He was sexually inadequate to the extent that he had to mutilate the corpses to achieve arousal. He was a sadist. He damaged the victims' eyes to stop them looking at him. He was a loner and he definitely worked alone. Bukhanovsky named him 'Citizen X'.

The pressure was on the officers, but all went quiet. Only one body in ten months, a woman killed near Moscow. Had the Maniac moved there?

Then, in August 1985, a dead woman, bearing the usual marks, was found near an airport. Officers checked flights and tickets, but found nothing. Checking other murders in the capital, however, they found three murders of young boys that seemed in all likelihood to have been committed by the man they were looking for – all had been raped and one had been decapitated.

But soon they were back at Shakhty where another young woman was found near the bus station, her mouth stuffed with leaves in the same way as one of the dead women in Moscow. Officers continued to work the train and bus stations, but without success.

Another profile of the killer provided some stark facts. Stabbing his victims was for him a way to enter them sexually. He might masturbate, either spontaneously or with his hand. He might damage the eyes because he believed the old superstition that the image of a killer is left on his victims' eyes. He cut women's sexual organs as a means of establishing control over them. Organs were often missing; he might have eaten them. He cut boys' sexual organs off to make them appear feminine. He would have had a difficult childhood, and had a vibrant fantasy life and a perverse response to sexuality.

Nothing happened until July and August, 1986, when a couple of women's bodies turned up, the second buried with only a hand pointing up out of the earth.

Burakov cracked under the pressure towards the end of 1986 and spent time in hospital. The killer, too, took a rest and no bodies were found until April 1988. A woman was discovered, the tip of her nose sliced off and her skull smashed. Her eyes had not been touched, however. Then a nineteen-year-old boy was found in May with his penis cut off. He had been seen entering the woods with a middle-aged man with gold teeth and a sports bag. Even with that lead, they turned up nothing and in April 1989 another boy's body was found and in July an eight-year-old boy. Elena Varga was killed in August and that same week, ten-year-old Aleksei Khobotov went missing, his body showing up four months later. A ten-year-old boy was found with his tongue bitten off; in July 1990, a thirteen-year-old was discovered mutilated in the botanical gardens. In fact there were thirty-two victims in a period of eight years.

The fall of communism meant newspapers were now free to report on the case and there was a feeding frenzy with officials threatening each other and people becoming desperate for the case to be solved and the killing to stop. When an eleven-year-old was stabbed forty-two times and castrated, the public were outraged.

Another couple of sixteen-year-old boys were murdered before Burakov's work at the stations, checking the names of passengers, began to bear fruit. Over half a million people had been investigated up to this point, but one name stood out.

Andrei Chikatilo had been at the station the day one of the recent murders had been carried out nearby. He had been seen emerging from the woods and washing his hands. On his cheek had been a red smear, his finger had been cut and his coat was covered in twigs. When checked out, it turned out he had resigned from a teaching job after molesting students. His travel records coincided with several murders and there had been no deaths while he had spent time in prison in 1984.

Chikatilo was arrested and a search of his house revealed twenty-three knives, but nothing linking him with his victims. At first, Chikatilo denied everything, but then he began to admit to 'sexual weakness' and 'perverse sexual activity', and to the fact that he was impotent.

He was persuaded that it would be best for him to admit everything but claim insanity. Days passed while

Chikatilo considered this, still denying he was the killer. Finally, however, he confessed, going through each of the thirty-six murders in detail. He explained that he was clearing the world of undesirables – vagrants, runaways and prostitutes. These were the people he killed. He told how he could not achieve an erection and used the knife as a penis substitute. He had also believed the story of the killer's image being imprinted on the victim's eyes, but had stopped believing it which explains why he stopped damaging the eyes at one point. He told how he could only get gratification if he committed violence. 'I had to see blood and wound the victims.' He talked about placing his semen inside a uterus that he had just removed and as he walked back through the woods, he would chew on it – 'the truffle of sexual murder', as he described it. He would tear at his victims' mouths with his teeth. He said it gave him an 'animal satisfaction' to chew or swallow nipples or testicles. In all, he confessed to fifty-six murders and said that being caught was a relief.

Why had he done it? Perhaps because of his chilling childhood: father a POW during World War II and desperate famine in Russia, a famine so bad that there were reported instances of cannibalism. Human flesh was bought and sold and Chikatilo was told by his mother that his ten-year-old brother had been taken and killed and eaten.

He was examined and found to be sane before being brought to a court in Rostov, where he was kept in a large iron cage. The court was full, some 250 people screaming at him when he was brought in. The trial was a fiasco and there was little doubt from day one that Chikatilo would be found guilty. His efforts at pretending to be mad, drooling and rolling his eyes, singing, speaking nonsense and claiming that he was being 'radiated' were to no avail.

He was found guilty on fifty-two counts of murder and five of molestation. The people in the courtroom cried out for him to be handed over to them so that they could do to him what he had done to his victims, and it is reported that the Japanese offered a million dollars for his brain so that they could study it.

However, on February 14, 1994, he was taken to a soundproofed room, told to face the wall and not turn round. He was then executed with a single shot behind the right ear.

ALBERT FISH

It was probably a good job that Delia Budd was illiterate because, in 1934, six years after her daughter, Grace, had been abducted, she received a letter containing these chilling words:

On Sunday June the 3, 1928 I called on you at 406 W 15 St. Brought you pot cheese–strawberries. We had lunch. Grace sat in my lap and kissed me. I made up my mind to eat her. On the pretense of taking her to a party. You said yes she could go. I took her to an empty house in Westchester I had already picked out. When we got there, I told her to remain outside. She picked wildflowers. I went upstairs and stripped all my clothes off. I knew if I did not I would get her blood on them. When all was ready I went to the window and called her. Then I hid in a closet until she was in the room. When she saw me all naked she began to cry and tried to run down the stairs. I grabbed her and she said she would tell her mamma. First I stripped her naked. How she did kick – bite and scratch. I choked her to death, then cut her in small pieces so I could take my meat to my rooms. Cook and eat it. How sweet and tender her little ass was roasted in the oven. It took me 9 days to eat her entire body. I did not fuck her tho I could of had I wished. She died a virgin.

The letter had been written by Albert Hamilton Fish, the man who had taken and killed Grace Budd. Fish, then fifty-eight years old, had arrived on the Budds' doorstep in May, 1928, pretending to be Frank Howard, a farmer from Farmingdale, New York. He was calling in response to an advert placed in the New York World by Edward Budd, Grace's eighteen-year-old brother. It read: 'Young man, 18, wishes position in country. Edward Budd, 406 West 15th Street.' Fish spun a story that he needed someone to work on his farm and Edward was eager for the work. Fish returned a few days later to confirm that Edward had the job and was asked to stay for lunch. While there, Fish befriended Grace. She sat on his lap at the dinner table. As he was about to leave, he said he was on his way to a children's birthday party at his sister's house and wondered whether Grace would like to accompany him. Grace's mother was unsure, but her husband Albert thought it would be fun for the girl and off Grace went with Albert Fish. It was the last they saw of their daughter.

Albert Fish was born Hamilton Fish in 1870 and his father was forty-three years older than his mother.

When his father died in 1875, the five-year-old Hamilton was put into St John's Orphanage by his mother. It was there that he changed his name to Albert to avoid the nickname 'Ham and Fish' that he had been given by the other children.

Life in the orphanage was harsh and cruel. There were regular beatings and whippings, but, perversely, Albert grew to enjoy the pain. He enjoyed it so much, in fact, that he would have erections for which the other children mocked him. His mother was able to look after him again when she found employment in 1879, but Albert was already scarred by his experiences at St John's. By the age of twelve, he was engaged in a homosexual relationship. His partner, a telegraph boy, introduced him to perverse practices such as coprophagia and drinking urine. He spent his weekends watching boys undress at the public baths.

Fish claimed that by 1890 he was working as a male prostitute in New York City and that he was raping young boys on a regular basis. In 1898 he married and six children followed. He was working as a house painter but was also molesting countless children, mostly boys under the age of six. At this time, he developed an interest in castration and tried it out on a man with whom he had been having a relationship; the man fled before Fish could carry it out.

In 1903, he was charged with embezzlement and was sent to Sing Sing. But it wasn't that much of a hardship for him as he could have sex with other inmates.

His life changed completely in 1917, when his wife ran off with another man. Fish began to behave even more strangely than before. He claimed to hear voices and once wrapped himself up in a carpet, saying he had been ordered to do so by Saint John. His children reported seeing him beat himself on his nude body with a nail-studded piece of wood until he was covered with blood. Once they saw him standing alone on a hill with his hands raised, shouting, 'I am Christ.'

He inserted needles into his body, in the area of the groin – twenty-nine were discovered by an X-ray following his eventual arrest – and inserted alcohol-covered balls of cotton wool into his anus; he would then ignite them. In this way, he thought he could cleanse himself of his sins.

Some four years prior to the abduction of Grace Budd, seven-year-old Francis McDonnell was playing with some friends near his home on Staten Island. His mother saw a man behaving oddly. He walked up and down the street, wringing his hands and talking to himself. She thought no more of him and went indoors. Later that same day, the same man lured Francis into some nearby woods. Next day his body was discovered, sexually brutalised, mutilated and strangled. It would be another ten years before they would discover who the killer was.

A year before Grace's murder, Fish abducted, tortured and killed another child, Billy Gaffney. Fish later confessed:

I brought him to the Riker Avenue dumps. There is a house that stands alone, not far from where I took him. I took the boy there. Stripped him naked and tied his hands and feet and gagged him with a piece of dirty rag I picked out of the dump. Then I burned his clothes. Threw his shoes in the dump. Then I walked back and took the trolley to 59 Street at 2 a.m. and walked from there home. Next day about 2 p.m., I took tools, a good heavy cat-o-nine tails. Home made. Short handle. Cut one of my belts in half, slit these halves in six strips about 8 inches long. I whipped his bare behind till the blood ran from his legs. I cut off his ears, nose, slit his mouth from ear to ear. Gouged out his eyes. He was dead then. I stuck the knife in his belly and held my mouth to his body and drank his blood. I picked up four old potato sacks and gathered a pile of stones. Then I cut him up. I had a grip with me. I put his nose, ears and a few slices of his belly in the grip. Then I cut him through the middle of his body. Just below the belly button. Then through his legs about two inches below his behind. I put this in my grip with a lot of paper. I cut off the head, feet, arms, hands and the legs below the knee. This I put in sacks weighed with stones, tied the ends and threw them into the pools of slimy water you will see all along the road going to North Beach. I came home with my meat. I had the front of his body I liked best. His monkey and pee wees and a nice little fat behind to roast in the oven and eat. I made a stew out of his ears, nose, pieces of his face and belly. I put onions, carrots, turnips, celery, salt and pepper. It was good. Then I split the cheeks of his behind open, cut off his monkey and pee wees and washed them first. I put strips of bacon on each cheek of his behind and put them in the oven. Then I picked 4 onions and when the meat had roasted about G hour, I poured about a pint of water over it for gravy and put in the onions. At frequent intervals I basted his behind with a wooden spoon. So the meat would be nice and juicy. In about 2 hours, it was nice and brown, cooked through. I never ate any roast turkey that tasted half as good as his sweet fat little behind did. I ate every bit of the meat in about four days. His little monkey was as sweet as a nut, but his pee-wees I could not chew. Threw them in the toilet.

Ultimately, it was Fish's arrogance that betrayed him. The letter he wrote to Mrs Budd was delivered in an envelope that bore the logo of the New York Private Chauffeurs' Benevolent Association. It turned out that a janitor of the association had left some stationery in a boarding house when he had moved out. Albert Fish had moved in after him but, the landlady told police, he had also since moved out. However, he had been expecting some money to be sent and had asked her to hold on to the cheque for him until he could call round to collect it. Detective William F. King waited at the house and when Fish arrived, asked him to accompany him to police HQ to answer some questions. Fish lunged at King with a razor, but the policeman easily overpowered him and arrested him.

Fish confessed to the premeditated murder of Grace Budd, launching a debate as to whether he was sane that raged both before his trial and throughout it. However, he was found to be both sane and guilty and was sentenced to death. He thanked the judge for his death sentence and after sentencing confessed to the murder of Francis McDonnell. It is speculated that as well as the three murders that can be ascribed to Albert Fish with certainty, he may actually have murdered at least fifteen children and assaulted hundreds more over the years.

At Sing Sing on January 16, 1936, at 11.06 a.m., he was strapped into 'Old Sparky', the electric chair, and three minutes later, was dead. He is reported to have said that the execution would be 'the supreme thrill of my life'.

CARL PANZRAM

He was escorted from his cell at 5.55 a.m. on Friday, September 5, 1930, and led to the gallows where the witnesses waited, a few newspapermen and about a dozen guards. He was six feet tall and 200 pounds of muscle. On his left forearm was a large tattoo of a boat's anchor, on his right another anchor with an eagle and the head of a Chinese man; underneath his shirt, on his massive chest were two eagles with the words 'Liberty' and 'Justice' tattooed underneath their wings. His eyes were a cold steel-grey, and a thick black moustache covered his top lip, lending his face the appearance of a perpetual sneer. He ran up the thirteen steps to the platform and just before the marshals placed the hood over his head, he spat in the face of the hangman and growled: 'Hurry up you bastard; I could kill ten men while you're fooling around!'

The executioner obliged and by 6.03 a.m., Carl Panzram's lifeless body was swinging in the early morning breeze.

A few thousand words can barely do justice to the evil that Carl Panzram wrought on the world. He was a killing machine like no other, a man without conscience or compassion. 'I was so full of hate that there was no room in me for such feelings as love, pity, kindness or honour or decency,' he once said. 'My only regret is that I wasn't born dead or not at all.'

Born in 1891, he was the product of a poor farming family in Minnesota. His parents split up when he was seven and by the age of eleven he was in reform school, the notorious Red Wing, near St Paul, Minnesota. There, he was beaten, whipped, abused and sodomised on a regular basis and it was there that he learned to hate religion, viewing it as the cause of most of his troubles. In truth, though, he hated everyone and everything, especially prison where he spent a large proportion of his life.

Released from Redwing, he went back to the arduous life on the farm, working from dawn to dusk and receiving endless beatings from his brothers. At the age of fourteen, however, he had had enough and hopped a freight train. Life's harsh realities were never far away though, and not long afterwards, he was gang-raped by four hobos riding in the same freight wagon as him. Then, he was incarcerated for burglary for a year in Butte, Montana. In 1907, he and another inmate escaped and began robbing and stealing their way around the Midwest. For good measure, they also set fire to every church they saw.

Later that year, Panzram lied about his age and enlisted in the army. However, the discipline was alien to a rebellious nature such as his and before too long, he was up before a court martial on three counts of larceny. He was sentenced to a dishonourable discharge and three years' hard labour at the forbidding Fort Leavenworth Penitentiary in Kansas. He was just sixteen and once again found himself in a regime of beatings and torture. Prisoners were chained to fifty-pound metal balls and the days were spent breaking rocks.

Released in 1910, he spent the next few years drifting across Kansas, Texas and across the South- West to California. As before, he stole and burned wherever he went. 'I burned down old barns, sheds, fences, snow sheds or anything I could, and when I couldn't burn anything else I would set fire to the grass on the prairies, or the woods, anything and everything,' he wrote later. He also raped countless men on his travels. 'Whenever I met one that wasn't too rusty looking I would make him raise his hands and drop his pants. I wasn't very particular either. I rode them old and young, tall and short, white and black. It made no difference to me at all except that they were human beings.'

In Fresno, in 1911, he was arrested and sentenced to six months but escaped within thirty days. Shortly afterwards, he spent three months in jail in Dalles in Oregon before again breaking out. A week later he was arrested in Harrison, Idaho. During his first night, he set one of the prison buildings on fire and escaped with a host of other prisoners in the direction of Montana. There, he was imprisoned for burglary and sentenced to a year in Montana State Prison at Deer Lodge. By November 1913 he had escaped, but was recaptured a week later.

His time at Deer Lodge was monotonous, but Panzram stayed busy. 'At that place I got to be an experienced wolf,' he said. 'I would start the morning with sodomy, work as hard at it as I could all day and sometimes half the night.' Unusually, he served his full sentence, including an extra year for escaping, eventually being released in 1915.

A few months later, he was arrested for larceny and sentenced to seven years at the Oregon State Penitentiary at Salem, another harsh and cruel correctional institute. Beatings and torture were rife and prisoners would be hung from rafters for hours on end. Panzram was hung on several occasions, once for ten hours a day for two days.

He escaped, of course, but was recaptured. Then, he left Salem for good by sawing through his cell bars with a hacksaw blade. He hopped a freight train out of the North-West, shaved his moustache and changed his name to John O'Leary. Once again, he began to leave a trail of burglary and burned churches in his wake.

He spent the summer of 1920 in New Haven, Connecticut, stealing and raping young men. On one occasion, he broke into a large house. It turned out to be the house of William H. Taft, former president of the United States. Panzram got away with goods and bonds worth around $3,000, money he used to buy a yacht, the Akista, which he sailed along the Connecticut coast, breaking into other boats en route. His other favourite pastimes of rape and murder were never far from his thoughts. 'I figured it would be a good plan to hire a few sailors to work for me, get them out to my yacht, get them drunk, commit sodomy on them, rob them and then kill them. This I done.' He would take on a couple of sailors, get them drunk, shoot them when they were asleep and drop their bodies into the sea. He killed around ten men in this way in three weeks, but in late August the Akista was sunk in a storm.

Following yet another jail sentence – six months for burglary and possession of a handgun – he was arrested again but jumped bail and stowed away on a ship bound for Anngola on Africa's west coast. There he was employed by the Sinclair Oil Company, but before too long he was up to his old tricks, raping and killing an eleven year-old boy. 'A little nigger boy about eleven or twelve years old came bumming around,' he wrote. He killed him by smashing his skull with a boulder. 'I left him there, but first I committed sodomy on him and then I killed him. His brains were coming out of his ears when I left him and he will never be any deader.'

Some weeks later, in the Congo, he hired six natives to take him crocodile hunting. As they paddled down-river, Panzram shot them all in the back and fed them to the crocodiles. He realised that too many people knew he had hired the men and had to flee, stowing away on a ship bound for Lisbon. Another ship took him back to the United States. It was 1922 and he was thirty-one.

In July of that year, while he was in Salem Massachusetts, thinking about stealing another boat, he saw a twelve year-old boy who was running an errand. George McMahon was Panzram's next victim. 'I grabbed him by the arm and told him I was going to kill him,' he confessed later. 'I stayed with the boy about three hours. During that time, I committed sodomy on the boy six times, and then I killed him by beating his brains out with a rock . . . I had stuffed down his throat several sheets of paper out of a magazine.' He was seen by a couple of witnesses who recognised him years later when he was arrested for the last time.

In Providence, Rhode Island, in the summer of 1923, Panzram stole a boat and sailed the coastline, stealing from boats at their moorings. He took on board a boy that he had befriended, George Walosin, and raped him that night. He tried to sell the boat and found a buyer but after a few drinks on board, he shot the man and threw him overboard. Next day, Walosin, who had witnessed the murder, jumped ship and told police in Yonkers that he had been sexually assaulted by Panzram.

A few days later, police boarded the yacht and arrested him on charges of sodomy, burglary and robbery. Facing more prison time, Panzram told his lawyer that if he could get him out of jail, he would let him have the boat. The lawyer arranged bail and Panzram was free. The yacht was found to be stolen, of course, and the lawyer was none too pleased to learn that he had worked for nothing.

Hoping to steal another boat and make his way to South America, Panzram headed for New London on the familiar Connecticut coast. There, searching for someone to mug, he found a boy begging. He dragged him into some woods and raped and strangled him.

Back in Manhattan, a short time after, he was taken on as a bathroom steward on the US Army Transport ship, US Grant, which was about to leave for China. The United States would not be free of him just yet, however.

Before the ship had even left port, he was thrown off for being drunk and fighting with other members of the crew.

He returned to Connecticut, arriving in the sleepy village of Larchmont on the south shore of Westchester County, looking for someone to rob. The Larchmont train depot looked like a good bet. Dozens of suitcases, belonging to passengers travelling on the next day's train, had been left in a room there. Panzram surmised there would be rich pickings in them. However, while he was rifling through the cases, a passing policeman spied him through a window. After a struggle he was arrested and taken into custody.

In the Larchmont village jail, Panzram began to confess to crimes. He told police interviewing him that he was a fugitive from prison in Oregon where he had been serving a seventeen-year sentence for shooting a police officer. They wired the penitentiary in Oregon who confirmed that Jeff Baldwin – the name Panzram had gone under – was, indeed, very much wanted in that state. There was even a $500 dollar reward for information leading to his capture. Panzram is reported to have tried to claim the reward.

Panzram was sentenced to five years in Connecticut, taken to Sing Sing prison and then moved on to the notorious Dannemora prison, one of the most brutal in the United States where some of the nation's most hardened criminals were incarcerated. Again, beatings, whippings and torture were the order of the day.

Within weeks guards found a firebomb that Panzram had made and not long after he attacked a guard who had been particularly brutal towards him, hitting him on the back of the head with a heavy implement while he slept. He tried to escape by jumping from a prison wall, but the thirty feet drop broke both his legs and ankles and damaged his spine. He was merely dumped in his cell without any kind of medical attention.

At this time, Panzram was fantasising about killing as many people as he could. He dreamt of blowing up a railway tunnel or dynamiting a bridge in New York. He plotted to poison the water supply in the nearby town of Dannemora, killing the population of the entire town.

In July 1928, he was released, bitter, crippled and even more insane than when he had arrived at Dannemora. He wanted to take revenge on the world for the way he had been treated. He resumed his previous existence, committing numerous robberies and killing at least one man. He was arrested again, in Washington DC, but for the first time in years gave his real name and his string of crimes began to emerge. One policeman asked him what his crime was. 'I reform people,' was the reply.

He tried to escape, of course, but was caught and

punished by being hoisted with his arms tied to a rafter above his head so that his toes just touched the ground. He was left like that for a day and a half, being beaten as he hung there. At some point he began to confess to the murder of young boys and talked about how much he enjoyed killing them.

One of the guards at Dannemora befriended Panzram and he agreed to write his life story for him. Over the next few weeks he spilled his sordid story onto paper provided by the guard, a 20,000-word confession detailing the thousands of crimes, numerous arrests and dozens of murders that had occupied him since Red Wing. He also reasoned that he had committed himself to a life of crime because of the way he had been treated. 'All my associates,' he wrote, 'all of my surroundings, the atmosphere of deceit, treachery, brutality, degeneracy, hypocrisy and everything that is bad and nothing that is good. Why am I what I am? I'll tell you why. I did not make myself what I am. Others had the making of me.'

He knew now there was no escape and, after being recognised as the killer of George McMahon, wrote in a letter to the District Attorney of Salem: 'I not only committed that murder but twenty-one besides and I assure you here and now that if I ever get free and have the opportunity I shall sure knock off another twenty-two!'

Panzram was sentenced to twenty-five years in the Federal Prison at Leavenworth, Kansas. He was almost back where it had all begun. The irony was not lost on him and, on hearing his sentence his face broke into a wide grin.

Arriving at the prison, he told the warden: 'I'll kill the first man that bothers me.' Sure enough, that's exactly what he did. He beat to death the supervisor of the laundry room in which he worked, a man who had, somewhat unwisely, treated him badly.

By now, his notoriety was widespread and the fact that he chose to defend himself during his trial, only added to this.

It was no great surprise that he was found guilty and sentenced to death by hanging. On hearing the sentence Panzram turned to the judge and said: 'I certainly want to thank you, judge, just let me get my fingers around your neck for sixty seconds and you'll never sit on another bench as judge!'

Panzram's body remained unclaimed after his hanging. It was dumped in a wheelbarrow and removed to the prison cemetery where it was buried in a grave marked only with the number '31614'.

'I hate all the f----ing human race,' he had written shortly before his execution. 'I get a kick out of murdering people.'

CHARLES
STARKWEATHER

Charles Starkweather stalks popular culture in much the same way as his hero, James Dean. The films, *The Sadist, Badlands, The Stand, Kalifornia* and, more recently, *Natural Born Killers,* as well as the Bruce Springsteen song, *Nebraska,* all make reference to or tell the story of the red-haired, slow-witted, bow-legged killer who slew eleven people during a road trip through Nebraska and Wyoming in 1958 with his girlfriend, Caril Ann Fugate.

Unlike most serial killers, there is nothing in Starkweather's upbringing that suggested he was going to turn into a murderer. He was undoubtedly born in hard times, in the town of Lincoln, Nebraska, in November 1938, but his parents, Guy and Helen, always managed to provide for their seven children and Starkweather did not recall growing up hungry or facing the kind of struggle to survive that some people did at the time. There was no abuse, no absent father, no booze, no drugs; just a well-behaved, clean-living, strong family unit. Guy was a quiet man, a carpenter, whose crippling arthritis and bad back sometimes led to bouts of unemployment, while Helen was a hard-working mother who sometimes supplemented her husband's income with work as a waitress.

School was another matter for young Charles, however. He was teased remorselessly for how he looked – he suffered from genu varus, a mild birth defect that caused his legs to be bowed – and the way he spoke; he also had a mild speech impediment. If that was not bad enough, he was a slow learner and never seemed to apply himself to his schoolwork. To make matters worse, it was discovered in his teens that he also suffered from severe myopia, or short-sightedness, making him almost blind.

Charles would escape to the gym, building up his body until he was strong enough to bully the bullies. Suddenly, this well-behaved boy from a good family turned into one of the town's most troubled and troublesome young men. As his friend Bob van Busch said: 'He could be mean as hell, cruel. If he saw some poor guy on the street who was bigger than he was, better looking, or better dressed, he'd try to take the poor bastard down to his size.'

It was around the time that James Dean was single-handedly inventing the moody American teenager on celluloid and Starkweather began to morph into Dean –

he dressed like him, and bought into the whole rebellion thing, body and soul. But Starkweather was, in reality, a seething mass of self-loathing; he saw himself as a failure, living in perpetual fear of being a loser with no future.

Caril Ann Fugate was just thirteen when she met Charles in 1957. Like Charles, she had a rebellious nature and was not a great scholar. She was a pretty girl with dark brown hair and an unpredictable temper and Charles immediately fell for her. He even left school so that he could work at the Western Newspaper Union warehouse near her school, loading and unloading trucks. He was not the most diligent of workers, however, and his boss at the time was distinctly unimpressed: 'Of all the employees in the warehouse, he was the dumbest man we had,' he later reported.

Meanwhile, the relationship between Charles and his father was deteriorating and when Caril crashed Charles's hotrod – insured by his father – Guy had had enough and threw Charles out of the house.

He moved into a rooming house and Caril became even more the centre of his world. He told friends that they were getting married and made up a story that she was pregnant. Her parents were not pleased when the story made its way back to them.

Starkweather took a job on a garbage truck, a job that only served to add to the desperate pessimism he felt about his life. It seemed to him that crime would provide the only way out of poverty and failure and he passed his time on the garbage truck planning bank robberies that would allow him to escape this life. During this time, a simple mantra ran through his head: 'Dead people are all on the same level.'

On November 30, 1957, while visiting a petrol station, Charles did not even have enough money to buy a stuffed toy dog for Caril. Robert Colvert, the twenty-one-year-old attendant, refused him credit and Charles resolved to take revenge.

He returned at three the next morning with a shotgun, but left the gun in the car when he went in to buy a pack of cigarettes from Colvert who was working on his own. Starkweather then drove off, but turned the car round and went back in for some chewing gum. Again, he left the gun in the car. He drove off again, but stopped the car a short distance away, put on a bandana and a hat to cover his red hair and walked back to the petrol station with the gun in a bag. Removing the gun, he held Covert up and took a hundred dollars from the cash register. He then made Colvert get into the car and drove him to a piece of wasteland. Colvert jumped him, trying to grab the gun, but it went off and Colvert fell to his knees. Starkweather blasted him in the head, making a widow of his young, pregnant wife. Telling Caril about the robbery later, he claimed that someone else had killed Colvert. She did not believe him.

The story of the murder made big headlines in the papers, but police believed the perpetrator to be a transient and it looked like Charles had got away with it. It made him feel empowered, someone who was beyond the normal laws and standards by which we live our lives. He felt like he could get away with anything.

Life, however, did not improve. He lost his job as a garbageman and was locked out of his room by his landlady when he failed to pay the rent. Meanwhile, Caril's family, as well as his own, were dead against their relationship. He was getting desperate.

On January 21, 1958, he drove to the squalid, litter-strewn hovel that was Caril's house, taking with him a borrowed .22 rifle and some ammunition. He later claimed that he had hoped to go hunting with Caril's stepfather, Marion Bartlett, with the aim of patching up their relationship. He also brought along a couple of discarded carpet samples he had found for Velda.

Velda opened the door. Also in the house were Marion and the couple's two-year-old daughter, Betty Jean. But it was not long before the talk developed into the same old argument. Velda did not want him to carry on seeing her daughter and Marion literally kicked him out of the house.

Starkweather found a payphone and called work to tell them that he was ill and would not be back for a few days. He then returned to the house to wait for Caril to come home from school. She argued with her parents on her return and, hearing the raised voices, Starkweather went back into the house. He claims that Velda began hitting him, screaming that he had got Caril pregnant. Starkweather went out and got his gun. When Marion threatened him with a clawhammer, Starkweather shot him in the head. Velda rushed him with a knife, he later claimed, and he shot her in the face. The baby was crying and when Velda, still alive, tried to reach it, he slammed the butt of the rifle into her head a couple of times. He went to the baby's bedroom to try to quieten her, but, unable to do so, threw Velda's knife at her, hitting her in the throat and killing her. He then returned to the room in which Marion was still moving around. Starkweather said later: 'I tried to stab him in the throat, but the knife wouldn't go in, and I just hit the top part of it with my hand and it went in.'

He dragged Velda's body to the outhouse and stuffed her down the open toilet. Meanwhile, the baby's body was put in a box in the outhouse and Marion was left in the chicken coop. Then Charlie and Caril cleaned up the mess and spent the remainder of the evening drinking Pepsi and eating crisps. For almost a week they stayed there, the corpses rotting outside. Visitors were turned away by a note Caril had pinned to the door telling people to stay away as everyone inside had flu.

Eventually, people became suspicious and the police were called but Caril fobbed them off with the flu story. When Caril's grandmother asked the police to visit again, they searched inside the house but found nothing untoward. Later that day, Bob van Busch and his brother made a search of the property and discovered the grisly remains of Velda, Marion and Betty. By this time, Charlie and Caril were long gone.

They headed for a farm, twenty miles from Lincoln, belonging to a Starkweather family friend, August Meyer, arriving there on January 27. The circumstances are unknown, but Starkweather shot Meyer in the head, claiming later, as he did for many of his killings, that it was in self-defence. They took his money and guns, had a meal and fell asleep.

The following day, their car having become stuck in the deep mud of a dirt track, they hitched a ride from seventeen-year-old Robert Jensen and sixteen-year-old Carol King. Before too long, Starkweather was holding them at gunpoint, demanding money. He made Jensen drive back to the Meyer farm where he fired six bullets into his head. Carol was shot once and then stabbed repeatedly in the abdomen and pubic area. When she was found, her jeans and panties were round her ankles, but she had not been raped. The couple disagreed later about Caril's role in the killings. She claimed she was sitting in the car during the shootings and mutilation, while he said she actually shot the girl when he was absent from the scene and helped in the mutilation of her body as she was jealous of Starkweather's attraction to her.

Bizarrely, the couple now drove back to Lincoln where everyone was looking for them. They even drove past Caril's house to see whether the bodies had been found, but the police cars outside the house were enough to tell them. They then slept in the car in another, more affluent part of town. By the time they awoke on January 29, the other three bodies had been found and a huge manhunt was under way.

Forty-seven-year-old C. Lauer Ward, president of the Capital Bridge and Capital Steel companies, was a good friend of the governor of Nebraska. That morning, his wife Clara was at home with Lillian Fencl, their hard-of-hearing, fifty-one-year-old maid.

Lillian opened the door to Charlie holding a gun. He soon realised she could not hear very well and wrote notes to tell her what he wanted. When Clara came into the kitchen to see what had happened to breakfast, Charlie assured her that nothing bad was going to happen. He called Caril in and she had some coffee and fell asleep in the library while Charlie ate breakfast.

Later, when Clara went upstairs to change her shoes, Starkweather followed her. He claimed she had a gun which she fired, missing him. After throwing a knife at her which stuck in her back, he stabbed her repeatedly in the neck and chest.

He then called his father and told him to tell Bob van Busch that he was going to kill him because he had been interfering in his relationship with Caril, and followed this with a letter addressed to 'the law only', an attempt to justify his and Caril's actions. 'I and Caril are sorry for what has happen,' he wrote. 'Cause I have hurt every body cause of it and so has caril. But I'n saying one thing every body than cane out there was luckie there not dead even caril's sister.'

They took Ward's black 1956 Packard, loaded it with food and got ready to leave, but not before shooting dead C. Lauer Ward when he came home from work that evening. Lillian Fencl was then tied to a bed and stabbed to death. Charlie later said Caril killed her but Caril blamed him. The bodies were discovered the next day and Ward's friend, Governor Anderson, called out the National Guard. Jeeps, armed with mounted machine guns, began to patrol the streets and parents taking their children to school carried guns. Meanwhile, in the sky, spotter planes scrutinised the roads below for the black Packard.

Starkweather and Caril now headed for Washington State, crossing into Wyoming on the morning of the 30th. They wanted to change cars and came upon a travelling shoe salesman from Montana, Merle Collison, asleep in his Buick at the side of the highway. He was shot in the head, neck, arm and leg. Charlie, gallant as ever, later blamed Caril for it.

But he was unable to work out how to release the car's emergency break and when a young geologist innocently stopped to offer help, Charlie thanked him by pulling his gun on him and telling him if he did not find out how to release the break, he would be killed. The geologist realised that the man seated next to Starkweather was in fact dead and tried to wrestle the weapon away from Starkweather. By some strange coincidence, just then a young Wyoming deputy sheriff, William Romer, pulled up in his car to see what was going on. Caril jumped out of the back seat of the car, shouting that she wanted him to take her to the police, that it was Starkweather in the car and he was a killer. Charlie, by this time, had jumped back into the Packard and gunned it in the direction of the nearby town of Douglas. The deputy set off in hot pursuit, radioing in that he was chasing a black Packard and ordering that a roadblock be set up. Douglas police chief, Robert Ainslie, and Sheriff Earl Heflin of Converse County happened to see Starkweather's car fly past them at speed and also set off in pursuit. Heflin took careful aim and shot out the back windscreen of the Packard. To their surprise, however, Starkweather came to an abrupt halt in the middle of the highway.

They pulled up behind him, cautiously waiting for him to get out. When he did, they told him to lie on the ground. It turned out that he had stopped because he thought he had been shot. But the blood was merely from a cut around his ear made by the broken glass of the windscreen. Heflin was appalled: 'He thought he was bleeding to death. That's why he stopped. That's the kind of yellow sonofabitch he is.'

He did look the part, though, when photographed later. Shaggy, swept back hair, cigarette dangling, Dean-like, from his lips, black leather motorcycle jerkin, tight black denims, cowboy boots – the very image of teenage rebellion.

Under arrest, their choice was stark. The gas chamber in Wyoming or the electric chair in Nebraska. They chose Nebraska and he and Caril were extradited in January 1958 where they were both charged with first-degree murder and murder while committing a robbery.

Starkweather's lawyers entered a plea of 'innocent by

reason of insanity', but Starkweather maintained that he was sane. He also said initially that Caril was innocent. Shortly after he was arrested, he told police officers: 'Don't be rough on the girl. She didn't have a thing to do with it.' He changed his tune, however, when he learned that Caril was saying that she had actually been held hostage by him and he began to implicate her, claiming she was responsible for some of the murders and all the mutilations.

Caril was found guilty but, being only fourteen, she was spared the electric chair and sentenced, instead, to life imprisonment. She was paroled in 1976, still claiming her innocence.

In Starkweather's case, it took the jury only twenty-four hours to reach a verdict of guilty and he was sentenced to death in the electric chair, a sentence carried out on June 25, 1959. His father raised money for his appeal by selling locks of his hair, but the appeal failed.

On the eve of his execution Charles Starkweather was asked if he would like to donate his eyes. He refused, saying: 'Why should I? Nobody ever gave me anything.'

RICHARD SPECK

It was unmistakably a man, but he had women's breasts and was wearing blue silk panties. He paraded around, took a bit of cocaine, had sex with another inmate of the prison and said: 'If they only knew how much fun I'm having, they'd turn me loose.'

The video tape had been sent anonymously to Chicago television news editor, Bill Kurtis in 1996. It had been made in Stateville Prison in 1988 and depicted scenes of sex and drug use. At the centre of it was the bizarre spectacle of nurse-killer Richard Speck who had died in 1991 and whose breasts were the result of hormone treatments that had been smuggled into the jail. Speck joked when asked why he had killed eight nurses on the night of July 14, 1966. 'It just wasn't their night,' he said. Then asked how he has felt since then, he replied coldly: 'Like I always feel. Had no feelings.'

Speck was born, the seventh of eight children, on December 6, 1941, in the small town of Kirkwood, Illinois. His parents, Benjamin and Mary, were religious people, but his father died when Richard was six years old and

Mary, having moved the family to Fair Park, near Dallas, Texas, remarried. Her new husband, Carl Lindbergh, was the antithesis of Benjamin Speck. He drank, was abusive and was often gone from the family for long periods. He hated Richard and Richard hated him.

By the age of twelve, Richard Speck was already going off the rails. He was a poor student, eventually dropping out in ninth grade, and had discovered alcohol. In his defence, however, it has been suggested that the alcohol was used to counter the headaches from which he suffered. These were apparently a direct result of head injuries he suffered throughout childhood – aged five, he was injured while playing in a sandbox with a claw hammer; he twice fell out of trees, and at fifteen he ran into a steel girder, injuring his head yet again.

Aged nineteen, he had a tattoo done which would become significant in later life. It read: 'Born to Raise Hell' and that is just what he did. By his mid-twenties, a drug-dependent alcoholic, he had thirty-seven arrests to his name. Charges included public drunkenness, disorderly conduct and burglary

At twenty he had married fifteen-year-old Shirley Malone and fathered a child, but the marriage ended in 1966. According to Malone, Speck often raped her at knifepoint, claiming that he needed sex four to five times each day. He spent a large part of their marriage in prison. He told people he wanted to kill his ex-wife, but he never got round to it and, heading back to Illinois, in a three-month period, he seems to have vented his anger on other women.

The first to die was Mary Pierce, a divorcee who had rejected his advances. On April 13, her naked body was found, strangled, in a shed behind the bar where she worked. A few days earlier, a sixty-five-year-old woman had been grabbed from behind and raped by a man with a southern drawl whose description matched that of Speck.

The cops were on to him and, tracing him to the Christy Hotel, they found jewellery and a radio belonging to the rape victim. Other items from burglaries he had carried out, were also discovered. But Speck was gone.

He landed work on the iron-ore barges of the Great Lakes, but was dismissed for repeated drunkenness on the job as well as his violent behaviour. On July 2, he was in the area of Indiana Harbor. Not far from there, that day, three young girls disappeared and their bodies were never found. All that remained were their clothes, left in their car.

On July 13, Speck was drinking heavily in the Shipyard Inn in south Chicago. As ever, he was angry and depressed. He had tried to get work on a ship bound for New Orleans but had been unable to do so. Therefore, having consumed quantities of pills and booze, he decided that it was time to 'raise some hell.' He set off towards one of the nearby student dormitories of the South Chicago Community Hospital. In his possession were a hunting knife, a pocket-knife and a .22 calibre pistol.

For the past several weeks, Speck had been watching the women coming and going from the buildings, sunbathing in a nearby park and leaving the building to attend their classes. He knew their schedules well enough to know that at that time of night they would be home and in bed.

Twenty-three-year-old Cora Amurao, a nursing exchange student from the Philippines, opened the door at Jeffrey Manor, a two-storey townhouse occupied by student nurses. In front of her stood Speck, dressed in dark clothing, reeking of alcohol, high as a kite and brandishing the pistol and the knife. 'I'm not going to hurt you,' he told the terrified woman. 'I'm only going to tie you up. I need your money to go to New Orleans.'

He went into the house and got the five other nurses there at the time out of bed. All six were herded into one room where he tied them up and sat them in a circle on the floor. In the next hour another three arrived home from evenings out. They, too, were tied up and sat on the floor.

Twenty-year-old Pamela Wilkening was the first to die. He took her into another room and stabbed her in the chest before strangling her with a torn piece of bedsheet. Returning to the room, he selected twenty-year-old Mary Jordan and twenty-one-year-old Suzanne Farris. He took them into another bedroom and stabbed Jordan in the heart, neck and eye. Turning to Farris, he stabbed her eighteen times and then strangled her already dead body. He also raped her.

Nina Schmale, twenty-four years of age, was now taken to a room where he told her to lie on a bed. He cut her throat and strangled her. Valentine Pasion, twenty-three, was stabbed in the throat and Nerlita Gargullo was stabbed four times and then strangled. He washed his hands before returning to carry Patricia Matusek into the bathroom where he kicked her in the stomach and strangled her.

For the next twenty minutes he raped Gloria Davy upstairs and then took her down to the ground floor where he raped her anally with an unknown implement. Then he strangled her, before leaving the house, thinking everyone was dead.

Unknown to Speck, however, Cora Amurao, who had first opened the door to him, had slithered under one of the beds in the room and pressed herself up against the wall. She lay there, terrified, until 6.00 a.m. to be certain that he had gone. Then she clambered out on to the balcony shouting: 'My friends are all dead! I'm the only one alive! Oh God, I'm the only one alive!'

When the police arrived on the scene, the property resembled a charnel house. The carpet squished underfoot from the amount of blood it had soaked up. Experienced policemen took one look and then ran outside to throw up. There was one strong clue, however, to the killer's identity. The neatness of the square knots used to tie the girls up suggested that he was, most likely, a seaman.

The cops went to work and within hours knew their killer was Richard Speck. Cora, although heavily sedated, had managed to give a description of the killer and a gas station attendant recalled that one of his managers had been talking about a guy of the same description who complained about missing a ship and losing out on a job just a couple of days before. A police sketch artist drew an uncanny likeness of Speck, which was taken to the Maritime Union Hall. Someone there remembered an angry seaman who had lost out on a double booking – two men had been sent for one job – and he was able to retrieve the crumpled assignment sheet from the wastebasket. The sheet gave the name of Richard Speck.

Speck was on the loose for the next few days, drinking

and crashing in cheap hotels in Chicago. The police were always close on his tail and at one point he was interviewed by a couple of them in his room because he had a gun. They did not realise who he was, however. Eventually, he stayed in a hotel in Skid Row, the Starr. He had drunk a pint of cheap wine and, feeling suicidal, he smashed the bottle and dragged its jagged ends across his wrist and inner elbow, severing an artery. He then lay bleeding on the bed in his tiny cubicle in the hotel, surrounded by newspapers carrying his picture. He called out for water and help, but was ignored.

Eventually, one of the down-and-outs Speck had been drinking with in the last few days recognised Speck's picture and, having returned to the hotel, discovered him, lying on the bed. He called the police anonymously to tell them where he was, but no patrol car was dispatched.

Instead, Speck was taken to Cook County Hospital, the very same hospital in which the nurses' bodies lay. Leroy Smith, a first-year resident, examined Speck and thought there was something familiar about him. He washed the blood off his arm and there it was – the tattoo saying 'Born to Raise Hell'. He found a newspaper and confirmed that it was Speck from the photo. When Speck asked for water, Smith held him tight by the neck and asked him: 'Did you give water to the nurses?'

The trial began on April 3, 1967, in the Peoria County Courthouse, in Peoria, Illinois, three hours south of Chicago. Cora Amurao testified at the trial and a dramatic and defining moment came when she was asked if she could identify the killer of her fellow students. She rose from her seat in the witness box, walked across the courtroom to stand in front of Speck. She pointed at him, almost touching him, and said: 'This is the man'.

On April 15, 1967, after forty-nine minutes of deliberation, the jury found Richard Benjamin Speck guilty of all eight murders. The court was cleared and Judge Paschen sentenced Speck to death in the electric chair. He avoided it, however, when the Supreme Court declared capital punishment unconstitutional. Instead, Speck was sentenced to fifty to 100 years in prison for each count of murder – a total of 400 to 1,200 years.

In 1973 a new statutory maximum of 300 years was introduced and he became eligible for parole in 1977, but his requests were denied seven times in the following thirteen years.

In Stateville Prison, in Joliet, he was known as 'birdman' after the Birdman of Alcatraz, due to the fact that he kept a pair of sparrows that had flown into his cell. He was often caught with drugs or distilled moonshine, however, and was far from a model prisoner. Punishment for such breaches never phased him. 'How am I going to get in trouble? I'm here for 1,200 years!'

He spent less than twenty years inside, however. A massive heart attack killed him on December 5, 1991. No one claimed his body. He was cremated and his ashes were dispersed in an unknown location.

HARVEY GLATMAN

Harvey Glatman was a serial killer before the term was coined by the author John Brophy. A rapist and killer, he was a complex human being who hated women because they threatened him and represented what he could not understand about himself. Violence and force were his only ways to get close to them and establish control over them.

Harvey had been different from birth. He was slow and never had any friends, but the first real sign his mother Ophelia had that there was something not quite right with her son, was when he was four years old. She walked into his room to find that he had tied a length of string around his penis, put the other end in a drawer and leaned back against the tugging string. The parents dismissed this as a bit of childish experimentation, but it was a lot more than that and, later, rope would replace string and become his means of conquest.

At school, Harvey was called names on account of his large ears and buck teeth. But, above all, he was afraid of girls and never joined in activities and games after school. He would rather go home and play his own game which involved his beloved rope. He would tie it round his neck, throw it over a pipe or rafter and pull on it while masturbating. He had discovered auto-erotic asphyxiation at an early age. When he was eleven, his parents found out about the game and took him to a doctor who just put it down to growing pains.

He did well at school, but girls were still an alien life form; he stammered and blushed whenever any came near him. Moreover, his confidence was not helped by a very bad case of acne. So, to get his thrills, he started to break into houses and take things, but not particularly for gain; more for the excitement.

His breaking and entering soon graduated into something different. He would follow a woman home from the centre of Denver, break into her house, force her into her bedroom and tie her with the rope he carried everywhere with him. He would also gag her with a piece of cloth. He had stolen a .25 pistol during one of his burglaries and it came in handy. The woman was at his mercy and he was free to touch her as he pleased. He would unbutton clothes and fondle their bodies, doing the same to himself. He never fully undressed them or raped them. However, it made him feel like a real man and not the loser he really was.

In May, 1945, however, when he was seventeen, he

was finally caught breaking into a house and the police discovered the rope and the gun on him. He confessed to some of the burglaries he had committed, but was careful to leave out the ones that had involved the women. Seeming not to have learned his lesson, although perhaps not able to control his desires even if he had, while awaiting trial he abducted a woman called Norene Laurel, tied her up and drove her to Sunshine Canyon. He performed his usual acts and then let her go. At the police station, she recognised his face in an album of mugshots and he was arrested again, this time without bail. He was sentenced to a year in Colorado State Prison but was paroled after eight months.

Ophelia, Harvey's mother wanted him to make a fresh start and set him up in a flat in Yonkers. He got a job as a TV repairman, a trade he had learned in prison, and she returned to Denver. Harvey, meanwhile, was on the lookout for excitement. He bought a toy gun – possession of a real one would mean a long prison-stretch if he was caught with it – and he carried his pocket knife and his trusty length of rope, made of the finest hemp.

At midnight on August 17, 1946, Thomas Staro and Doris Thorn were accosted by a man with a gun. They were marched into a grove of trees and the man tied Staro's legs together and made him lie down. The man with the gun began to touch Thorn's breasts. However, unknown to Glatman, Staro had worked himself free of his ropes and was tiptoeing up behind him. There was a struggle and Glatman slashed Staro's shoulder with the knife before running away into the night.

He fled to Albany where he rented a flat and prepared for his next attack. It came on the night of August 22. He pushed off-duty nurse Florence Hayden into a yard where he bound her wrists together. As he did this, however, she screamed and Glatman fled. Next evening, he tried it on with two women walking together, but lost his nerve, eventually just taking their purses.

The Albany Police Department was, by this time, becoming interested in this man who targeted women. The descriptions given by the women all matched; so they knew the crimes were being perpetrated by the same man.

Within two days, he was arrested and he confessed. In spite of the pleas of his mother who all this time had believed him to be leading a quiet life in Yonkers, he was sentenced to five to ten years in prison; he was in the big league now. At Elmira, where he spent the first two years of his sentence, he was diagnosed as a 'psychopathic personality – schizophrenic type'. He was then moved to maximum security at Sing Sing. As is reported often to be the case with sociopaths like Glatman, he played the system well and got time off for good behaviour, being released after serving only two years and eight months. There were conditions though; he had to return to the care of his mother, get a job and be under court supervision for four and a half years.

He behaved himself, and in 1956 he was free of all restrictions. He moved to Los Angeles and went crazy.

Harvey had enjoyed photography in his art classes at high school and now he took it up again, but with a more sinister purpose. He intended to use it to photograph girls from the modelling studios that had sprung up everywhere in LA. Girls who had arrived in Hollywood dreaming of being stars like Marilyn Monroe offered themselves to be snapped clothed, semi-clothed or naked, according to how much they were paid.

He worked as a TV repairman again and rented a small apartment on Melrose Avenue, saving enough to buy a used 1951 Dodge Cornet and some expensive photography equipment. He invented a name, Johnny Glenn, for his photographer identity and spent months hanging around the modelling studios, taking thousands of photographs.

But, it was not quite enough for Harvey.

Judith Ann Dull was a nineteen-year-old divorcee working to fund a child custody battle she was waging with her ex-husband. Glatman called her on the morning of August 1, 1957, and asked if she would be interested in posing for a true crime magazine layout. She was wary, but agreed to pose for him at her own apartment at two o'clock that afternoon. He asked her to wear a tight skirt and sweater.

Arriving at her apartment, he told her the light was not good enough and suggested they go to his studio. Once there, he explained that the pictures were to illustrate a story about bondage and she would have to be tied up. Innocently, she allowed him to tie her wrists and ankles, at which point he pulled a .32 Browning automatic pistol from his pocket. He undid the ties on her wrists and ordered the now terrified Judith to strip off, slowly. He photographed her all the while, barking out instructions as to how he wanted her to pose.

He then raped her several times and forced her to sit beside him while he watched television. He said he would take her home afterwards.

Of course, he had no intention of taking her home.

When he told her he would drop her on the outskirts of town, she presumed that was to allow him to make his escape. They got in the car and he drove 100 miles out of town before stopping the car. He made as if to untie her and for a moment she must have thought it was going to be alright, but quickly he put the rope round her neck, pushed her down onto her knees and ran the other loop of rope around her ankles. Pulling up on the rope, her neck snapped and she was dead. He finished the evening off by using his flash attachment to take photos of the dead girl, arranging her body in a variety of poses.

He stuck the photos all over his bedroom walls.

It was seven months before he killed again.

He met twenty-four-year-old Shirley Ann Bridgeford, a divorced mother of two children, through the Patty Sullivan Lonely Hearts Club. 'George Williams' promised to take her square dancing on March 7, 1958. Williams – in reality Harvey Glatman – picked her up at her home where, to his surprise and concern, a houseful of people greeted him. He suggested to her that rather than go dancing, they go for a drive in the country and get some dinner somewhere en route. She agreed and they stopped in Oceanside.

After dinner they drove on. Somewhere near Anza State Park he stopped the car and pulled his gun out, ordering Shirley to undress. He raped her and then took photographs of her. He then waited until the sun came up to take pictures of her in daylight before garotting her. As with Judith Dull, he then photographed the corpse in different poses. Four months later, it was the turn of Ruth Mercado, her body photographed and dumped near to Shirley Bridgeford's remains.

In the summer of 1958, Glatman went to the Diane Studio, one of the better agencies on Sunset Boulevard. It was arranged for him to work with Lorraine Virgil, a woman who had signed on with the agency only the previous week. He was to pick her up at eight that evening

But the owner of the studio, Diane, was suspicious of the man with the big ears, unkempt hair and smelly body odour. She phoned Lorraine and told her to be careful.

As soon as Lorraine got into his car and he started heading in the wrong direction alarm bells began to ring in her head. When she questioned him, he told her someone had already booked the studio and they were actually going to his own private studio.

As they sped down the freeway, she became even more anxious. Again, she asked him where they were going. He said 'Annaheim'. However, she knew that they had already sped past the Annaheim turn-off. As she became more and more concerned, he began to shout at her to shut up. He swung the car dangerously into an exit ramp, crossing two lanes to get to it. Off the freeway, he stopped the car and asked her to put her arms out.

He told her he was going to tie her up to keep her quiet and to emphasise his point, he pulled out his gun. Lorraine reached for the door handle, trying to escape, but he grabbed her and they struggled. He tried desperately to wrap a coil of rope around her but, unlike the other women, Lorraine fought back.

She grabbed the gun barrel and the gun went off, the bullet burning her thigh as it skimmed past. Suddenly, Glatman released his hold on her and she wrenched open the car door and fell out. He climbed out behind her, trying to haul her back into the car, but just as he grabbed her sweater, the pair were bathed in a pool of light. It came from the headlights of a patrol car.

She stumbled towards them, still holding the gun and fell at their feet. Glatman, meanwhile, cowered by his car, sobbing and whimpering that it was not his fault.

When Glatman's mother left the prison after visiting her son, she said to the assembled press: 'He is not a vicious man – he is sick.' And that was his only hope of escaping the gas chamber; to prove that he was not of sane mind. Harvey did not want to be examined, though; he wanted to die. However, he was persuaded to undergo psychiatric tests. There was no point. The report said: 'he shows no evidence of a psychosis. He knows right from wrong, the nature and quality of his acts and he can keep from doing wrong if he so desires.'

Harvey pleaded guilty and on December 15, 1958, he was sentenced to die in the gas chamber.

On September 18, 1959, he entered San Quentin's notorious 'green room'. The chamber door was locked shut at a minute past ten. He was strapped in by two minutes past ten. The cyanide pellets were released a minute later and by twelve minutes past ten, Harvey Glatman was dead.

He might have enjoyed it a bit more if he had been hung on the end of a rope of the finest quality hemp.

CHARLES MANSON

By the time he was thirty-two years old, Charles Manson had spent less than half of his life outside prisons and institutions. In fact it is reported that when he was about to be released from prison in 1967, he pleaded with the authorities: 'Don't let me out, I can't cope with the outside world.' When questioned about this in a 1981 interview, he claimed that what he really meant was: 'I can't handle the maniacs outside, let me back in.'

Had they complied with his request, the web of mayhem that he spun in the late 1960s would have been prevented.

Charles Milles Manson was born in 1934 to sixteen-year-old Ada Kathleen Maddox in Cincinnati General Hospital. He took his name from a man to whom his mother was briefly married, but his biological father could have been any one of a number of men. Ada was feckless and promiscuous and a big drinker, and she may even have been a prostitute. When she and her brother were sent to prison in 1939 for robbing a petrol station,

Charles was sent to West Virginia to stay with an aunt and uncle, returning to his mother when she was paroled in 1942. He returned to a life of alcohol and the comings and goings of his mother's men, lived out in cheap, dilapidated hotel rooms.

Ada tried, without success, to have Charles fostered, and he ended up in Gibault School for Boys in Terre Haute, Indiana. After ten months he fled, going back to his mother. But she did not want him and he had to rob a grocery store to get enough money to rent a room.

Burglary and theft became his way of life, but he was soon caught and sent to a juvenile centre in Indianapolis. He escaped but was recaptured and placed in another institution from which he again escaped, this time with another inmate. They committed a couple of armed robberies as they made their way to the home of the other boy's uncle.

Captured once again, Manson was sent to the Indiana School for Boys from which he escaped in 1951 with a couple of other boys. The trio were caught in Utah, driving a stolen car after carrying out a string of robberies. Driving a stolen car across a state line constituted a federal crime and Manson was sent to Washington DC's National Training School for Boys. He was illiterate and, as was noted by a caseworker, dangerously antisocial.

In 1952, only a month before he was due to attend a parole hearing, Manson held a razor to the throat of another inmate and sodomised him. They moved him to the Federal Reformatory in Petersburg, Virginia and, as he was now considered 'dangerous', he was transferred to a more secure institution in Ohio. He played the game there, winning parole in May, 1954.

January 1955, saw him married to a hospital waitress, Rosalie Jean Wills. He worked at poorly paid jobs and supplemented his income by stealing cars. However, in March 1956 his career as a car thief caught up with him and he was sentenced to three years at Terminal Island in San Pedro, California. When he tried to escape, again shortly before a parole hearing, five years' probation was added to his sentence and, needless to say, parole was denied.

By the time Manson was finally paroled in 1958, Rosalie had divorced him and disappeared with the son, Charles Manson Jnr., who had been born shortly after he went to prison. He changed career and started pimping a sixteen-year-old girl, but it was not long before he was in court again, charged with trying to cash a forged US Treasury cheque. The judge was lenient, however, and Manson received a ten-year suspended sentence and the usual probation. Eventually, his problems built up – he was investigated for violation of the Mann Act, transporting women over a state line for immoral purposes and he had breached his probation. He was arrested and ordered to serve the ten years.

In March 1967, he was released.

He headed for San Francisco. It was the 'Summer of Love' and the city's Haight-Ashbury was a mecca for hippies and drop-outs. Manson had learned to play guitar in prison and he busked around the area. Meeting a girl, Mary Brunner, who was an assistant librarian at the University of California in Berkeley, he moved in with her. He persuaded Brunner to let other women move in and soon there were no fewer that eighteen girls living in the house with them, most of them emotionally troubled young women rebelling against their parents and society in general.

Manson was a charismatic individual and took on the role of a kind of guru to these young women, sprinkling his philosophy with bits of scientology and other religious references. He could manipulate them very easily and LSD, amphetamines and other drugs helped him establish further control over them.

With a group of them, he took off in a renovated school bus and travelled to Washington State and then down through Los Angeles and into Mexico. Returning to the LA area, the Family, as they were calling themselves, settled in Topanga Canyon.

While out hitch-hiking, one day, two of the girls were picked up by Beach Boy, Dennis Wilson. He took them back to his house and before long the rest of the Family had moved in, costing Wilson around $100,000 over the next few months. He even paid for studio time for Manson to record the songs he had written in prison and introduced him to music business acquaintances who might help him get on, one of whom was Doris Day's record producer son, Terry Melcher.

Wilson managed to clear the Family out of his house and they settled at Spahn's Movie Ranch near Topanga Canyon before moving to a couple of ranches close to Death Valley.

It was round about this time, December 1968, that Manson first heard the newly released Beatles' *White Album*. He had been an obsessive Beatles fan when they first exploded onto the American scene and now he assimilated them into his philosophy, a philosophy that said that the blacks in America's cities would shortly rise up and slaughter the whites.

He described The Beatles as 'the soul' and 'part of the hole in the infinite', announcing to his followers that the album was predicting the social upheaval he had been telling them about – The Beatles were talking directly to the Family.

They were soon on the move again, back to Topanga

Canyon. In a canary-yellow building that Manson called the Yellow Submarine, he finessed his vision and began to call the impending apocalypse 'Helter Skelter' after a track on the White Album. The Family would be safe while the killing was going on, he said; they would go into hiding in 'the bottomless pit', a secret city beneath Death Valley.

He decided that they should write an album of songs that would send coded messages out, triggering the turmoil he had predicted. They invited Terry Melcher to come to the house to hear the songs. Melcher failed to turn up and Manson was furious.

In March 1969, Manson paid a visit to a house at 10050 Cielo Drive. He thought Melcher lived there, but the record producer had actually moved out and since February it had been leased by film director Roman Polanski and his pregnant young wife, the actress Sharon Tate. Manson was told that Melcher had decamped.

A few months later, on the night of August 9, Manson unleashed Helter Skelter. He had come to the conclusion that he would have to show the blacks the way and ordered Family members Charles 'Tex' Watson, Patricia Krenwinkel, Susan Atkins and Linda Kasabian to go to Cielo Drive and 'totally destroy everyone in it as gruesome as you can.'

Arriving at the quiet, secluded house, they cut the

phone lines and climbed into the grounds. A car's headlights approached and Watson instructed the girls to hide in some bushes. Pulling out a gun, he shot dead the car's driver. It was eighteen-year-old Stephen Parent, who had been visiting William Garretson, a caretaker living in the nearby guest-house on the property. Watson then cut a hole in a screen at an open window and told Kasabian to wait at the gate. He and the two other girls climbed in through the window.

Wojciech Frykowski, a friend of Polanski, was wakened from sleep on the couch in the living room. 'I'm the devil, and I'm here to do the devil's business,' Watson chillingly told him. The other occupants of the house were rounded up: Tate, Jay Sebring, America's top men's hair stylist and twenty-five-year-old Abigail Folger, an heiress to a coffee fortune.

Watson tied Tate's and Sebring's necks together and threw the other end of the rope over a beam so that they would choke if they tried to escape. Folger went to get her purse and they took the seventy dollars she had in it. Watson then stabbed Folger a number of times. Frykowski had freed his hands from the towel they had used to tie him up and tried to escape but Watson hit him on the head a number of times with his gun and then shot him twice. At this point, Kasabian appeared, trying to bring a halt to proceedings, saying that someone was coming.

Folger ran to the pool area where Krenwinkel stabbed her repeatedly along with Watson. Frykowski, trying to crawl across the lawn, was also stabbed by Watson. He was found later to have fifty-one stab wounds. Meanwhile, in the house, Sharon Tate was pleading for her life and that of her unborn baby. Atkins told her she did not care about her or her baby and she and Watson stabbed her sixteen times.

Manson had asked them to leave a sign when they left. So Atkins grabbed a towel and wrote the word 'pig' on the front door in Sharon Tate's blood.

The following night it was the turn of Leno LaBianca, a supermarket executive, and his wife Rosemary. This time Manson went himself, 'to show them how to do it'.

They broke in and woke the sleeping couple, covering their heads with pillow cases. Manson left at this point and instructed Krenwinkel and Leslie Van Houten to go into the house and kill the couple. Watson began stabbing Leno with a chrome-plated bayonet, but in the bedroom Rosemary was putting up a fight. Watson stabbed her, however, and she fell. Returning to the living room, he carved 'war' on Leno's stomach. In the bedroom, Krenwinkel was stabbing Rosemary with a kitchen knife and Watson ordered Van Houten to stab her, too. Rosemary LaBianca received a total of forty-one stab wounds.

Krenwinkel wrote 'Rise' and 'Death to pigs' on the walls and misspelled 'Healther Skelter' on the refrigerator door, using the couple's blood. She stabbed Leno's corpse a further fourteen times, leaving a carving fork sticking out of his stomach. She stuck a steak knife in his neck.

Bizzarely, the LAPD did not link the Tate and LaBianca murders. They thought the Tate case was probably the result of a drug deal gone wrong and they even ignored connections with a group of hippies led by 'a guy named Charlie'. Neither did they link them with the murder of Gary Hinman, whom, with the help of other Family members, Bobby Beausoleil had murdered a few weeks previously.

It was not until the end of August that the team investigating the LaBianca case enquired about similar crimes. They learned of the Hinman killing and how the words 'Political piggy' had been written on the wall in the victim's blood. If LAPD had paid attention to LA sheriff's office detectives, they would have learned that Beausoleil, known to have been hanging out with Manson's group, had been arrested.

Finally, it began to be clear that the two cases were connected and it was decided to investigate the similarities with the Hinman case. The investigation led straight back to the Family and Charles Manson.

In October, the desert ranches were raided and a couple of dozen people, including Manson, were arrested. Meanwhile, Susan Atkins confessed to detectives that she had been involved in the Hinman killing and she also told the women with whom she shared a cell in prison what had been going on.

Warrants were issued for Watson, Krenwinkel and Kasabian in the Tate case and they were noted as suspects in the LaBianca case. Soon, after Kasabian had handed herself in to police, they were all under arrest. Kasabian had not taken part in the actual killings and was granted immunity in exchange for testifying against the others.

The girls tried to twist their stories to take all the blame themselves and spare Charlie, but, on January 25, 1971, Manson, Krenwinkel and Atkins were found guilty of all seven charges of murder and Leslie Van Houten was found guilty of two counts of murder. Watson was found guilty on all seven counts later in the year. They were sentenced to death, but their sentences were commuted to life after the US Supreme Court declared the death penalty unconstitutional in 1972.

But at least they had been stopped before their mayhem was able to spread further. Susan Atkins told her cellmates that other celebrities on their list included Richard Burton and Elizabeth Taylor, Frank Sinatra, Steve McQueen and Tom Jones.

She told them she had planned to carve the words 'helter skelter' on Elizabeth Taylor's face with a red-hot knife. Then she would gouge her eyes out. Richard Burton was to be castrated and his penis and Taylor's eyes were to be put in a bottle and mailed to Eddie Fisher, Taylor's ex-husband. Sinatra was to be skinned alive while his own music played; the Family would then make purses from his skin and sell them. Tom Jones would have his throat slit, but only after having sex with Atkins.

As a bizarre footnote to the story, a Family member, Lynette 'Squeaky' Fromme, tried to assassinate President Gerald Ford in 1975.

EDMUND EMIL KEMPER III: THE CO-ED KILLER

Edmund Emil Kemper III had always been a little odd, but had been behaving increasingly strangely since the break-up of his parents' marriage. At the age of nine, he had buried the family cat alive in the back garden of his house in Burbank, California. He had then dug it up, decapitated it and mounted its head on a stick. He dreamt of murdering people and would cut up his sister's dolls and engage in strange sex games with them. His behaviour was not helped by his mother locking him in the basement at night for eight months, fearing that he would molest his sisters.

In 1963, aged fifteen, his mother was finding it impossible to control him, and after he had run away from his father's house, he was sent to live with his father's parents on their remote Californian farm at North Fork, high in California's Sierra Mountains. Life there was very boring for Kemper. He was away from school and isolated from his normal life. One day there was an argument when his grandmother insisted that he stay home and do housework instead of going into the fields to work with his grandfather. He picked up a rifle to go outside and shoot something but when she told him not to shoot any birds he turned round and fired a bullet into her head before shooting her in the back. He heard his grandfather arrive and killed him with a single shot as he got out of his car. Kemper said to police interviewing him: 'I just wondered how it would feel to shoot Grandma.'

He was diagnosed as suffering from paranoid schizophrenia and detained in Atascadero State Mental Hospital for the criminally insane.

In 1969, aged twenty-one, standing six feet nine inches tall and weighing 300 pounds, he was released into the care of his mother, Clarnell. The doctors considered Clarnell to be at the root of most of Kemper's problems and warned him not to go back to her, but he did. Needless to say, life with her was no better than it had been before. They argued violently and she would blame him because she could not get any dates. Indeed, she seemed to get on better with the students at the University of Santa Cruz where she worked as a secretary than she did with her own son. He eventually moved out, to Alameda near San Francisco, sharing a rented flat with a friend. Most of his time was spent cruising around the California highways, picking up young, female hitch-hikers.

Kemper held down a job at a Green Giant canning factory and, still a virgin, worked out his sex and violence fantasies with pornography and detective magazines. In 1971 he had a motorcycle accident for which he received $15,000 in compensation. He was unable to work and now had time and money on his hands.

In spring 1972 Kemper, after yet another tempestuous argument with his mother, went out looking for a victim on whom he could vent his anger. He quickly picked up two hitch-hikers, Mary Anne Pesce and Anita Luchessa, eighteen-year-old students making their way back to Stanford University. He pulled a gun on them and informed them that he was going to rape them. Pulling off onto a side road, he made one girl climb into the boot of the car. He handcuffed the other one and then stabbed and strangled her. Opening the boot, he stabbed the other girl. He then drove the bodies back to the apartment where he decapitated them and cut off their hands.

Returning to his apartment that night, he removed the clothing from the bodies and had sex with them. Next day he buried the heads and bodies in different places in order to make it difficult for them to be identified if discovered. He got rid of the clothes in remote parts of the Santa Cruz mountains. One of the girls' heads was found the following August, but without the remainder of her body it was impossible to prove how she had died.

In September he struck again. He picked up a fifteen-year-old Asian ballet student, Aiko Koo, and told her she was being kidnapped. When she became hysterical, he pulled his gun out and told her to be quiet. North of Santa Cruz, he smothered her until she lost consciousness and then strangled her and had sex with her dead body. He then visited his mother and chatted with her while the body lay in the car's boot. Returning to his apartment, he had intercourse again with the corpse and in the morning he cut it up and drove it out into the country where he buried the hands and the torso in different places again. This time, he kept the head in the boot and it was still there when he visited a psychiatrist.

Around this time, in November 1972, Kemper's records were sealed, meaning that they no longer existed as a blemish on his character. His mother had been fighting for this and he had been examined by two psychiatrists who agreed that he had made good progress. Little did they know what kind of progress he had really been making and it was not long before his murderous instinct forced him to strike again.

He picked up a girl one afternoon and killed her with a single shot from the new gun he had purchased; with his records sealed he could now own a gun. He drove her back to his mother's house and hid her in the closet of his bedroom. Next morning, when his mother left for work, he dismembered the corpse, removing the bullet from the head in case it was found. He tossed the parts off a cliff into the sea, some of them being found within days. He buried the head in the garden under his mother's window. 'She always wanted people to look up to her,' he later joked.

By now, of course, there was panic and security was heightened everywhere. Papers spoke of the Co-ed Killer and girls were warned to be careful, but he still managed to pick two up on the UCSC campus less than a month later. He had shot them even before he had driven off university property. The guards at the gate failed to spot the bodies slumped inside the car and he drove them to his mother's where he decapitated them in her driveway while she was in the house. It gave him a thrill to have her so close when he did it. He took the heads into his bedroom and masturbated over them. For a couple of days he drove around with the bodies in the car before disposing of them in the usual way, taking care to remove the bullets.

A few months later, he bought another gun, a .44, but

a sheriff noted the name on the record of the sale of the gun and decided to pay Kemper a visit. He asked Kemper for the pistol and said it would be retained by the authorities until a court decided whether it was lawful for him to own a gun. Kemper went to the boot of the car and took the pistol out, handing it to the officer who then left. But Kemper was shaken. He had come very close to being found out. The car, after all, had a bullet hole in it and had been awash with blood very recently. He realised that it was time for the endgame; he would kill his mother and then give himself up.

On April 20, Kemper and his mother had their usual argument and, as usual, she humiliated him. At five next morning, while she slept, he smashed her skull with a claw-hammer and slit her throat. He raped the corpse and cut her head off. He placed it on the mantelpiece and used it as a dartboard. He then called Sally Hallett, a friend of his mother, and invited her to the house for a surprise dinner. When she arrived he clubbed her, strangled her and decapitated her. He then slept in his mother's bed before going out and driving for miles through a number of states. He stopped in Colorado, called the police and gave himself up. It was over.

Ed Kemper confessed to everything, waiving his right to an attorney. He told them that he had kept hair, teeth and skin of some victims as trophies. He also told them that he had sliced some flesh off two of his victims' legs and cooked it in a macaroni casserole. When asked what punishment would fit the crimes he had committed, he replied: 'Death by torture.'

The trial was over very quickly. Psychiatrists testified that he had been sane when committing the murders and he was found guilty of eight counts of first-degree murder and sentenced to life imprisonment. He has proved to be a quiet, well-behaved inmate.

KENNETH ALLEN MCDUFF: THE BROOMSTICK KILLER

Texan Kenneth Allen McDuff has the rare distinction of being the only American ever to have been condemned to death, had his sentence commuted and then sentenced to death again for an entirely different crime.

He was born in Rosebud, a small town in central Texas, in 1946 and was nothing but trouble from the start. His schooldays were a constant battle with authority and he was a relentless bully. As is often the case, though, he was also a coward, backing off if a victim of his bullying stood up to him. His antisocial behaviour was not helped by the fact that his mother Addie, believed her six foot three, 230-pound son could do no wrong, even later in his life when he had done a great deal of wrong.

Dropping out of school at an early age, McDuff worked with his father, pouring concrete. His spare time was spent hell-raising. He drank, fought and womanised, wrecking a succession of cars while he did it. He was often in trouble with the authorities and, aged nineteen, he was sent to prison on fourteen counts of burglary.

In less than a year, he was out, picking up where he had left off. On August 6, 1966, McDuff was cruising in his car with an associate, Roy Dale Green. Driving through a suburb of Fort Worth, they spotted a car parked at a baseball park. Robert Brand, seventeen, his girlfriend Edna Louise Sullivan, sixteen, and Brand's cousin, Marcus Dunnam, fifteen, were taking a break after giving Louise some driving lessons.

McDuff and Green climbed out of their car and ordered the three teenagers at gunpoint to get out. They locked them in the boots of the two cars. Green drove one, McDuff the other, to a secluded area where, as they begged for mercy, McDuff shot the two boys in the head at point-blank range. Louise was then raped by both men a number of times; they also abused her with a broken broomstick handle. McDuff then slowly strangled her by pressing the broomstick across her throat.

Green was not as ruthless as McDuff and confessed to police the following day. McDuff was arrested and Green testified against him in exchange for a lighter sentence. At his trial, Falls County sheriff Brady Pamplin, a former Texas Ranger, described McDuff as the most remorseless and sadistic killer he had ever met, while Green said that McDuff once boasted to him: 'Killing a woman's like killing a chicken. They both squawk.'

McDuff was sentenced to death.

He was lucky though. In 1972, the United States Supreme Court declared execution to be unconstitutional and his sentence was overturned. At the same time, Texan prisons were under fire for the terrible and oppressive conditions in which inmates were being held. Reforms were introduced which meant that few prisoners served out their full term, even killers such as Kenneth McDuff. Consequently, he was given parole in October 1989, having served twenty-three years. This was in spite of the fact that, while incarcerated, he had offered a member of the parole board a bribe of $10,000 and, in spite of his denials, was convicted for it while inside. There are some who believe another bribe got him his release, but, to this day, it has never been proved and McDuff never said.

Three days after he was released, the body of a prostitute, Sarafia Parker, was found near Temple, Texas. It was never proved conclusively that McDuff was the murderer, but it seems too much of a coincidence that his parole officer was located in Temple.

Out of prison, he returned immediately to his old ways. He was picked up by police on a number of occasions - for making terrorist threats when trying to start a fight with some black youths, for drunk driving and for public drunkenness. He also became addicted to crack cocaine. He was supposed to be studying to be a machinist at Texas State University, but spent most of his time hanging out with the dregs of society.

In October 1991, a woman was seen in the passenger seat of his car, her hands behind her, shouting and seemingly attempting to break the windscreen with her feet. The woman, thirty-seven-year-old prostitute Brenda Thompson, was never seen again. A few days later another prostitute, Reginia 'Gina' Moore, also disappeared.

In December of the same year, McDuff and a friend, serial alcoholic Alva Hank Worley, were out looking for drugs when they spotted Colleen Reed, an attractive twenty-eight-year-old accountant, alone at a car wash. McDuff grabbed hold of her and pushed her into his car. The police were called when witnesses heard screams, but McDuff and Worley had gone by the time they arrived.

They drove her out of town, taking turns raping her as they drove north along Interstate 35 towards a site near Lake Belton, continuing with their attacks when they arrived. Then McDuff tied her hands behind her back, raped her on the bonnet of the car, beat her and tortured her sexually with lit cigarettes. He then struck her hard, according to Worley, certainly breaking some of her bones and possibly killing her. He dropped Worley and disposed of the body.

By this time he was working at a supermarket in Waco. He took a shine to a woman who worked there, Melissa Northrup, telling friends that he wanted to rob the store and 'take' the girl. On March 1, he did just that. When his car was found near the store and the girl's was discovered in a wooded area in Dallas County, police launched an investigation. Witnesses said that McDuff had been in the area and near the site of Melissa's kidnapping. Her body was found by a fisherman a month later in a gravel pit close to where her car had been abandoned. She had been tied up and strangled. She was two months pregnant.

Around this time, the body of another prostitute was found. She had last been seen in February on the Texas State University campus, looking for McDuff's dorm room.

By now, though, McDuff was working as a garbage-man in Kansas City. On May 1, 1992, he made it onto America's Most Wanted list and within a day, one of his work colleagues had contacted the police to tell them where he was. He was arrested.

He was tried first for the murder of Melissa Northrup and, trying to defend himself, created a very bad impression in court. He was unable to provide an alibi for the night of the murder and was sentenced to death.

He then stood trial for the murder of Colleen Reed, even though no body had been found. His behaviour was even worse during this trial, partly because the judge was black and McDuff was a racist bigot. He was convicted and given a second death sentence on the basis of Worley's testimony and the fact that five of Reed's hairs that found in his car.

To this day, no one really knows how many women Kenneth McDuff actually killed and a body discovered near Rosebud in October 2006 is suspected to be another of his victims.

By the time he was sentenced, McDuff was dying anyway. He had been diagnosed with hepatitis C and cirrhosis. When interviewed on death row, he said nonchalantly: 'I consider myself dead. I'm just waiting to be buried.'

The McDuff case launched a torrent of soul-searching about the Texas prison system, the third largest criminal justice system in the United States. There was an outbreak of prison construction, and parole reforms were introduced that were collectively known as the

'McDuff Rules' to prevent anyone ever being able to do again what McDuff did.

On November 17, 1998, just after 6.00 p.m., Kenneth Alan McDuff was put to death by lethal injection in Huntsville prison. Thirty-two years too late, most people said.

JEFFREY DAHMER

The night of July 22, 1991 was an oppressively hot one in Milwaukee, Wisconsin's largest city. Sweat dripped from the two police officers as they sat in their patrol car around the area near Marquette University at around midnight. Suddenly, they spied a short black man wearing what looked like a pair of handcuffs. The cuffs suggested he might have escaped from police arrest and they apprehended him. When questioned, however, Tracy Edwards started to tell them about a 'weird dude' who had invited him up to his apartment, put the handcuffs on him and threatened him with a knife.

It sounded to the officers like a lovers' tiff, but they decided to investigate just the same and knocked on the door of apartment 213 in the Oxford Apartments at 924 North 25th Street. The door was opened by a well-groomed, good-looking thirty-one-year-old man with blond hair.

The blond man seemed very calm and rational and his apartment looked reasonably tidy. However, a strange smell pervaded the place. Without any fuss, he said he would go and get the key to the handcuffs which was in the bedroom. Edwards warned the officers that the knife he had been threatened with was also in there. So one of the officers went to check, but, on his way, saw that there were photographs lying around showing dismembered bodies and skulls in a refrigerator. He shouted back to his colleague to cuff the blond man and arrest him. The blond struggled and screamed as the other cop tried to put the cuffs on him, but the officer quickly managed to subdue him.

The first officer at this point decided to have a look in the fridge but when he opened the door he froze in horror. A pair of eyes stared out at him from a dis-embodied head. 'There's a fucking head in the refrigerator,' he screamed.

The freezer contained a further three heads, wrapped tidily in plastic bags. In the closet in the bedroom he found a stockpot containing decomposed hands and a penis. On the shelf above were two skulls. There were male genitalia preserved in formaldehyde and a range of chemicals – ethyl alcohol, chloroform and more formaldehyde.

There were also photographs in a filing cabinet, taken as the victims died as well as afterwards. A man's head was shown in one, lying in the sink; another depicted a victim cut neatly open from neck to groin; others showed victims still alive, in erotic and bondage poises.

Jeffrey Dahmer was born in Milwaukee in May 1960, to Joyce and Lionel Dahmer. The family later moved to Iowa, where Lionel was working on his Ph.D. at Iowa State University, and then on to Akron, Ohio.

At first, Jeffrey was an ordinary, happy little boy. At the age of six, however, he had surgery for a double hernia and his father believes he was never the same again. 'He seemed smaller, somehow more vulnerable . . . he grew more inward, sitting quietly for long periods, hardly stirring, his face oddly motionless,' he later wrote. And it did not get better as Jeff grew older and became tense and extremely shy. At his trial it was revealed that, as a child, he would collect dead animals and strip the flesh from them, on one occasion mounting a dog's head on a stake.

In his late teenage years, as others began to carve out notions of what they were going to do with their lives, Jeff seemed completely unmotivated. Instead of thinking about girls and a future career, he was locked into a gruesome fantasy world that featured death and dismemberment. By now he was drinking a lot and was considered a loner and an alcoholic by classmates.

When Jeff was almost eighteen his parents got divorced, Lionel remarrying a few months later. It was around this time that Dahmer committed his first murder, killing Steven Hicks, an eighteen-year-old hitch-hiker. He invited Hicks back to his house, and killed him by hitting him over the head with a barbell because he 'didn't want him to leave.' He cut up his body and buried it in the woods behind his house.

Jeff enrolled for Ohio State University in 1978, but his drinking got in the way of his studies and he dropped out after just one term. His father had now had enough of this strangely morose and monosyllabic son of his and gave him a stark choice; either he got a job or joined the army. There was no way he was getting a job, so Lionel drove him to the army recruiting office in January 1979.

Again, however, Dahmer's drinking made life impossible and, after being stationed in Germany for a couple of years, he was discharged early for drunkenness, moving in with his grandmother back in Milwaukee and getting a job.

A string of offences followed – drunkenness, disorderly conduct and then indecent exposure and, in 1989, child molesting; he was reported to have masturbated in front of two boys. He persuaded the judge that he had, in fact, just been urinating and was put on probation for a year.

His father wrote later that his son had become 'a liar, an alcoholic, a thief, an exhibitionist, a molester of children. I could not imagine how he had become such a ruined soul ... There was something missing in Jeff ... We call it a 'conscience' ... that had either died or had never been alive in the first place.'

Dahmer had, by this time, already killed his second victim, Steven Toumi, in a hotel room in September that year. He had picked him up in a gay bar and the two went to a hotel to drink and have sex. When he woke up next morning, Dahmer found Tuomi dead. He stuffed his body into a large suitcase, took it to the basement of his grandmother's house, had sex with it and masturbated over it before dismembering it and disposing of it in the rubbish.

His third victim was fourteen-year-old Native American, Jamie Doxtator and the fourth was Richard Guerro in March, 1988.

His grandmother began to object to the noise and partying in Dahmer's room in the basement and so he moved into his own apartment in September 1988. Next day he picked up a thirteen-year-old Laotian boy called Sinthasomphone, who agreed to pose for photographs for fifty dollars. By grim coincidence, he was the older brother of a boy Dahmer would kill in 1991.

But he did not kill Sinthasomphone, and when the boy returned home, his parents realised he had been drugged. The cops picked up Dahmer on charges of sexual exploitation of a child and second-degree sexual assault. He pleaded guilty, claiming he thought the boy was older.

However, even as he awaited sentencing, he struck again, killing Anthony Sears, a handsome black model. Dahmer boiled the skull to remove the skin and painted it grey. He still had it when he was arrested.

In court, Dahmer put on the kind of manipulative performance only a psychopath can and he escaped the prison sentence being demanded by the prosecution, receiving five years' probation. He was also ordered to spend a year in the House of Correction under 'work release', which meant he went to work during the day and returned to jail at night. In spite of a letter from Dahmer's father, pleading with the judge not to release him without treatment, he was released after just ten months and went to live with his grandmother, before moving into his rooms in the Oxford Apartments in May, 1990.

Exactly a year later, a naked fourteen-year-old Laotian, Konerak Sinthasomphone, was found wandering on the streets of the Milwaukee neighbourhood in which Dahmer's flat was located. He talked to a couple of women, but was largely incoherent, having already been drugged by Dahmer. The police were called and took the boy back to Dahmer's flat to investigate. Dahmer told them, however, that Konerak was his nineteen-year-old boyfriend and that they had had a drunken argument. The police handed the boy over to Dahmer, noting a strange smell in the apartment. Dahmer killed Konerak a few hours later.

From September 1987, to July 1991, Jeffrey Dahmer killed sixteen men, the majority of them black. Their ages ranged from fourteen to thirty-one and they all had high-risk lifestyles.

The killing process was always the same. He picked his victim up at a gay bar, lured him back to the basement to pose for photographs, usually in return for payment, and then he would offer him a drugged drink, strangle him, masturbate on the body or even have sex with it. He would then cut the corpse up and get rid of it. He would take photographs throughout and would also sometimes boil the skull to remove the flesh and then paint it grey to look like plastic, keeping it and other body parts as mementos. He began experimenting with various chemical methods and acids to dispose of the flesh and bones which would be poured down a drain or flushed away in the toilet. He often preserved the genitals in formaldehyde.

He told police that he also ate some of the flesh of his victims, claiming that by doing so they would come alive in him again. He experimented with seasoning and meat tenderisers. Eating human meat gave him an erection, he said, and his fridge contained strips of human flesh.

Before they died, he sometimes tried to perform a kind of lobotomy on his victims. After drugging them, he would drill a hole in their skulls and inject muriatic acid into their brains. He was trying to create a functioning zombie-like creature that he could exercise ultimate control over and control, after all, was really what it was all about. Needless to say, most died during this procedure, but one apparently survived for a few days.

On January 29, 1992, the jury was selected for Dahmer's trial. He was indicted on seventeen charges of murder, later reduced to fifteen, to which he pleaded guilty, against the advice of his legal team, but claiming insanity. His counsel had to pursue the argument that only a person who was insane could have committed Dahmer's crimes. The prosecution, on the other hand, had to prove that he was legally insane, an evil psychopath who murdered his victims in cold blood and with malice aforethought.

Security in the courthouse was unlike that for any trial in Milwaukee's history. A sniffer dog was brought in to search for bombs and everyone entering the courtroom was searched and checked with a metal detector. A barrier, eight feet high, made of steel and bullet-proof glass was erected around the place where Dahmer would sit, to protect him from the public.

The jury deliberated for five hours before deciding that Jeffrey Dahmer should go to prison and not hospital. He was found sane and guilty on all fifteen charges.

On the day of his sentencing, he read out a statement, an apology of a kind. 'Your Honor, it is now over. This has never been a case of trying to get free. I didn't ever want freedom. Frankly, I wanted death for myself. This was a case to tell the world that I did what I did, but not for reasons of hate. I hated no one. I knew I was sick or evil or both. Now I believe I was sick. The doctors have told me about my sickness, and now I have some peace. I know how much harm I have caused . . . Thank God there will be no more harm that I can do. I believe that only the Lord Jesus Christ can save me from my sins...I ask for no consideration.'

He got none. He was given fifteen life sentences, a total of 957 years in prison.

They sent him to the Columbia Correctional Institute in Portage, Wisconsin where, for his own safety, he was kept apart from the general prison population. The segregation was not entirely successful, however, as he was attacked by a razor-wielding Cuban one day while leaving the prison chapel. His wounds, however, were superficial.

On the whole, though, he was a model prisoner, becoming a born-again Christian and gradually persuading the prison authorities to allow him more contact with other inmates. This proved costly for him.

One day he was paired with two other dangerous inmates on a work detail. One was Jesse Anderson, a white man who had murdered his wife and blamed it on a black man. The other was Christopher Scarver, a black schizophrenic doing time for first-degree murder, who suffered from delusions that he was God. It was a volatile combination, Scarver being partnered with one man, Dahmer, who had killed so many black men, and another, Anderson, who had tried to finger a black man for a murder he had committed.

On the morning of November 28, 1994, the guard left the three men to get on with their work. He came back twenty minutes later to find Dahmer and Anderson lying in pools of blood. Dahmer's skull had been smashed in with a broom handle and he was pronounced dead at eleven minutes past nine in an ambulance on the way to hospital.